Intellectuals and Reform in the Ottoman Empire

This book uncovers Young Turk political and social ideas at the end of the nineteenth century, during the intellectual phase of the movement.

Analysing the life in exile of two of the most charismatic leaders of the Young Turk movement, Ahmet Rıza and Mehmet Sabahattin, the book unravels their plans for the future of the Ottoman Empire, covering issues of power, religion, citizenship, minority rights, the role of the West, and the accountability of the Sultan. The book follows Rıza and Sabahattin through their association with philosophical circles, and highlights how their emphasis on intellectualism and elitism had a twofold effect. On the one hand, seeing themselves as enlightened and entrusted with a mission, they engaged in enduring debates, leaving an important legacy for both Ottoman and Republican rule. On the other hand, the rigidity resulting from elitism and intellectualism prevented the conception of concrete plans for change, causing a schism at the 1902 Congress of Ottoman Liberals and marking the end of the intellectual phase.

Using bilingual period journals, contemporary accounts, police archives and political and philosophical treaties, this book is of interest to students, scholars and researchers of Middle East and Ottoman History, and Political Science more broadly.

Stefano Taglia is Fellow at the Oriental Institute of the Academy of Sciences of the Czech Republic. His research interests are in the fields of nationalism and minorities in the Ottoman Empire.

SOAS/Routledge Studies on the Middle East

Edited by Benjamin C. Fortna, *SOAS, University of London* and Ulrike Freitag, *Zentrum Moderner Orient and Freie Universität, Berlin, Germany*

This series features the latest disciplinary approaches to Middle Eastern Studies. It covers the Social Sciences and the Humanities in both the pre-modern and modern periods of the region. While primarily interested in publishing single-authored studies, the series is also open to edited volumes on innovative topics, as well as textbooks and reference works.

1 Islamic Nationhood and Colonial Indonesia
The *umma* below the winds
Michael Francis Laffan

2 Russian–Muslim Confrontation in the Caucasus
Alternative visions of the conflict between Imam Shamil and the Russians, 1830–1859
Edited and translated by Thomas Sanders, Ernest Tucker and Gary Hamburg

3 Late Ottoman Society
The intellectual legacy
Edited by Elisabeth Özdalga

4 Iraqi Arab Nationalism
Authoritarian, totalitarian and pro-Fascist inclinations, 1932–1941
Peter Wien

5 Medieval Arabic Historiography
Authors as actors
Konrad Hirschler

6 Ottoman Administration of Iraq, 1890–1908
Gökhan Çetinsaya

7 Cities in the Pre-Modern Islamic World
The urban impact of religion, state and society
Edited by Amira K. Bennison and Alison L. Gascoigne

8 Subalterns and Social Protest
History from below in the Middle East and North Africa
Edited by Stephanie Cronin

9 Nazism in Syria and Lebanon
The ambivalence of the German option, 1933–1945
Götz Nordbruch

10 Nationalism and Liberal Thought in the Arab East
Ideology and practice
Edited by Christoph Schumann

11 **State-Society Relations in Ba'thist Iraq**
Facing dictatorship
Achim Rohde

12 **Untold Histories of the Middle East**
Recovering voices from the 19th and 20th centuries
Edited by Amy Singer, Christoph K. Neumann and Selçuk Akşin Somel

13 **Court Cultures in the Muslim World**
Seventh to nineteenth centuries
Edited by Albrecht Fuess and Jan-Peter Hartung

14 **The City in the Ottoman Empire**
Migration and the making of urban modernity
Edited by Ulrike Freitag, Malte Fuhrmann, Nora Lafi and Florian Riedler

15 **Opposition and Legitimacy in the Ottoman Empire**
Conspiracies and political cultures
Florian Riedler

16 **Islam and the Politics of Secularism**
The Caliphate and Middle Eastern modernization in the early 20th century
Nurullah Ardiç

17 **State-Nationalisms in the Ottoman Empire, Greece and Turkey**
Orthodox and Muslims, 1830–1945
Edited by Benjamin C. Fortna, Stefanos Katsikas, Dimitris Kamouzis and Paraskevas Konortas

18 **The Making of the Arab Intellectual**
Empire, public sphere and the colonial coordinates of selfhood
Edited by Dyala Hamzah

19 **Orthodox Christians in the Late Ottoman Empire**
Ayşe Ozil

20 **A Provincial History of the Ottoman Empire**
Cyprus and the Eastern Mediterranean in the nineteenth century
Marc Aymes

21 **Urban Governance Under the Ottomans**
Between cosmopolitanism and conflict
Edited by Ulrike Freitag and Nora Lafi

22 **Ottoman Notables and Participatory Politics**
Tanzimat reform in Tokat, 1839–1876
John K. Bragg

23 **Intellectuals and Reform in the Ottoman Empire**
The Young Turks on the challenges of modernity
Stefano Taglia

Intellectuals and Reform in the Ottoman Empire

The Young Turks on the challenges of modernity

Stefano Taglia

LONDON AND NEW YORK

First published 2015
by Routledge
2 Park Square, Milton Park, Abingdon, Oxon OX14 4RN

and by Routledge
711 Third Avenue, New York, NY 10017

Routledge is an imprint of the Taylor & Francis Group, an informa business

© 2015 Stefano Taglia

The right of Stefano Taglia to be identified as author of this work has been asserted by him in accordance with sections 77 and 78 of the Copyright, Designs and Patents Act 1988.

All rights reserved. No part of this book may be reprinted or reproduced or utilised in any form or by any electronic, mechanical, or other means, now known or hereafter invented, including photocopying and recording, or in any information storage or retrieval system, without permission in writing from the publishers.

Trademark notice: Product or corporate names may be trademarks or registered trademarks, and are used only for identification and explanation without intent to infringe.

British Library Cataloguing in Publication Data
A catalogue record for this book is available from the British Library

Library of Congress Cataloging in Publication Data
Intellectuals and reform in the Ottoman Empire : the Young Turks on the challenges of modernity / Stefano Taglia.
    pages cm. – (SOAS/Routledge studies on the Middle East ; 23)
Includes bibliographical references and index.
    1. Ittihat ve Terakki Cemiyeti–History. 2. Ahmet Riza, 1859-1930. 3. Sabahaddin, Prens, 1877-1948. 4. Intellectuals–Turkey–Biography. 5. Political activists–Turkey–Biography. 6. Exiles–Biography. 7. Social change–Turkey–History–19th century. 8. Liberalism–Turkey–History–19th century. 9. Turkey–Intellectual life–19th century. 10. Turkey–Politics and government–1878-1909. I. Title.
    DR572.5.T34 2015
    956.1'0154–dc23
                    2014041640

ISBN: 978-1-138-82545-1 (hbk)
ISBN: 978-1-315-73998-4 (ebk)

Typeset in Times New Roman
by Taylor & Francis Books

Printed and bound by CPI Group (UK) Ltd, Croydon, CR0 4YY

Contents

	Acknowledgements	viii
	Introduction	1
1	The Ottoman Empire under Sultan Abdülhamit II	13
2	Young Turk émigrés, the press and the Parisian *milieu*	29
3	Ahmet Rıza and *Mechveret*	52
4	Mehmet Sabahattin and social science	80
5	The end of an idea, the 1902 Congress of Ottoman Liberals in Paris	107
	Conclusion	129
	Afterword	139
	References	154
	Index	164

Acknowledgements

There is a long list of people who have contributed greatly to making this book a reality. They are all listed below, save those for whom my memory is failing now.

Professor Benjamin C. Fortna has endured my presence as a doctoral student for some time but never showed any signs of impatience. Instead, he has encouraged and promoted me all along. Without his precious suggestions on my dissertation and his inspiration as a scholar, my path to this book would have been arduous, if not impossible. Apart from all the academic and intellectual help Professor Fortna has provided me, the calmness and tranquillity he has instilled in me in moments of anxiety were fundamental.

Dr Yorgos Dedes's Turkish and Ottoman teachings, as well as his valuable comments on some of my work, were also crucial factors enabling me to complete my dissertation, first, and turn it into a book, later. Suggestions and comments of my examiners, Professor Ali Ansari and Dr Frederick Anscombe, were crucial to make me think broader than my contained topic.

My archival research would not have been as fruitful without the help of Professor Şükrü Hanioğlu, who provided me with guidance to Young Turk sources at Firestone Library, of Princeton University. There, I also received immense help from Dr James W. Weinberger. The Director of the Police Archives in Paris was constantly ready to hear my further requests for material and made sure I was able to consult everything I was interested in. In terms of content, an informal discussion with Professor François Georgeon proved to be a turning point in my understanding of the links between Ahmet Rıza and positivism. Sincere thanks also go to Professor Palmira Brummett, Dr Marc Aymes and Dr Vangelis Kechriotis who commented at length on one of my draft chapters and provided me with great ideas.

In its primitive form, the manuscript was read and commented upon by Catherine Cornet, Roland Belgrave and Dr Daniel Grey who provided interesting and valuable feedback and proofread the whole dissertation. In its latest form, the manuscript was carefully read by Professor Eberhard Kienle who, with his incredible dedication, has provided extremely valuable comments. However, Professor Kienle deserves to be mentioned also as a constant source of friendship and support dating back a long time, now. More comments and suggestions have been provided by my two new colleagues, Gabriela Özel-Volfova and Dr Jan Zouplna. They have spent time and effort not only on my academic work, but also in making me feel at home in my new place. Many thanks also go to a number of people who have helped me with some of the translation and with whom I have also spent time discussing my topic during evenings out: Nilay Afet Seyranoğlu, Taylan Güngör, and Dr Yoannis Moutsis. I am also extremely grateful to Ayşe Ebru Akçasu for her help on parts of the translation and comments on the manuscript. I would also like to thank Dr Ondrej Beranek, Director of the Oriental Institute of the Academy of Sciences of the Czech Republic, for providing support and tranquillity in the last, crucial, months of writing. I would also like to extend my gratitude to the two external reviewers of Routledge who were really sharp in catching some incongruities in my initial work; if this book has grown from its embryonic state, is also thanks to them. Thanks also to Joe Whiting, Ruth Bradley, Kris Wischenkamper and Kathryn Rylance at Routledge for their patience and help.

This book, however, would surely not have been possible without the dedication and fundamental help of Valeria (Mosini): thank you!

Introduction
Locating reform in the nineteenth century Ottoman Empire

The object of enquiry

On the 23rd September 1912, while fighting against the Italians in North Africa, Enver,[1] a young Ottoman officer *en route* to become one of the most influential statesmen of the Ottoman Empire, wrote to a friend in Europe:

> C'est un poison votre civilisation, mais c'est un poison qui éveille et on ne veut, on ne peut plus dormir. On sent que si on refermait les yeux, ce serait pour mourir. Et la grande différence c'est que vous autres avec tout votre 'Erkenntnis' [knowledge] vous prenez la vie légèrement tandisque [sic] nous, quand nous avons la 'Erkenntnis' nous nous rendons la vie plus difficile qu'elle ne l'est en vérité, surtout si nous changeons les principes que nous sommes habitués.[2]

The dilemma articulated by Enver Paşa represents what Ottoman reformers had been asking themselves for a very long time, at least since the reign of Sultan Süleyman in the mid sixteenth century.[3] Since then, the pressing question 'How can the state be saved?' had been approached in different ways, but never so radically as during the last quarter of the nineteenth century. When Enver wrote these lines, ten years had passed since the first Congress of Ottoman Liberals held in Paris in 1902 and four years since the Young Turk Revolution of 1908 that had reinstated the constitution. However, as framed by Enver, the solution to close one's eyes and absorb the influence of Western European civilisation, without dying in the process had not yet been decisively defined. Death here takes the form of cultural annihilation, loss of traditional aspects of society or the collapse of the Empire as political entity.

The question of how Ottoman statesmen and intellectuals in the late nineteenth century translated their visions of the Empire's identity into strategies for reform, shifts the question 'how to reform the Empire to save it' from the context of political action to the context of historical analysis. Discussing, in a historical context, how specific political ideas were transformed into plans for reform, in the late nineteenth century, in connection with the question of the relation between the Empire and the West, is the object of inquiry of this book. Historians have widely analysed the impact of Western influences on attempts at reform in the Ottoman Empire. Some attribute the relative success of the reforms implemented to the level of 'Westernisation' that Ottoman modernisers achieved, reaching the conclusion that, the more aspects of Western culture the reform had borrowed, the more successful and effective it was.[4] That narrative, though, emphasises the "adoption of Western European institutions and attitudes ... [rather] than the process of adaptation".[5] A more balanced approach suggests that the crucial reforms of the Empire resulted from the interplay, and mutual reinforcement, of borrowed and indigenous features. A case in point is, for example, the *Hatt-ı Şerif* of Gülhane – the symbol of Ottoman reform that paved the way to the *Tanzimat* – which drew as much from Western liberal thought as from Islamic principles of social justice.[6] There has also been criticism of the excessive cultural Westernisation of some strata of Ottoman society in the early twentieth century, exposed as a form of dandyism, if not of supine mimicking.[7] To fully appreciate the relevance of Enver's dilemma to an historiographical discourse that aims at reconstructing the intellectual processes behind the turn of events that characterise the last decades of the Ottoman Empire (which, as shown in the Afterword, are relevant to, and may be helpful in addressing, contemporary debates), it is appropriate, first of all, to spell out the framework in which the question was inscribed.

The need to reform the Empire

Modern reform in the Ottoman Empire had started with the first attempts to renovate the military in the late eighteenth century – under Sultan Selim III (1761–1808) – yet these attempts were neither complete nor consistent. Much of the difficulty of the endeavour resided in the nature of the Empire itself, which was ethnically, religiously, and culturally so diverse that it proved extremely difficult to formulate coherent ideas and plans for its organisation. In the nineteenth century, the ethos of reform picked up momentum under Sultans Mahmut II (1803–1839), Abdülmecit (1839–1861), and Abdülaziz (1861–1876); communication, education, the military and government improved, particularly during the *Tanzimat* period (1839–1876) initiated with the *Hatt-ı Şerif* of Gülhane, when some civil liberties were granted to all citizens of the Empire, and with the *Islahat Fermanı* of 1856, with which the state began to be construed as having a duty of care towards its citizens.

In the face of military defeats and increased Western involvement, the threat of the Empire's collapse became more tangible, and, therefore, winning Europe's confidence became a pressing objective. Some minorities began to see the appeal of a nationalistic discourse that the West had long been instigating, which, giving prominence to linguistic, ethnic, and religious definitions of the various identities, challenged what seemed to some of them a rather bland, and unrealistic, identity the central government insisted on imposing throughout the Empire. Additionally, a liberal philosophical approach emerged as some statesmen, members of the military, the bureaucracy, and the new elite began to study more widely European languages and to take an interest in scientific subjects – hitherto marginalised due to their alleged incompatibility with Islam. This approach was influenced by positivism, materialism, and various strands of social science, and, above all, by the French Revolution as an ideologically defining event.[8] The time was ripe for the intellectual elite to come forward with requests for more representation in government, and more rights for the citizens, identified as *reaya*, 'the flock'.

These developments pushed some Ottomans who still believed in the possibility and feasibility of living in an imperial framework to look for their own version of (inclusive) nationalism. This translated into the formulation of *Osmanlılık*, Ottomanism, a proto-nationalist political project aimed at promoting:

> the notion of one Ottoman nation, consisting of individuals with equal rights, sharing the same mother country, and loyal to the state and the sultan ... The policy of Ottomanism was developed particularly to prevent the development of nationalism in non-Muslim communities.[9]

Ottomanism was a strategy for reducing inter-ethnic and inter-religious tensions by acknowledging in full the mixed ethnicity and multi religious character of the Empire (which included Albanians, Arabs, Armenians, Bulgarians, Greeks, Kurds, Serbs, Syrians, Turks, as well as Muslims, Orthodox Christians, Gregorian Catholics, and Jews, among others), and by making that very acknowledgment the glue that would hold it together. It implied a form of patriotism intended to provide a barrier against the centrifugal forces represented by the emerging local nationalisms, in turn caused, at least in part, by the unequal status of Muslim and non-Muslim citizens. In fact, non-Muslims were politically, though not economically, second class citizens, exempted from military service in return for payment of a poll tax until the *Tanzimat*. In 1895–1896, when the Young Turks were most passionately defending Ottomanism as a political project, 73.5% of the total population of the Empire was Muslim.[10] The relationship between the central power and the Ottoman ethnic minorities was further complicated by two main factors: the relative animosity between the various minorities, and the exploitation of their grievances on the part of the foreign powers with a view to making territorial gains at the expenses of the Empire.[11]

The first ideologues of Ottomanism belonged to the bureaucracy created during the *Tanzimat*. In the 1860s came the Young Ottomans who criticised what they regarded as too broad an adoption of Western institutions and social arrangements in the *Tanzimat* period. Most significantly, the Young Ottomans promoted the view that constitutionalism was fully compatible with the true spirit of early Islam, which defended the sovereignty of the people and their right to be consulted by the rulers according to the practice of *shura*.[12] The conjunction between the men of the *Tanzimat*, the Young Ottomans and an increasing European pressure to introduce reforms prioritising non-Muslim elements of the Empire resulted in the proclamation of the Constitution and the beginning of the First Constitutional Period, *Birinci Meşrutiyet* (1876–1878) under the rule of Sultan Abdülhamit II (1876–1909). It is indeed interesting to note that the Constitution was announced during the Istanbul Conference, on 23rd December. In theory the conference had been convened to press onto the Empire drastic reforms in Bulgaria; however, the Ottoman statesmen made clear that, having then just adopted a Constitution which translated into equal rights for all, reform specific to a group could, therefore, not possibly be conceived of, and that the conference itself had no point in going ahead. The result was a declaration of war on the part of Russia that gave way to the Russo-Turkish War of 1877–1878. After two years of Constitutional rule, Sultan Abdülhamit II made a sudden turnaround, suspending the Constitution, allegedly because of the extraordinary crisis affecting the Empire as a result of the war with Russia. Abdülhamit started a period of absolute rule, and pursued a strategy of reform driven by far-reaching centralisation, the elimination of intermediary bodies and a reliance on 'traditional' Islamic values mixed with a political use of religion. Abdülhamit's rule brought about progress in matters of education[13] and communication[14] in the Empire and, as an ironic by-product of these, the emergence of a politically more active and aware cadre of students, now trained in the new Hamidian schools and able to use new means of communication for learning and dissemination. Overall, it is with the advent of Sultan Abdülhamit II that attempts to establish a feasible plan of reform and modernisation reached a peak and came from many sides.[15] While previously the impetus to reform had generally come from the state, with the sole exception of the Young Ottomans, Abdülhamit's rule witnessed a sort of popularisation of the voices of reform – even if this was limited to the members of the elite. This led to the formulation of a spectrum of competing ideas so rich and dynamic that the usual and rigid characterisation of the Ottoman society of the time as divided between Islamists, Modernists and Westernists is unhelpful. The intellectual, political, and social themes discussed at the time were syncretic and complex, making the period in question one of the most formative in the history of the Empire and definitely one for which rigid labels do not explain the complexity of its dynamics. Although the Ottomanist reformers of the Young Turk movement failed to formulate a unidirectional plan that would translate into tangible policies, they nonetheless produced the intellectual ferment that would prepare the political, social and cultural foundations of the Republic and whose debates are, to some extent, still discussed today.

The Young Turk movement and reform

Time has come to introduce the political entity that best represented a concerted attempt at envisaging a future for the Empire that sharply differed from the one planned by the Sultan; this political group – that is the Young

Turk movement – emerged in Istanbul in 1889 and was active until the 1920s, functioning as an umbrella organisation under which a number of smaller groups operated. The general ideas that held it together included: the full endorsement of the rule of law, an urge to reintroduce a constitutional system that would extend the same rights to all Ottomans, and an orientation towards rationality (as rigorous, clear and logical thinking) in decision-making. The resulting mix was a movement that came to "[s]imultaneously include a tendency toward technocratic authoritarianism and toward trans-mutation of liberal political forms into those of a tutelary regime."[16] This movement was the direct product of the various entities that, over time, had provided sources of inspiration.

In the historical literature, the Young Turk movement has often been portrayed as an agent of change only during the revolution of 1908, while its earlier stages have been regarded as marginal,[17] if not altogether irrelevant;[18] accordingly, attention has been given to Young Turk members as precursors of Mustafa Kemal Atatürk, with emphasis on the militarist phase of the movement.[19] Studies of the movement that looked beyond its militaristic aspect revealed a multiplicity of approaches, some historians emphasising continuity in the cultural, ideological and social traits that characterised it from its inception to its demise,[20] others focussing on identifying different periods in it,[21] and analysing the interplay between continuity and change in each period.[22] Taking into account the different influences on the Young Turk movement – from the intellectual exchanges of the Translation Office, the ideas of the Young Ottomans, the principles of the First Constitutional Period, the interaction with religious organisations and Freemasonry, through to nineteenth-century European philosophical and political thinking – it is not surprising that its trajectory was indeed diverse, and consisted in phases that spoke with different, sometimes conflicting, voices.

This book concentrates on the 1889–1902 period, which goes from the birth of the Young Turk movement to the first Congress of Ottoman Liberals held in Paris; I identify it as a specific, extremely important, and distinctive period in the history of the movement, one which it is appropriate to refer to as the 'intellectual phase'.[23] I reconstruct its salient developments through the works of two of its leaders, Ahmet Rıza (1859–1930) and Prince Mehmet Sabahattin (1878–1948), who, thus far, have been mentioned in the historical literature only briefly,[24] and mainly with respect to their involvement in post-1908 political activities.[25]

In fact, as I discuss throughout the book, Rıza and Sabahettin have a lot to say since, as the architects of the intellectual phase of the movement, they most effectively debated issues of crucial relevance to the survival of the Empire – relating, in particular, to the relationship between the central power and minorities, the role of religion in the reformed state, and, most importantly, the relationship with the West, which, all together, form the core of the Ottoman identity to which Enver's question quoted earlier relates. Hence, they must be credited for providing in good time genuine and well thought-through attempts at addressing that all-important question, and, by doing so, offering useful guidelines for reforming the state according to their respective visions of the future.

The intellectual phase of the Young Turk movement

Ahmet Rıza left the Empire in 1889, on the pretext of attending the *Exposition Universelle* to be held in Paris in the same year, but with the real intention to organise the opposition to Sultan Abdülhamit II from abroad.[26] Once in Paris, he embarked on a series of publishing projects, which, in different ways, reflected his deep commitment to positivism. They included the foundation, together with Ottoman Lebanese Halil Ganem, of *Meşveret* (Consultation), a fortnightly journal in Ottoman with a supplement in French, *Mechveret Supplément Français*,[27] and regular contributions to prominent international journals.[28] In 1922, out of his experience in Europe, Rıza published a book, *La Faillite morale de la politique occidentale en Orient*.[29] Throughout this book, Rıza's work will be used as a source on his overall ideology as well as on more specific events. Even though, as stated above, the book was published in 1922, the same thoughts expressed then, had been previously and constantly expressed through the pages of his earlier publications.[30]

Prince Mehmet Sabahattin joined the diasporic community of Young Turk intellectuals in Paris in 1899, following an overnight escape from the Empire together with his father *Damat*[31] Mahmut, and his brother Lutfullah. In Paris, Sabahattin befriended Edmond Demolins (1852–1901), joining the latter's school of social science,[32] and becoming an admirer of British liberalism, which he appreciated for its emphasis on private initiative and *laissez-faire* approach to economic matters. He would summarise in a monograph his views for reforming the state according to a federal structure, and restructuring the Ottoman society from its deepest roots.[33]

A crucial element in the story I am telling is the fact that Rıza and Sabahettin, like many other members of the Young Turk movement, left the Empire voluntarily and re-settled abroad, just like some Young Ottomans had done in the 1860s, but in much greater numbers and for much longer; the choice the Young Turk émigrés made provided them with intellectual and practical opportunities that would have been unthinkable within the borders of the Empire.[34] In particular, life in exile provided them with first-hand experience of what the 'West' had to offer, for the good and for the bad, putting them in a privileged position for addressing effectively the question of the Ottoman identity. On top of providing a wealth of intellectual contributions for discussion among Young Turk members and their sympathisers, Rıza and Sabahattin were most active towards the organisation of the first Congress of Ottoman Liberals held in Paris in 1902, and in relating its day-to-day developments through the press. Not too surprisingly perhaps, a well-conceived, but exceedingly diverse, *modus pensandi* did not give rise to a *modus operandi*. The Congress, convened with the explicit aim to create a united front against the rule of Abdülhamit, resulted instead in the positioning of the movement's factions – most notably, Rıza's and Sabahattin's – against one another, miserably failing its goal, and bringing to an end a remarkable phase in the history of the Young Turk movement.

Analysing Rıza's and Sabahattin's contributions, one comes to appreciate the 1889–1902 period as a *per se* entity, and one worthy of attention.[35] Those theoretical contributions could easily appear sterile, in terms of political achievements, particularly when compared to the 1908 Revolution, as some historians claim.[36] However, Rıza's and Sabahattin's discussions addressed debates that would resurface in the Republican period, and that have burning relevance today, particularly in relation to the role of religion in politics, the meaning of identity, and the relationship of Turkey with the West. Even if, as some historians contend, the relevance of the intellectual phase of the movement on the 1908 Revolution was negligible or zero, the point would still need explaining, and its consequences addressed.[37] Among those consequences may well be that "this revolution did not completely fulfil its historical mission, confining itself to the proclamation of a constitution; it did not abolish semi-colonial and feudal relations."[38] Hence, as events narrated in this book show, rather than thinking of the history of the Young Turk movement as being mainly defined by the 1908 Revolution and the emergence of the Turkish Republic, it is more appropriate to see it as consisting in two phases, with the Paris Congress of 1902 marking a hiatus between the liberal, and pluralistic, intellectual phase which preceded it, and the pragmatic, and militaristic one that followed it.

This first, rough, division of the period conveys the abstract nature of the political discourse of the intellectual phase of the movement, which addressed more the kind of society the Ottoman Empire should become once Abdülhamit's despotic rule had been brought to an end, than the way, and the means – negotiations or violence – to transform the political regime.[39] It also shows that the road to the 1908 Revolution was convoluted and nuanced, and that the opposition mounted to the Sultan was a multi-faceted endeavour that slowly, tortuously, and painstakingly, achieved incremental improvements – such as the re-instatement of the Constitution in 1908, and the shift from the Sultan's despotic rule to the Unionist nucleus's (only) authoritarian one.[40] The two-fold division described above, however, represents only a first approximation to an adequate description of the period in which the Young Turk movement was active because there was no unity of vision, or intent, within the movement prior to, and during the preparation for, the 1902 Congress.

Interestingly, the most contentious issue for the Congress delegates turned out to be the question of the relationship with the West, one of the essential components of the question of the Ottoman identity which, ten years later, Enver would find still unresolved (and so it is today). This was not only because the delegates could not agree on the desirable (or acceptable) degree of involvement or military intervention on the part of the West with matters internal to the Empire, but because it became apparent that the Western political, social and cultural heritage was not unified. In other words, it became apparent that different conceptions of the West were possible, which, taken as sources of inspiration for reform, would correspond to different conceptions of Ottoman identity, each of which would lead to a different sociopolitical arrangement of the Empire. In particular, it became apparent to the 1902 Congress delegates that the two rival conceptions of the West, presented to them by Rıza and Sabahattin, respectively, the former inspired by Comte's positivism, the latter by social science and British liberalism, were mutually incompatible, making not just unity of action, but also unity of vision, an impossibility.

This book is organised into five main chapters. Chapter 1 'The Ottoman Empire under Sultan Abdülhamit II', provides an overview of the historical period and a general presentation of Sultan Abdülhamit II's rule and policies in promoting a specific vision of Ottomanism. Chapter 2 'Young Turk émigrés, the press and the Parisian *milieu*', provides an assessment of the emergence of the Young Turk organisation, its connections with other contemporary organisations – such as the religious establishment and Freemasonry – and some of its sources of inspiration. Further on, the chapter discusses the role of exile and of the press in exile; Paris, as the specific centre of exile is looked at in conjunction with the idea of intellectualism. Together, space and experience constitute central lenses that help us understand the writings and ideas of the two ideologues in question. Chapters 3 'Ahmet Rıza and *Mechveret*', and 4 'Mehmet Sabahattin and social science', explore the ideologies of Rıza and Sabahettin through their own writings – both monographs and journal articles. The two chapters shed light on the sources of inspiration of the two men, positivism, and social science and British liberalism, respectively. The chapters examine how they envisaged reform and how they perceived previous attempts at reform, including those of the contemporary regime of Abdülhamit II. Moreover, Chapters 3 and 4 discuss Rıza's and Sabahattin's understanding of modern political systems and their suggestions on the role of religion in a reformed state as well as their opinion of what constituted an acceptable degree of external help. This last issue becomes pivotal in light of its link with the thinkers' respective stance on the fate of ethno-religious communities. These chapters also discuss the ambiguities and tensions that emerge in the works of the two intellectuals, and which give us important clues into the level of intellectual enthusiasm that characterised the members of the Young Turk movement in exile. What will emerge is a picture of two individuals who, even though they shared a disdain for the despotic nature of Hamidian rule, adopted distinct angles through which to imagine reform. Influenced by two different philosophical currents through the study of social science, Rıza and Sabahattin shared the feeling of a mission as exponents of enlightened intellectual elites but ended up disagreeing on the future organisation of the Empire: Mehmet Sabahattin emphasised federalism, in which diversity was institutionalised to ensure a balanced distribution of rights. Ahmet Rıza, on the other hand, was convinced that ethnic or religious difference should not feature centrally in organisation for the sake of a supra-ethnic, supra-religious Ottomanist project. These divergent visions resulted in a rupture between the members of the Young Turk movement that is investigated in detail in Chapter 5, 'The end of an idea, the 1902 Congress of Ottoman Liberals in Paris'. This chapter looks at the Congress of Ottoman Liberals that was held in Paris from the 4th to the 9th of February, 1902. I argue that this Congress represents a critical moment in the history of the Young Turk movement as a whole, as it is the moment when the two major groups, headed by Rıza and Sabahettin, were supposed to unite into a coherent and strong opposition faction. Instead, as the divergence between the two leaders became apparent, their two groups clashed and decided to go their own way. In fact, the failure of the Young Turk delegates at the Congress to agree on a united programme marks the end of the intellectual phase of the Young Turk movement. Lastly, as it will be argued in the Conclusion, however unfeasible their plan might look today, the two men and their numerous followers were fully invested in the feasibility of Ottomanism and actively worked towards its attainment. Even though it took very little time to turn their promising visions into a missed opportunity, their intellectual legacy lived on past their time and survives to this day in the heated negotiation of the identity of modern Turkey. The last chapter, the Afterword 'The enduring legacies of the Young Turk intellectuals', highlights the continuity of the debates, initiated by Rıza and Sabahattin, between 1890s and today's Turkey with a view to make links across periods and stress the importance of these debates.

Notes

1 Enver Paşa (1881–1922) took command of the Ottoman forces fighting the Italians in Libya in 1911; following the defeat in the Balkan Wars in 1912, he took the position of War Minister in 1913. During the Second Balkan War, he achieved important victories, and acquired enough power to establish a triumvirate with his two closest associates, Talat (1874–1921) as Minister of Interior Affairs, and Cemal (1872–1922) as Minister of the Navy. By 1914, he had become commander-in-chief and, with his two associates, masterminded the Ottoman entry into the First World War on the side of Germany. However, his military skills proved insufficient, and the Ottoman army in north-eastern Anatolia suffered a major defeat at the hands of the Russians. Following clashes with the Armenians and with defeat in sight, on 2nd November 1918, Enver, Talat and Cemal fled the Empire on board a German vessel. Talat, who had been most involved in the war with the Armenians, was killed in Germany in 1921 by an Armenian activist; Enver was killed in battle in August 1922, while Cemal was killed in Tbilisi, in the same year, by another Armenian activist. Justin McCarthy has given a synthetic, but telling, definition of Enver: "[He] was convinced he was a strategic genius, but really he was a cowboy." Justin McCarthy, *The Ottoman Turks: An Introductory History to 1923* (London: Longman, 1997), 359.
2 *Kendi Mektuplarında Enver Paşa*, edited by Şükrü Hanioğlu (Istanbul: Der Yayınları, 1989), 188.

10 *Introduction*

3 Bernard Lewis, "Ottoman Observers of Ottoman Decline", *Islamic Studies* 1, no. 1 (1962), 71–87.
4 See, for instance, Bernard Lewis, *The Emergence of Modern Turkey* (London: Oxford University Press, 1961), and Ernest E. Ramsaur, *The Young Turks: Prelude to the Revolution of 1908* (New York: Russell & Russell, 1970).
5 Benjamin C. Fortna, *Imperial Classroom: Islam, the State, and Education in the Late Ottoman Empire* (Oxford: Oxford University Press, 2002), 9–10.
6 See, for instance, Butrus Abu Manneh, "The Islamic Roots of the Gülhane Rescript," *Die Welt des Islam* 34 (1994), 173–203, and Frederick F. Anscombe, "Islam and the Age of Ottoman Reform," *Past and Present* 208, no. 1 (2010): 159–89.
7 See, for instance, Nora Şeni, "Fashion and Women's Clothing" in Şirin Tekeli (ed.), *Women in Modern Turkish Society: A Reader* (London: Zed Books, 1995), 25–45; and François Georgeon, "Ottomans and Drinkers: the Consumption of Wine and Alcohol in Istanbul in the 19th Century," in Eugene Rogan (ed.) *Outside In. Marginality in the Modern Middle East* (London: I.B. Tauris, 2002), 17–18.
8 For discussion, see Bernard Lewis, "The Impact of the French Revolution on Turkey," *Cahiers d'Histoire Mondiale* 1, no. 1 (1953), 106; and Erik J. Zürcher, *The Young Turk Legacy and the National Awakening: From the Ottoman Empire to Atatürk's Turkey* (London: I.B. Tauris, 2010).
9 Selçuk Akşin Somel, *Historical Dictionary of the Ottoman Empire* (Oxford: The Scarecrow Press, 2003), 221.
10 Accordingly, Christians were often better educated and richer than Muslims. Mete Tunçay, "In Lieu of a Conclusion," in Mete Tunçay and Erik J. Zürcher (eds), *Socialism and Nationalism in the Ottoman Empire 1876–1923* (London: I.B. Tauris, 1994), 157.
11 In the eyes of Western powers, Ottomanism represented a stumbling block to their ambitions of establishing mandates and protectorates through the Empire, and, whenever possible, making proper territorial gains.
12 The Young Ottomans formed in 1865; they consisted, mainly, of civil servants, mostly from the Translation Office, with a religious background; among them, Namık Kemal (1840–1888), Ziya Bey (1825–1880), and Ali Suavi (1838–1878) reached prominence.
13 Fortna, *Imperial Classroom*.
14 Lewis, *Emergence*, 181.
15 Contrary to what some historians claim, the Hamidian period was not a setback in the reform of the Empire but the moment in which some of these changes reached maturity and fullness. This issue is treated more in-depth in the next chapter.
16 Carter V. Findley, "The Advent of Ideology in the Islamic Middle East – Part II," *Studia Islamica* 56 (1982), 147–180.
17 Feroz Ahmad, *The Young Turks, the Committee of Union and Progress in Turkish Politics, 1908–1914* (Oxford: Oxford University Press, 1969).
18 Erik J. Zürcher, *The Unionist Factor: The Role of the Committee of Union and Progress in the Turkish National Movement, 1905–1926* (Leiden: E. J. Brill, 1984).
19 Zürcher, *The Young Turk Legacy*.
20 Niyazi Berkes, *The Development of Secularism in Turkey* (New York: Routledge, 1998).
21 Hanioğlu, *The Young Turks in Opposition* (Oxford University Press, New York, 1995); *Preparation for a Revolution* (New York: Oxford University Press, 2001).
22 Şerif Mardin, "Continuity and Change in the Ideas of the Young Turks," in Şerif Mardin *Religion, Society and Modernity in Turkey* (New York: Syracuse University Press, 2006), 164–81.
23 Interesting analogies with the intellectual and political endeavours of early twentieth-century Iranian modernisers may be found in Cyrus Schayegh, *Who is*

Knowledgeable is Strong – Science, Class, and the Formation of Modern Iranian Society, 1900–1950 (Berkeley, CA: University of Los Angeles Press, 2009).
24 Hanioğlu, *Young Turks in Opposition*; and *Preparation for a Revolution*.
25 Ahmad, *The Young Turks, the Committee of Union and Progress in Turkish Politics*; Berkes, *The Development of Secularism*, and M. Naim Turfan, *Rise of the Young Turks: Politics, the Military and Ottoman Collapse* (London: I.B. Tauris, 2000).
26 Ahmet Rıza, *Ahmed Rıza Bey'in Anıları* (Istanbul: Arba, 1988).
27 For reasons of clarity and brevity, from now on, the group and its publication will always be referred to in the French spelling, *Mechveret*, apart from reference to specific articles that are cited and appeared in the Ottoman or French issue.
28 Such as the *Positivist Review* and *La Revue Occidentale*.
29 Ahmet Rıza, *La Faillite morale de la politique occidentale en orient* (Paris: Librairie Picart, 1922).
30 Ideas such as the fact that Europe had its eyes set on the dismemberment of the Empire as well as the bankruptcy and hypocrisy of its political involvement are constant features of Rıza's writings, in his book, as much as in his earlier articles and editorial pieces. Regarding the first issue, see, for example, the following articles: "Avrupa Matbu'atı Niçin Türkler Aleyhindedir ve Bulgarlar Leyhindedir?" *Şûra-yı Ümmet*, no. 35 (August 1903); "Question de Macedoine," *Revue Occidentale* 27, no. 4 (1st August 1904), 211–212; "Memorandum aux Puissances," *Mechveret Supplément Français* 3, no. 201 (1st July 1908).
31 *Damat* was used as a honorary title by sons-in-law of the sultans.
32 This was called *École des Roches*, from the locality near Verneuil where it was based.
33 Mehmet Sabahattin, *Türkiye nasıl kurtarılabilir?* (İstanbul: Kader Matbaasi, 1334/ 1918).
34 The literature on Young Turks in exile is scarce; a notable exception is Hans-Lukas Kieser, *A Quest for Belonging* (Istanbul: Isis Press, 2007). James McDougall, *History and the Culture of Nationalism in Algeria* (Cambridge: Cambridge University Press, 2006), instead provides an interesting parallel with other groups in exile and how these formulated a new idea of nationalism/proto-nationalism.
35 "It is perhaps in its intellectual and cultural life that the Young Turk period is most interesting and most significant." Lewis, *Emergence*, 225.
36 "However great the indirect contributions of the centres abroad may have been in preparing the climate of the revolution of 1908 ... [this] was the result of the work of groups working inside the Empire. Generally the members of those opposition groups do not seem to have been much concerned with theoretical approaches to the reforms they wanted, nor with the building of a coherent ideology," Zürcher, *The Unionist Factor*, 21. Notably, opinion on the relevance (or lack thereof) of the intellectual phase of the Young Turk movement (1889–1902) on revolutionary events is divided: "The 'Young' Turks, or party of reform, whom diplomats had hitherto been wont to regard as dreamers, had long carried on a secret propaganda, which had made great headway in the army." William Miller, *The Ottoman Empire and its Successors, 1801–1927* (Cambridge: Cambridge University Press, 1927), 475; and: "The almost bloodless revolution of the Young Turks had 'Ottomanism' as password and 'Liberty, Equality, Justice' as motto," Anahide Ter Minassian, "The Role of the Armenian Community in the Foundation and Development of the Socialist Movement in the Ottoman Empire and Turkey, 1876–1923," in Mete Tunçay and Erik Ian Zürcher (eds), *Socialism and Nationalism in the Ottoman Empire 1876–1923* (London: I.B. Tauris, 1994), 138.
37 Şerif Mardin, *Continuity and Change*.

12 Introduction

38 Ibrahim Yalimov, "The Bulgarian Community and the Development of the Socialist Movement in the Ottoman Empire During the Period 1876–1923," in Tunçay and Zürcher (eds), *Socialism and Nationalism in the Ottoman Empire*, 90.
39 Notably, at the 1902 Paris Congress, both Rıza and Sabahattin were adamant in stating that the Young Turk movement housed no intention to harm the Sultan in any way, or achieve regime change by violent means.
40 There is a lively debate around the assessment of Unionist rule. Some historians see it as an authoritarian regime, and highlight the similarities with the previous rule of Sultan Abdülhamit II; some others view it as, broadly speaking, a fairly liberal system in which liberties were finally granted to the population. There are two considerations to be made on this specific matter. The first is a matter of interpretation and sources. The same view that I put forth in my book is shared by a number of people: Fatma Müge Göçek, "What is the Meaning of the 1908 Young Turk Revolution? A Critical Historical Assessment in 2008," *İstanbul Üniversitesi Siyasal Bilgiler Fakültesi Dergisi* 38 (2008), 179–214; Şükrü Hanioğlu, "The Committee of Union and Progress and the 1908 Revolution," in François Georgeon (ed.), *'L'Ivresse de la liberté' La révolution de 1908 dans l'Empire ottoman* (Leuven: Peeters, 2012), 15–26; and Nader Sohrabi, "Illiberal Constitutionalism. The Committee of Union and Progress as a Clandestine Network and the Purges," in Georgeon (ed.), *L'Ivresse de la liberté*, 109–120. In all these, the Unionist regime is at best defined as illiberal and autocratic, and at worst as fully dictatorial. In the former, the argument is supported with the escalation of violence, an overall curb on freedoms, and the carrying out of purges, intimidations and repressions following the events of 1909. The latter argument of the Committee of Union and Progress being fully dictatorial is frequently supported with the claim that it was a regime that systematically assassinated those who were its political opponents. Aside from secondary sources, there is a host of primary material that corroborates the view of an authoritarian regime, so defined by contemporary observers. The second consideration has to do with political views today. The imprint left by the Unionist regime, and its memory in history, is a matter of judgement according to political views, and is therefore debatable on either side.

1 The Ottoman Empire under Sultan Abdülhamit II

Background

In 1299, a Turkic splinter group of the *Oğuz* tribal confederation based in Central Asia occupied part of Anatolia and proclaimed it an independent *Beylik* (Principality); in a matter of 150-odd years, this spread North- and South-wards, and became a powerful empire, which, in 1453, took Constantinople and made it its capital. By the late seventeenth century, at its territorial apogee, the Ottoman Empire stretched North to South from the outskirts of Vienna to Yemen, and West to East from modern Algeria to Iraq. Its 'golden age', as it is usually regarded, which coincided with the beginning of its difficulties, may be identified with the daring move that was the second siege of Vienna in 1683. Defeat ensued, and the first peace agreement unfavourable to the Ottomans – the Treaty of Karlowitz – was signed in 1699: a sense that "something fundamental had changed"[1] spread around. Ottoman statesmen started comparing the unsatisfactory state of affairs of the Empire to past moments of difficulty and attempted to find a solution to this situation. Their response to try and improve the situation took very different shapes: first came a wave of defensive wars, aimed at tightening the Empire's grip on lands that, in one way or another, were falling out of control due to battles against local rebels and European invaders; then, the realisation that problems could not be halted by war alone brought about a more constructive reaction – reform – which took, yet again, a variety of shapes, and underwent several stages.

Probably the first document treating the issue of the need to reform the Ottoman Empire was a memorandum – the *Asafname* – written as far back as the mid-1500s by Lutfi Paşa, the Grand Vizier of Sultan Süleyman.[2] Referred to as "more than a Mirror of Ministers, of the kind common in Muslim literature since early times,"[3] it was directly concerned with the deterioration of a state that, because of its adhering to the principles of Islam, had hitherto been thought to be free from the danger of downfall. The publication of the memorandum triggered a wave of criticism at the administration of the state: some blamed the neglect of true Islamic principles from the governing elite, others appreciated that the Empire stood on pillars that belonged to an ideologically and politically by-gone age, and that the negative state of affairs could be reversed only by modernising it.

Actually, England, France and Russia, which, for political and economic ambitions, all had expansionist tendencies over the Empire, had devised techniques to stir up trouble in its dominions. One such technique consisted in instilling nationalistic tendencies in some ethnic and religious minorities,[4] and requesting reform, allegedly to relieve excessive pressure on, or mistreatment of, those minorities. The Great Powers' requests to reform the Empire were not genuinely directed at safeguarding the rights of its ethnic and religious components, nor at modernising it, and least of all at including the Ottomans into the world market as partners of equal status. Requesting reform on the part of the Great Powers was often nothing but a pretext to claim a right to intervene directly into Ottoman affairs either to make territorial gains (particularly in Russia's case), or to secure economic advantages (in the case of the European countries, Britain in particular), had their requests not been met.[5] In the case of Russia, for instance, it had tried to stir up rebellions in Greece during the temporary occupation of Morea in 1770, while, in 1797, Bonaparte's France had pushed his generals to foster ideas of independence throughout the Ionian Islands.[6] A further series of foreign-inspired upheavals and secessions followed in the nineteenth century, which led to the independence of Greece, to the Serbians pushing for autonomy in the 1830s, the Wallachians and Moldavians revolting in 1848 and acquiring autonomy in 1859, and the Romanians reaching independence in 1861. As to the insurrections of the 1870s in Bosnia, Herzegovina and Bulgaria, we know that Russia had worked towards stirring them for some time: "… il y a quinze ans que la Russie préparait cette insurrection."[7]

By the last quarter of the eighteenth century, almost all the major ethnicities of the Empire – Albanians, Arabs, Armenians, Bulgarians, Greeks, Kurds, Romanians, and Serbs – had expressed their grievances,[8] making the emergence of nationalisms a dramatic reality, a severe political blow, and a long-lasting challenge, which increased the Ottomans' already deep sense of insecurity and failure. When the nationalistic feelings of the Empire's minorities acquired a religious basis, the result was the shake-up of Ottoman society from its foundations: what was the meaning of an Ottoman sentiment of affiliation in a state that was slowly losing its non-Muslim sectors? The question represented an enormous challenge in political, social and ideological terms, one that assigned Ottoman reformers the task of re-shaping the term Ottomanism according to a new political and social definition. Considering that all attempts to reform thus far – the *Hatt-ı Şerif* of Gülhane of 1839, the *Islahat Fermanı* of 1856 and the Constitution of 1876 – were based on the assumption that a common affiliative sense of Ottomanism among all ethnic and religious groups that composed the Empire did exist, the task facing Ottoman reformers was an extremely difficult one indeed. If the often foreign-inspired challenge represented by emerging nationalisms was not enough of a problem for Ottoman reformers, there was another way in which the involvement of Europe and Russia with the Empire's internal affairs proved highly problematic; this related to economic matters, and caused the stratification of its populations in 'classes' created along religious lines. This is because Europe and Russia favoured Christian merchants and businessmen, particularly the Greeks, as trading partners:

> [t]rade is from the first almost entirely in their hands [the Greek minority]. Even where the capital is foreign, the practical working is to a great extent directed by Greeks. Soon the land, too, passes into their hands. Your village Turk is helpless and improvident. It is a point of honour with him to make a great show at a marriage. He borrows money ... then his ruin is speedy, and the land on whose security he has borrowed passes out of his possession.[9]

The concentration of trade in the hands of ethnic minorities brought to full fruition the situation created by the Capitulations of 1541 when, as part of an alliance between Sultan Süleyman I and Francis I of France:

> French merchants and other residents in the Ottoman state were given privileges ... which were later extended to other European states, and which had the effect of placing Europeans in the Ottoman state outside local jurisdiction.[10]

The essence of the Capitulations was not only that Europeans could operate their own courts and postal services within the Empire, but also that Ottomans were denied the right to use tariffs to protect their agricultural goods and the output of their emerging manufacturing sector; this had serious detrimental consequences, particularly for the Muslim Arabo-Turkish section of the Ottoman society:

> there is no peasant who is unhappier than the Turkish peasant. He suffers more than his Christian equivalent because of the situation whereby he is placed in an inferior position with regard to the latter and cannot rely on the protection of consuls, ambassadors and foreign governments.[11]

Moreover, when members of the minorities entered the bureaucracy, they attained advancement and promotion faster than the Muslims because of their knowledge of foreign customs and command of foreign languages, French in particular. Not surprisingly, the Christian middle-class that had emerged rapidly outdid the Turkish one: "[t]he Turkish-Muslim segment of society did not have a middle class (merchants, intellectuals, clergy) which could compete politically with the Christian one."[12] The moment the state itself suffered economic difficulties, due to an unfavourable balance of payments, things became even worse for the Muslims, who formed the bulk of the military and bureaucratic machines, because monthly pay was always late and frequently missed. This worsening of the economic situation of civil servants and bureaucrats reached the top of the pyramid, as indicated, for instance, by the fact that the foreign ministers' salaries fell drastically from the early 1860s to the mid-1890s from a peak of 75,000 kuruş to a low of 30,000 kuruş.[13]

In short, the multi-faceted nature of foreign involvement within the Empire benefited the non-Muslim sectors of society the most; its overall impact was to fragment it socially creating a gap constructed along confessional lines, and strangling the Muslim component economically as a nineteenth-century Ottoman reformer noted:

> Istanbul might well become orderly and prosperous like Paris or London, but 'we would not be the ones who would profit from or taste these delights ... Rather, we would turn up from time to time as sellers of firewood and charcoal and gaze at it sadly'. The question which haunted Muslim Turks was not whether the country would survive, but whether they would survive in it.[14]

Among the many difficulties facing Ottoman reformers was the fact that their Empire was lagging behind in specific areas: scientifically and technologically backwards when confronted with the West, the Empire was de facto in a position of perennial weakness vis-à-vis external challenges, and of inertia in answering internal demands for change aimed at its modernisation in political, economic and social terms.

Abdülhamit's way to look at reform

Abdülhamit II had come to the throne at a very critical time: European entanglement had reached its peak, the economic situation had worsened in unprecedented ways, and the Empire had never been socially so fragmented:

> [the] second half of the 1870s was one of the lowest points of the entire nineteenth century for the Ottomans, a fact evidenced especially in the government bankruptcy and the Russo-Turkish War, which brought the Russian army to the outskirts of Istanbul, flooded the city with refugees, and left the Ottoman government saddled with a huge indemnity.[15]

The Sultan was well aware of the fact that, to halt the apparent demise of the Empire, elements of modernity had to be introduced in it, and there is no doubt that, by the end of the 1870s, he was convinced of the necessity to reshape the structure of power, and the make-up of the society. Accordingly, he became an "avid reformer"[16] of the administrative system, and "a willing and active modernizer"[17] deeply engaged in the attempt to formulate a new discourse that would ensure the survival of the Empire. It would be simplistic, therefore, in analysing the history of the Ottoman Empire in the late nineteenth century, to assume that the Young Turk opposition movement expressed the only modernising force.

In terms of the weakening of the state, the Sultan identified three entities – some sectors of the religious establishment, the bureaucracy, and the foreign powers (Europe and Russia) – as primarily responsible for the worsening of the situation the Empire was in, particularly for shifting power away from the centre, and, consequently, creating new allegiances not embodied in the Ottoman Caliphal-Sultanic structure. He would have wished to go back to pre-*Tanzimat* times, as his close collaborator Grand Vizier Mahmut Nedim Paşa stated:[18]

> In the early days, when the sultans had personally tended to the affairs of government, and when the laws and regulations were kept within the bounds of the *şeri'at*, religious and communal zeal were real, and 'the union of hearts [that bound together] the sultanate and [the Muslim] community, as well as Ottoman power, increased day after day'. Moreover, when sultans managed the affairs of state themselves, Muslim power grew, the Janissary corps and the ulema were kept under control, and the interests of the state were kept apart from the private interests of its ministers.[19]

Abdülhamit's main recipe for improving matters was to further centralise power by incorporating the whole of the religious establishment in his own circle, decrease the autonomy of the bureaucracy,[20] and play foreign powers against each other in an attempt to turn their conflicting interests to his own benefit. The emphasis on centralised power to the detriment of local administrations is often indicated as an element of continuity in the reforming period of the Empire from the *Tanzimat* through to Abdülhamit's time; another, perhaps more interesting, element of continuity may be identified in the reformers' recurrent attempts at framing a new conception of Ottoman citizenry, although those attempts differed considerably over time.

In Abdülhamit's case, the new conception of Ottoman citizenry proposed, relied on instilling in the population a sense of tight affiliation to the state identified with his own *persona* as the Sultan, whose authority should be seen as the only legitimate one against newly created intermediary bodies such as parliament or representative councils, and as the Caliph entrusted with a sacred mission.[21] He thought that the key to bring about this new conception of Ottoman citizenry was Islam, to be used as a tool to unite all Muslims, upper and lower strata, irrespective of their ethnic identity. Abdülhamit set out to achieve this in different ways. Banners bearing the phrase '*Padişahım çok yaşa*' (Long live my Sultan) were circulated and affixed throughout the Empire, while he made sure to take part in the long, convoluted and sumptuous procession of the *Selamlık* – the Friday prayer. He intended to be seen by Ottomans and foreigners alike as powerful and as the pious ruler, so that everyone would be reminded of the might, effective and symbolic, of his office, but also of his God-given right to it.[22] Abdülhamit's public appearances at Friday prayers were thus aimed at reaffirming the central power by giving himself and his entourage visibility; however, this was limited to the population of Istanbul, the more affluent Ottomans, and the bureaucracy: other ways to enhance the Sultan's position by making his presence visible in the periphery had to be devised. Mosques and clock-towers 'signed' with the *tuğra* of the Sultan were erected all over the Empire, even in the most remote locations, to remind everybody of the Sultan's authority in connection with the religious sphere – through the mosques – and with the temporal and modern sphere – through the clock-towers which symbolised progress and celebrated the advancements of science.

In an attempt to penetrate with his own persona almost all aspects of everyday life, Abdülhamit had the Ottoman genealogical lineage – used to reinforce the sacred nature of the Sultan and the House of Osman – printed in the state almanacs, the *Salname*:[23]

> Such manifest official fiction was an ancient tradition in Islamic court panegyrics, but what is interesting here is that it should be featured in a state almanac which is a creation of bureaucratic modernization and features such mundane data as the names of the various ministers, agricultural produce, and main geographical features of the area.[24]

An important document in Abdülhamit's reforming endeavour was issued on 11th May 1879; it was in the form of a memorandum, probably written by the *Baş Kâtib* (the Chief Scribe) to describe the vast work towards the regeneration of the Empire the state had embarked on. The Sultan himself re-affirmed its contents in a private discussion with Sir Henry Layard, the British ambassador to the Ottoman Porte, who, in his turn, informed Lord Salisbury – the then Foreign Secretary – during a meeting on the 28th of the same month.[25] Among the various issues mentioned in the memorandum, emphasis was on the importance of tightening central control on representative bodies and provincial agencies,[26] while regulating those in terms of criteria for choosing and appointing officials in the ministries and provinces, moralising and making more responsible government officials, and, more generally, setting up the duties and limits of governmental bodies and functions in an unambiguous manner.

Reform of the educational system was another issue touched on in the memorandum, which Abdülhamit regarded as a necessary step to modernise Ottoman society and, mixing tradition with innovation in the process, turn education into an engine to bring about economic development. The spirit of his educational reform, which expanded widely the state-funded educational activity initiated during the *Tanzimat* period, consisted of inscribing the curriculum in a European-blueprinted framework, while keeping it predominantly Ottoman and Muslim in content.[27] Yet another initiative was the creation of an Academy of Sciences,[28] but the memorandum also promised the establishment of new schools, whether academic or vocational. Among those, *Ziraat Mektebi* (Agricultural School) and *Ticaret Mektebi* (Trade School) to be established in Istanbul and the provinces; industrial and veterinary schools to be set up in Istanbul; a law School and Imperial *Lycées* in Istanbul, Bursa, Kastamonu, Konya and Diyarbakır. In sum, Abdülhamit's reign marked the quantitative expansion of schools with the opening of "approximately 9147 primary schools, 219 middle schools, 104 secondary schools and 18 higher or professional schools,"[29] but education was ameliorated also qualitatively, in an effort to improve the training of future government officials so that they would administer the Empire well, and in a modern way, while safeguarding its characteristic features against foreign influences.[30] But the Sultan's reform faced problems: one consisted in the lack of competent instructors; a more serious one related to the penetration of spies in most schools,[31] who reported the presence of students dangerously propagating liberal ideas, which led to a u-turn in educational matters, aimed at controlling the youth and moulding it according to the new conception of Ottoman citizenry revolving around Abdülhamit's own *persona*.

Religion as propaganda

Abdülhamit was persuaded that a clever use of religion could work in three positive ways: reinforce his position in the eyes of the Ottoman Muslim population, strengthen the role of the Ottoman Sultan-Caliph as the rightful and most powerful Muslim ruler in the world, and use his influence on Muslims abroad to harass European powers in their Muslim colonies. Religious zeal, appearance at important religious functions, strict adherence and promotion of Hanefi Sunni Islam, and devotion to old traditions were part of a wider, far-reaching, strategy aimed to ensure that the Palace would regain legitimacy and prestige against alternative sources of power.

In the book, *Avec mon père le Sultan Abdulhamid*,[32] Aïché Osmanoglu (1887–1960) recalls the daily life and habits of her father, the Sultan. She mentions the importance he attributed to religious ceremonies, not just the Friday prayer, but also the festivities commemorating the birth of the Prophet. During the rituals at the *Hamidiye* mosque, processions were organised which ministers, troops and other important government officials had to attend. The aim of those processions was to show the importance the Sultan attributed to religion, while displaying his might, wealth, and proximity to his people:

> Il était obligatoire que la Sultane Mère, avec la première dame du palais, vînt à la prière du vendredi … De l'extérieur, venaient les sultanes mariées et les épouses des ministres … La présence des princes impériaux et des fils du souverain au défilé était une règle absolue, parce qu'ils devaient se trouver à la tête de leur régiment et saluer le souverain … Dés que la voiture de Papa apparaissait à la porte impériale du Palais, la marche

impériale retentissait, les trompettes sonnaient le salut, et les soldats saluaient d'un hourra ... le Cheikh-ul-Islam accueillait le souverain à la porte de la mosquée ... Les hadjis venus de l'extérieur, les musulmans venus du Yémen et d'Arabie étendaient des nattes de paille dans la cour de la mosquée et faisaient le prière en même temps que le souverain.[33]

Two attentive and insightful observers of the time, Andrew Ryan and Halil Halid, give similar accounts of the pomposity orchestrated by the Sultan for the *selamlık* procession. Ryan, who worked as a dragoman for the British government in the Ottoman Empire between 1899 and 1924, recalls in his autobiographical book that:

> the Friday *selamlik*, as it was called, was an elaborate ceremony, attended by many dignitaries and surrounded by an imposing military display, which served the double purpose of show and of protection for the person of a timorous ruler. I never saw him at this function without thinking how much power was vested in this remote personage.[34]

Halid, a scholar and diplomat who spent some time in Britain, mentions in his own biography that "the present sultan [Abdülhamit II] is much more careful than any of his immediate predecessors in fulfilling this obligation of going to the mosque on Fridays," and that during the processions "the troops of the first and second divisions of the army of the capital flood the neighbourhood of that mosque [the *Hamidiye*]."[35]

The ceremony associated with dispatching the annual procession to Mecca to commemorate the birth of the Prophet was another occasion to display and emphasise the piousness of the Sultan and of his entourage. It included the sending of the *Très Noble Coffre* and of the Noble *Mehmel* to the holy city of Mecca.[36] The *Mehmel* was brought to the palace in a procession – watched by thousands – headed by the Grand Eunuch, attended by women wearing the *oustoufas* (traditionally embroidered tissues) who made offerings of presents and money to relatives and acquaintances. The ceremony was intended to display the maximum degree of pomposity: "Le Noble Coffre, qui attendait à l'appartement du Grand Eunuque, était chargé sur un grand chameau tout chamarré ... Quand le coffre avait traversé le Bosphore, et atteint Uskudar, on faisait tonner le canon."[37]

This emblematic gesture, and all the show constructed around the Mecca procession, served the Sultan in the ways already mentioned; it also provided some entertainment for the people in Istanbul and for the pilgrims en route, and the opportunity for them to marvel at the magnificence of the Noble *Mehmel*, enhancing Abdülhamit's popularity in his double authority as Sultan-Caliph. But religion-related activities served also another purpose: that of positioning the Empire on the world stage in a two-fold manner. Firstly, reminding foreign governments that the Sultan was solidly in power, and had the population fully behind him, as the Friday prayers, attended by large crowds, showed. Secondly, enhancing his position among the Muslim rulers of other countries, who could, if they so wished, resort to Istanbul as the capital of the most powerful and territorially independent Muslim state for help against interference from the Great Powers. In this way, Abdülhamit hoped to encourage rebellions in the Muslim countries of Asia and Africa, which had fallen under the colonising sway of European powers.

Transport and communication

Another way in which Abdülhamit increased the power of the central government – whether intentionally, or as a by-product of his modernising efforts – was through the impetus he gave to improve transport, whether by road or railroad, and communication, whether by post or telegraph, all of which gave important results in terms of commerce, trade, and the circulation of ideas and information. This is because, prior to the bettering of the transport system, many crucial state functions (collecting taxes, running schools, and legal affairs) had, out of necessity, been devoluted to local governors who had become more and more influential as time went by.

The most important, ambitious, and expensive infrastructural work undertaken under Abdülhamit was the construction of the *Hicaz* Railway, which started in 1900, following the establishment of two *ad-hoc* commissions; by 1908, the railroad had reached Medina. Its total estimated cost was to be extremely high, and was to be accompanied (at a further cost) by the creation of an *ad-hoc* fleet entrusted with the defence of the coast of the province along the railroad. The sum involved was phenomenal, and raising it was extremely difficult especially as this grand project was to be solely an Ottoman Muslim venture, in line with the Sultan's policy to forbid foreigners, whether Muslim or not, from sending offerings to the holy cities of Mecca and Medina, and/or fund the construction of buildings or other infrastructures in the *Hicaz*, as the British consul in Jeddah in the early 1880s reported:

> a silver ladder for the door of the Ka'ba 'worth 45,000 rupees' sent by the Nawab of Rampur had been turned down because 'the Sultan ... objected to a foreign subject [making such gifts] and sent orders that no such a one should have the privilege ... All such gifts can only be made by the Exalted Personage of the Caliph who alone holds the august title of Protector of the Holy Places. No foreign ruler has the right to partake of this glory.[38]

The policy in question did not directly pertain to the religious sphere, but, keeping for himself the exclusiveness to charitable gifts and improvements in the holy area, Abdülhamit re-iterated his strategy of using the power of religious motivation to reinforce his own position and diminish that of any potential opponent, whether Ottoman or non-Ottoman Muslim, or non-Muslim. The Sultan made the first donation towards the construction of the

Hicaz Railway; his example was soon followed by the most affluent Ottoman politicians and bureaucrats who contributed generously. But, unless the difficulty created by Abdülhamit's policy to forbid non-Ottoman Muslims from making donations was by-passed, the moneys necessary for the work would not have been raised. A solution was found, whereby donations would be accepted, even if coming from non-Ottoman Muslims, as long as these were channelled through the commissions for the railway construction; actually, foreign donations were implicitly solicited when the project was presented as aimed to "protect the Hijaz from Christian threats," and, therefore, offered a service to all the Muslims of the world; hence, "present[ing] gifts for [its] realisation ... is to demonstrate the love for God and His Prophet."[39] Large sums of money came from Egypt, India and present-day Pakistan. So, in the end, the funds necessary for the project were gathered from contributions from three sources: private Ottoman autonomous donations, non-Ottoman Muslim donations, and three new taxes introduced for this special purpose: a poll tax on all male Muslim family heads, a special stamp tax, and a tax levied on every *haci* (pilgrim) who was not too poor, upon arrival at Jidda. Bearing in mind that, at the time, the Empire was often forced to resort to foreign lending for any activity that entailed large sums of money,[40] the *Hicaz* Railway was a miracle of a success. It came to be seen as "a symbol of an attempt to resist European control and influence," and represented "the epitome of the Hamidian method to achieve traditional goals and oppose Western values."[41] Hence, the construction of the *Hicaz* Railway turned out to be a tremendous achievement for Abdülhamit, and represents a considerable part of his legacy; but, initially, it must have represented a huge effort, almost a gamble, for the administration.[42] Yet, apart from improving communication, and showing the external world what the Empire could do, the Sultan had a further, serious, reason to embark on the railway project, which related to the fact that authority in the *vilayet* of the *Hicaz* was divided among the central government and the *emir* of Mecca, who, although chosen in Istanbul, was not necessarily submitted to the central government. In fact, it had happened several times that the *emir* was chosen because of his links to the Bedouin tribes, to ensure control of the area, especially in terms of pilgrims' safety, which the Ottoman military on its own was not always able to guarantee. Relying on keeping on good terms with the Bedouin tribes through the *emir* implied leasing out a degree of authority over certain sections of the territory, which created a rather fragile balance of power and stability that was a constant worry for Istanbul.

The construction of the *Hicaz* Railroad had the effect of increasing the visibility of the central authority with respect to the *emir* and the Bedouin tribes, re-balancing the power sharing between them, while allowing troops to move fast to the area, in case of need, for instance, to secure protection for the pilgrimage caravans. Last but not least, the construction of the *Hicaz* Railroad, difficult as it had been technically and financially, was the perfect way to re-assert the Sultan's sovereignty on Mecca and Medina as the *Hadim-ül haremeyn* (Protector of the Holy Places), in case any other Muslim ruler may consider attempting to overshadow his power. Abdülhamit's determination with regard to the railway project, which made possible its completion, testifies to his pragmatic approach, which enabled him to compromise on the question of donations from non-Ottoman Muslims. Regrettably, for him, and for the Empire, he would not be able to display the same degree of pragmatism whenever he felt threatened, which he always did when the opposition movement was somehow involved, or he believed it might be, with his reform attempts.

Abdülhamit and the internal opposition

Abdülhamit's attempts at reform revolved around his centralised view of power, inspired by his conviction that widening his citizens' individual liberties was secondary to defending the integrity and stability of the Empire, his conception (and use) of religion as a reminder of his role and importance as Sultan-Caliph, and his obsession with dispossessing of power all governmental agencies other than those directly emanating from the Palace, all of which testify to a conservative approach. However, his legacy is mixed, as some of the reforms he introduced were genuine attempts at catching up with Europe on modernity and technological advancements: "[He] expanded the educational system, made serious attempts to train the bureaucracy, instituted administrative controls, and paid closer attention to trade and crafts. All in all, he tried to promote material advances while conserving the established order."[43]

Given that the problems that haunted the Empire were structural, and sprung out of new political, social and economic realities – to which the Sultan's faith in saving the state through a revival of old traditional values could provide temporary improvements, at best – a new world-view, capable of bringing about a new conception of the state and the redistribution of power, was bound to arise, especially due to the widening and improvement of the education system and the expansion of communication, which made news travel faster. A variety of opposition groups gathered under the umbrella term of Young Turk movement had conceptualised, in various, sometimes mutually conflicting, ways, that new world-view. Those groups had come about also as a result of the cultural influence the West had exerted on increasingly larger sections of the Ottoman society particularly through the philosophical ideas and social and political movements of the eighteenth and nineteenth centuries. The Young Turk movement was antagonistic to the Sultan's conception of reform, had roots in the past while being projected towards the future, and was ready to engage in techniques seldom employed before. Its emergence represented the coming on the scene of a formidable enemy from within, which interfered with, and further complicated, Abdülhamit's reforming attempts. The very fact that members of the Young Turk movement had cultural and ideological links with the West, which inspired their liberal attitudes to individual freedom, represented a direct challenge to Abdülhamit's attempts at halting Western ideological influence. The fact that the movement combined demands for more freedom with strict adherence to the Ottomanist goal of keeping the Empire together by recalibrating the rules regulating the rights and duties of all the ethno-religious groups in it, was not enough to reassure Abdülhamit, nor was the conciliatory tone the movement initially used in addressing him. He remained deeply concerned by their requests to increase individual liberties, and the degree of autonomy of the non-Muslims, which, for him, constituted a direct threat to the integrity of the Empire:

> [t]he Arabs, Albanians, Jews, and Christians ... had aspirations and goals 'specific to their nation and race'; the Christians and Jews wanted to reach these goals by establishing free nations ... It was therefore essential to maintain the supremacy of the state in order to thwart the rise of ethnic and national consciousness among the various minority groups, to prevent individual freedom from undermining the integrity of the state, and to give the government time to raise the economic, cultural, and political level of the Muslims, particularly the Turks.[44]

To make his intentions crystal-clear, after the first two years on the throne, Abdülhamit took a harsh line to the opposition in political terms with the suspension of the Constitution, and in security terms with a series of waves of arrests. From then on, it was all-out war between him and the Young Turk movement; he portrayed its members as aiming at re-enacting the Western-influenced *Tanzimat* period, which, in his view, had brought the Empire into decay, and intent on achieving economic and social advancement for themselves; briefly, as ambitious cheats greedy for power, disguised as liberal and modern political activists.

The juxtaposition between the Sultan and the opposition movement could not have been more radical: for the former, the fortunes of the Empire should be revived using Pan-Islamism to hold it together around tradition; for the latter, the idealistic attraction of the Enlightenment, the French Revolution, but also the lure of British liberalism, created a wealth of options from which to choose in terms of regenerating the Empire, to be firmly kept within the political (and social) project represented by Ottomanism. However, as it often happens of the fiercest of enemies, Abdülhamit and the Young Turk movement shared some convictions; for instance, that Islam had been "open to progress and science,"[45] and, therefore, had brought about economic development, well-being, and made the Empire superior to the West for a good deal of time; similarly, both were convinced that in the last years, Islam had been left to stagnate, and that this had caused the decay of Ottoman lands.

In his almost desperate attempt to keep the Empire together in the face of structural difficulties of all sorts, and increasing interest in it on the part of the Great Powers, Abdülhamit vented his frustration on the opposition, escalating matters at great speed. Soon after the suspension of the

Constitution, scores of Young Turk members, following the example set decades earlier by the Young Ottomans, fled the Empire for Europe, Greece, Egypt, with the effect of internationalising their struggle, and making the Sultan's position even more precarious in the eyes of external observers. Although France and Britain were very cautious, and ambivalent, in their attitude to the Young Turk movement, for fear that the Empire would collapse too soon, and in ways they would not be able to control, the international image of the Empire suffered a great deal from Abdülhamit's persecution of his political enemies. More than anything else, the treatment of the opposition movement on Abdülhamid's part attracted and justified internal and external observers of the time, whether historians or political and social commentators, who, in the main, gave a totally negative assessment of his rule as backwards, despotic, traditionally Islamic, and staunchly opposed to changes and modernity. This remained the received view among Ottomans into the first decades of the twentieth century; in Republican Turkey, it became part of the Kemalist approach aimed at creating a definite break with the Empire seen as an entity from which it was paramount to get away, and be seen as doing so. Unlike the Greeks[46] and Arabs, who had reworked their respective roles, legacies and cultures in the Empire prior to entering the twentieth century, the Turks had to wait until the second half of the twentieth century to see a different evaluation of the Empire's history in general, and of Hamidian rule in particular, one that looks at the period through a new lens and fewer prejudices.[47]

European commentators of the late nineteenth and early twentieth centuries also gave a negative assessment of Abdülhamit's reign; this is not surprising if one accepts the premise that Europe had vested interests and was actively engaged in promoting the fall of the Empire, and would benefit from it. The perseverance of a totally negative picture of Abdülhamit's rule in the Western literature up until a few decades ago may be seen as the continuation of that cultural and political legacy. Recently, though, new scholarly approaches have emerged that contextualise the spreading of the opposition movements in the full understanding of their demands and grievances, but also Abdülhamit's rule, crediting it with making genuine, however limited in scope, attempts at regenerating the Empire.[48] Perhaps the most striking aspect of those reforming attempts is the degree to which they were affected by the Sultan's constant dread of the opposition movement, which, on the one hand, interfered with, and spoiled, those attempts,[49] and on the other hand, shaped and modified the opposition in ways Abdülhamit had not anticipated, which were contrary to his interests.

Notes

1 Justin McCarthy, *The Ottoman Peoples and the End of Empire* (London: Arnold, 2001), 9.

2 The *Asafname*, Book of Asaf, took its name from the biblical figure of King Solomon's loyal and honest minister.
3 Lewis, "Ottoman Observers of Ottoman Decline," 71.
4 In contrast with the Empire's minorities, the Turkish community started to conceptualise its nationalistic discourse only in the early twentieth century, for instance, with Yusuf Akçura's *Üç Tarz-ı Siyaset* (Ankara: Türk Tarih Kurumu Basımevi, 1976).
5 This explains why reforming the Empire was paramount from an Ottoman perspective as a means to take away a pretext for direct foreign intervention in its dominions.
6 Ercüment Kuran, "The Impact of the Turkish Elite in the Nineteenth Century," in William Polk and Richard Chambers (eds), *Beginnings of Modernisation in the Middle East* (Chicago, IL: University of Chicago Press, 1968), 109.
7 Louis Antoine Léouzon Le Duc, *La Turquie est-elle incapable de réformes?* (Paris: E. Dentu, 1876), 7.
8 Roderic Davison, "Nationalism as an Ottoman Problem and the Ottoman Response," in William Haddad and William Ochsenwald (eds), *Nationalism in a non National State – the Dissolution of the Ottoman Empire* (Columbus: Ohio State University, 1977), 25–26.
9 William Mitchell Ramsay, *Impressions of Turkey during Twelve Years' Wanderings* (London: Hodder & Stoughton, 1897), 131.
10 Andrew Mango, *Atatürk*, 8th edn (London: John Murray, 2004), 6. Recall that it was only in 1923, following the Lausanne Treaty, that the Capitulations were abolished.
11 Şerif A. Mardin, "Libertarian Movements in the Ottoman Empire 1878–1895," *The Middle East Journal* 16, no. 2 (1962), 173.
12 Kemal Karpat, "The Transformation of the Ottoman State 1789–1908," *International Journal of Middle East Studies* 3, no. 3 (1972), 249.
13 Carter V. Findley, "Economic Bases of Revolution and Repression in the Late Ottoman Empire," *Comparative Studies in Society and History* 28, no. 1 (1986), 85–86.
14 Mango, *Atatürk*, 22.
15 Findley, "Economic Bases of Revolution and Repression in the Late Ottoman Empire," 97.
16 Carter V. Findley, *Bureaucratic Reforms in the Ottoman Empire – The Sublime Porte 1789–1922* (Princeton, NJ: Princeton University Press, 1980), 227.
17 Lewis, *Emergence*, 174.
18 Appointed Grand Vizier at various times (from 1871 to 1872 and from 1875 to 1876), Mahmut Nedim Paşa (1818–1883) was a staunch opponent of the *Tanzimat* reforms, convinced as he was of the need of a strong and absolute sultanic rule as the only antidote to decline, and, thus, an admirer and supporter of Sultan Abdülhamit II.
19 Butrus Abu Manneh, "The Sultan and the Bureaucracy: The Anti-*Tanzimat* Concepts of Grand Vizier Mahmud Nedim Paşa," *International Journal of Middle East Studies* 22, no. 3 (1990), 262.
20 Part of this attempt was to take power away from the Porte and reinforce the Palace bureaucratic establishment, the *Mabeyn*. Tanvir Wasti, "The Last Chroniclers of the Mabeyn," *Middle Eastern Studies* 32, no. 2 (April 1996), 1–29.
21 Selim Deringil, "The Invention of Tradition as Public Image in the late Ottoman Empire, 1808–1908," *Comparative Studies in Society and History* 35, (1993), 3–29.
22 François Georgeon, *Abdulhamid II, Le sultan calife, 1876–1909* (Paris: Fayard, 2003).
23 The *Salname*, introduced after the *Tanzimat* period, was a yearbook in which all important events of a given year were listed; it covered all areas of the Empire:

Anatolia, Syria, Palestine, Iraq, the Arabian peninsula, Egypt, Libya, Tunisia, Thrace, Greece, Macedonia, Albania, Kosovo, Bosnia Herzegovina, Yugoslavia, Bulgaria, part of the Aegean Islands, and extended into the Eastern Black Sea. The *Salname* are an invaluable source of information on matters concerning history, geography, administrative structures and institutions; the most perfected ones, published between 1847 and 1922, included as detailed information as postal charges, departure/arrival times of steamers, plans of bridges, reproductions of banners, etc. Hasan Duman, *A Biography and Union Catalogue of Ottoman Yearbooks* (Ankara: Foundation for Information and Documentation Services, 2000), 19–20.

24 Selim Deringil, *The Well-Protected Domains: Ideology and the Legitimation of Power in the Ottoman Empire 1876–1909* (New York: I.B. Tauris, 1998), 27.
25 The memorandum is kept at the *Yıldız* collection, Stanford J. Shaw, "A Promise of Reform: Two Complimentary Documents," *International Journal of Middle East Studies* 4, no. 3 (July 1973), 359–365.
26 In general, the preparation of laws, the establishment of regulation and the organisation of committees were devoted to tightening central control over the state branches.
27 Fortna, *Imperial Classroom*.
28 In another memorandum of 1901, the Sultan wrote to his ministers denouncing "the sorry state of Islamic schools and *madrasas* compared to the much greater number and superior conditions of Christian churches and schools." Selim Deringil, "Legitimacy Structures in the Ottoman State: The Reign of Abdulhamid II (1876–1908)," *International Journal of Middle East Studies* 23 (1991), 347.
29 Elizabeth B. Frierson, "Unimagined Communities: Women and Education in the late Ottoman Empire, 1876–1909," *Critical Matrix, Princeton Journal of Women, Gender and Culture* 9, no. 2 (1995), 77.
30 Some aspects of Abdülhamit's educational reform survive to this day, as testified by the fact that the Gülen boarding schools share several, important features in common with the secondary schools created under Abdülhamit. Berna Turam, *Between Islam and the State: The Politics of Engagement* (Stanford, CA: Stanford University Press, 2007).
31 "Les professeurs espionnent les élèves et les élèves espionnent les professeurs. Les pions [sic] fouillent les pupitres dans le but de trouver des écus ou des livres dont les mots: liberté, justice, Arménie, Bulgarie, autonomie, constitution, etc., etc., n'ont pas, au préalable, reçu le biffage (sic) de la censure. La possession d'un bouquin condamné par la censure équivaut à cinq ans de bagne." Youssouf Fehmi, *Tablettes Révolutionnaires d'un Jeune Turc* (Paris: A. Michalon, 1903), 58.
32 Aïché Osmanoglu, *Avec mon père le Sultan Abdulhamid* (Paris: L'Harmattan, 1991).
33 Ibid., 85–86.
34 Andrew Ryan, *The Last of the Dragomans* (London: Geoffrey Bles, 1951), 29.
35 Halil Halid, *The Diary of a Turk* (London: Black, 1903), 171.
36 The *Mehmel* refers to palanquins sent by rulers with their caravans on the pilgrimage to Mecca. Sending one to the holy pilgrimage was not only a sign of piousness but also signified political standing and might.
37 Aïché Osmanoglu, *Avec mon père*, 91–92.
38 Deringil, *The Well-Protected Domains*, 57.
39 William Ochsenwald, *The Hijaz Railroad* (Charlottesville: University Press of Virginia, 1980), 70.
40 Cf. The Ottoman economic situation in the nineteenth century and the establishment of the Ottoman Public Debt Administration. See, for example, McCarthy, *The Ottoman Turks*, 308–314; Erik J. Zürcher, *Turkey – A Modern History*, 6th edn

(London: I.B. Tauris, 2004), 88–90; Donald C. Blaisdell, *European Financial Control in the Ottoman Empire* (New York: Columbia University Press, 1929).
41 Ochsenwald, *The Hijaz Railroad*, 1, 4.
42 Incidentally, the *Hicaz* Railway, as construction or administration of communication in Ottoman lands by Ottomans, or at least Muslims, and not by Europeans, represents yet another sign of continuity between Abdülhamit's reign and previous ones. A predecessor of this is, in fact, to be found in the 1850s: the founding of the *Şirket-i Hayriye*. This was a water-transport corporation founded in 1851, as a response to two foreign steamboat companies operating on the Bosporus. "All Ottoman citizens could buy its shares; and Ottoman citizenship was required of all employees with the exception of the engineers. The first shareholders were, nevertheless, the members of the ruling elite: among them were the Sultan himself, the *Valide* Sultan (the Sultan's mother), Grand Vizier Reşit Paşa, Minister of War Mehmet Ali Paşa, banker M. Camondo, and the mayors of Bursa, Aydın, and Silistre ... Immediately after its formation, foreign boats were prohibited from carrying passengers between Istanbul, Üsküdar, and the Asian and European sides of the Bosporus – the routes of Şirket-i Hayriye's first six boats ... The 1888 regulation, which remained in effect until 1919, outlined seven routes." Zeynep Çelik, *The Remaking of Istanbul: Portrait of an Ottoman City in the Nineteenth Century* (Seattle: University of Washington Press, 1986), 84.
43 Kemal Karpat, "The Mass Media, Turkey," in Richard Ward and Dankwart Rustow, *Political Modernisation in Japan and Turkey* (Princeton, NJ: Princeton University Press, 1964), 265–282.
44 Kemal Karpat, *The Politicization of Islam*, 2nd edn (New York: Oxford University Press, 2002), 176.
45 Ibid., 173.
46 Michael Herzfeld, *Ours Once More: Folklore, Ideology, and the Making of Modern Greece* (Austin: University of Texas Press, 1982).
47 See, for instance, Deringil, *The Well-Protected Domains*; Engin Akarlı and Gabriel Den-Dor (eds), *Political Participation in Turkey: Historical Background and Present Problems* (Istanbul: Boğaziçi University Press, 1974); Kemal Karpat, "The Transformation of the Ottoman State, 1789–1908," 243–281.
48 See, for instance, Benjamin Fortna, *Imperial Classroom*; Frierson, "Unimagined Communities"; Roderic Davison (ed.), *Essays in Ottoman and Turkish History, 1774–1923: The Impact of the West* (Austin: University of Texas Press, 1990); Findley, *Bureaucratic Reform*; and Justin McCarthy, *The Ottoman Peoples and the End of Empire*.
49 As in the case of his filling the most prestigious schools of the Empire with spies to detect any anti-governmental activity that might be going on.

2 Young Turk émigrés, the press and the Parisian *milieu*

Early days

The Military Medical College in *Gülhane* was the birthplace of the first nucleus of organised opposition to the Sultan, which would soon develop into the Young Turk movement; its founding members were four students coming from different areas of the Empire: İbrahim Temo (1865–1939), an Albanian from Macedonia, İshak Sükûti (1868–1903), a Jew born in Diyarbakır, Mehmet Reşit (1873–1919) from the Caucasus, and Abdullah Cevdet (1869–1932) of Kurdish origin. The date of their first meeting was 2nd July 1889.[1]

Temo's memoirs provide an account of their first meeting, in the form of a conversation with İshak Sükûti during recess, which appears to have been very informal, almost accidental:

ME: Come, friend, let me share my thoughts with you a little. We all know that with its present condition and manner of administration, the beloved *vatan* (fatherland) will perish and vanish. Regarding this matter, all the time, nearly all of our free hours, we continuously express our grievances to one another; alas, we are unable to think of or discover a remedy to eliminate this danger. I think that instead of whining with these dry thoughts and occupations, it is necessary we switch to action.

İSHAK: What type of action?

ME: By working in the form of a society.

İSHAK: That's well and good, but, who do you think we can trust to undertake such a dangerous enterprise?!

ME: First of all, you, one; pointing at Mehmet Reşid (scarface, who, having exited the dormitory, was heading towards us), and this is two; we are now three. Behold, it means a society has commenced!

Signalling Mehmet Reşid, we called him over. We told him our thoughts. Meanwhile, when Abdullah Cevdet, who at the time was very devout, exited the school's mosque having completed his afternoon prayer and came up to us: and there you have the fourth, I said … Four hands united. This initial contractual pact was made on a coincidental day of May 1305 (1889) and the society was established.[2]

The name given to the newly founded society was *İttihad-ı Osmani Cemiyeti* (Ottoman Union Society). More details on the participants, and on the profile of prospective members, are in Temo's memoir:

> This was the first meeting of the society and it was composed of these people: one of the then high court civil servants Hersekli Ali Ruşdi, one of the newspaper writers, İzmirli Ali Şefik, medical student Asaf Derviş (Paşa) (university professor and *mamoş*), Muharrem Girid (lecturer at Damascus Faculty of Medicine), Dr. Abdullah Cevdet, İshak Sükûti, Şerafeddin Mağmumi, Çerkes Mehmed Reşid (the one who committed suicide), me and three more individuals whose names I cannot remember.
> ... due to his being the eldest and a hoca, [Hersekli] Ali Ruşdi Efendi [was appointed] chief, Şerafeddin [Mağmumi] secretary of minutes, Asaf Derviş treasurer. As for me, I became head of the 1/1 series of the sequence of numbers that would be used.
> On this first meeting of this national and secret society we knew that some decisions were to be taken and especially that the course of events [would lead to] discussion about who we were to accept into this national [and] secret society ... rather cautiously and [after] going through all sorts of trials, we reached the point of view that every Ottoman who is able and trustworthy could be accepted.[3]

Initially, and for a number of years, the *İttihad-ı Osmani Cemiyeti* grew slowly, expanding mainly in other schools such as, for instance, the Military Academy of Pangaltı, the Veterinary School, the Civil College, the Naval Academy and the Artillery and Engineering Schools. Following the clandestine circulation of a programmatic brochure in 1894, the Society started expanding broadly, reaching even some functionaries of the Porte and the administration.[4]

A member of the society, Dr Selânikli Nâzım (1870–1926), was sent to Paris to invite Ahmet Rıza, then the most representative person there, to join the society and head its first branch abroad; Rıza accepted on condition the society be re-named as *Nizam ve Terakki* – a translation of Auguste Comte's motto *Ordre et Progrès* – to reflect his commitment to positivism. Eventually, and not without heated discussion, the name chosen was *Osmanlı İttihad ve Terakki Cemiyeti* (Ottoman Committee of Union and Progress, CUP).

Intellectual predecessors and allies

One of the first channels of transmission of progressive ideas to the CUP was the Translation Office, *Bab-ı Âli Tercüme Odası*, established within the Foreign Ministry in 1833 under Sultan Mahmut II.[5] Referred to by some as "a literary club;"[6] this Office "[b]ecame the training ground for Ottoman diplomats, and also for the new intelligentsia who played a major role in ideological developments during the nineteenth century."[7] Some of the most influential reformists of the time worked at the *Tercüme Odası*: from men of the Tanzimat, such as Ali Fuad (1814–1869), to Mithat Paşa (1822–1884); from Young Ottomans, such as Namık Kemal (1840–1888), to Young Turks, such as Murat Bey (1854–1917).[8] The Office gradually increased in prestige and, by 1871, it had acquired as high an importance as the *Chef de Protocole* and the Secretary for Foreign Affairs, second only to the Foreign Minister. Among the various people and groups that passed through the Translation Office, the Young Ottomans had a remarkable influence on the Young Turk movement:

> [t]he name 'Jeune Turc' was also used at the time of the Young Ottoman movement, of which even the members applied the term to themselves when writing in French. The application of the term to the activists of the Committee of Union and Progress (*İttihad ve Terakki Cemiyeti*) and its various offshoots thus signifies, not the recognition of some difference between the Young Turks and the earlier movement, but rather the opposite.[9]

Notably, *Mechveret*, the fortnightly journal Rıza founded in Paris in 1895, explicitly mentioned Cairo born Young Ottoman Mustafa Fazıl Paşa (1829–75) as "chef du parti de la Jeune Turquie,"[10] and praised him in connection with Namık Kemal:

> [Mustafa Fazil] ... grand homme d'Etat qui, en Turquie, contribua largement à la diffusion de l'instruction, au développement des idées libérales en envoyant à Paris et à Londres, soit des étudiants, soit des administrateurs et des poètes tels que l'illustre Kémal, et en créant le parti de la Jeune-Turquie dont nous sommes aujourd'hui si fiers de porter le nom.[11]

Mechveret also praised Mithat Paşa,[12] particularly for his contribution to the Constitution of 1876 – which the Young Turk movement regarded as a pillar in the development of the political opposition to Abdülhamit II. Mithat Paşa held a number of official posts, as member of state councils, provincial governor and twice grand vizier, and travelled to Europe, to Vienna, Paris, London and Brussels.[13] He was also the drafter of the 1864 *Vilayet* Law and, when appointed governor of the *Tuna* (Danube) province, he oversaw the construction of extensive public works there.[14] His greatest achievement, however, was the approval and adoption of the Constitution by Abdülhamit, the sultan-to-be.[15] This was, in the eyes of the Young Turk members, Mithat's greatest legacy to a modern and reformed Empire. Mithat was revered in the Young Turk movement for his general ideas of reformism, "Ottoman patriotism and suppression of separatism, but just treatment of minorities within the Ottoman framework, and for absolute honesty."[16] Young Turks were also inspired by Mithat for his view that nations should be built on territorial basis rather than on religious creeds, that checks and balances should be imposed on governments to guarantee the well-being of the population, and that citizens should become more than the mere recipients of decisions taken, allegedly on their behalf, at higher levels.[17] The English supplement to the *Osmanlı* (Ottoman), the influential journal edited by Cevdet (which would later be influenced by Sabahattin), also praised Mithat: "[t]he spirit of the noble Mithat Pasha inspires all true Mussulmans, 'the Constitution' is not dead, it sleeps, but it will arise the stronger from its sleep, to become a living fact in a regenerated empire,"[18] and presented his exile and assassination as evidence of the Sultan's treachery and unwillingness to compromise.[19]

Among Western philosophical ideas, those that most attracted Young Turk members were the same that had inspired the French Revolution and positivism; accordingly, the ideas of liberty, equality and nationality, reconciled with Islam, featured prominently in the proto-nationalist ideology of Ottomanism. The idea of liberty required the creation of a representative government and the adherence to the rule of law;[20] equality required that all citizens of the Ottoman state, regardless of religion and ethnicity, should be treated in the same way; and nationality required that the rights granted by citizenship in Istanbul should be extended to all provinces, so that the centre and the periphery of the Empire should be on a level-plane.[21]

Besides intellectual heritages from the past, the Young Turk movement benefited from the patronage, both logistic and ideological, of other organisations, most notably, of Freemasonry. This, through the lodge system, provided the movement with the blueprint for an organisational structure capable of fostering the circulation of the Ottomanist project as broadly as possible, while channelling the transmission of Western political ideas,[22] and facilitating the efforts of Young Turk émigrés to join European intellectual circles.[23] The CUP also adopted from the *Carbonaro*-Freemasonry organisations the practice of secrecy, hierarchical structure, and the limited knowledge of the identity of the lodges' members. It has also been postulated that Freemasonry helped spread socialist and internationalist ideas within the Young Turk movement.[24] Evidence of the close links existing between the Young Turk movement and Freemasonry comes from Cléanthi Scalieri, an Istanbul-born Greek banker who, in 1865, joined the French Masonic lodge *L'Union d'Orient*. He actively supported the anti-Abdülhamit campaign,[25] and contributed to efforts to bring back Sultan Murat V, who, apparently, had been initiated to the Freemason lodge of *Italia Risorta*, in Scalieri's presence.[26] In the mid-1870s, Scalieri founded the lodge known as the *Envâr-ı Şarkiye* (Lights of the East),[27] and was an influential member of two more lodges, the French *Union d'Orient*, and the Greek *I Proodos* (Progress).

Freemasonry became more established in the Empire between 1863 and 1874, under the leadership of French lawyer Louis Amiable (1837–1896), who opened membership rights to the Turkish component of the Empire, and translated the Masonic regulations and rites into Ottoman, widening the appeal of Freemasonry to intellectuals, high officials, army officers and statesmen interested in the circulation of liberal ideas, who had been discouraged from joining it by the lack of Turco-Muslim participation in it. The effect of the inclusionary move Amiable introduced was almost immediate: between 1865 and 1869 Turkish membership in Masonic organisations in Istanbul rose drastically, going from a low of three to a high of 53 members. The new members were mostly intellectuals from circles close to the Sultan, "Ottoman high officials, army pashas and statesmen"[28] interested in the introduction of liberal laws into the Empire. Around the same time, in the late 1860s, Istanbul witnessed a boom not only in membership, but also in the number of lodges. According to Dumont:

> there were about 15 lodges in the Imperial capital, all connected to various European orders. Four were dependent on the Great Lodge of England, four others on the *Grand Orient* of France, at least five on the *Grande Oriente* of Italy, one on the German Great Lodge of Hamburg, one on the Great Lodge of Ireland, and one or two on the *Meghali Anatoli* of Greece.[29]

Notably, with the advent to power of Sultan Abdülhamit II, the Freemason lodges in the Empire came close to disappearing due to a clampdown, while remaining in communication with Ottoman émigrés.[30] It is unclear whether Rıza became a member or not; Dumont states that this was the case,[31] while Hanioğlu doubts it, on account of Rıza's positivist leanings.[32] Whatever the case, in 1892 Rıza acknowledged that "la Franc-Maçonnerie a joué un rôle positif dans la lutte contre le cléricalisme et pour la liberté de conscience."[33] The Freemasons also provided Young Turks with protection in safe houses, and economic help to sustain their publishing endeavours and to fund trips to Europe for advocacy and fundraising purposes.[34]

Besides the Freemasons, Young Turk members found allies in their struggle against the Sultan also in some religious quarters – both among the ulema and the Sufi orders – though the nature and ultimate motives for their mutual involvement are not fully clear. The controversial point relates, in the main, to whether the convergence between the Young Turk and the religious establishment was genuine, or merely strategic. Some evidence suggests that some influential ulema and many Islamic students had supported the efforts of the Young Ottomans and greeted the promulgation of the First Constitution in 1876 with enthusiasm:

> Chakir Effendi, one of its [the Constitution] warmest partisans, was one of the most learned, distinguished and highly esteemed Ulema at Constantinople; it was he who headed a deputation of Ulemas and doctors of the law, to congratulate Midhat immediately after the ceremony of promulgation was over. The most enthusiastic champions of both Midhat and the Constitution were the Softas, or body of students, numbering several thousands, of all the *medreses* ... in Constantinople, the future generation of the educated mind of the nation.[35]

There is also evidence that the religious establishment became deeply involved with the CUP:

> Les Softas ... faisaient fonction de boucs émissaires du parti libéral au temps de Midhat-Pacha. Aujourd'hui ils se sont enrôlés dans les cadres mêmes du parti libéral. Ils ont leurs places entre l'élite de la nation et les convertis aux idées nouvelles. Ils peuvent être très utilement employés, car ils trouvent auprès des masses plus de crédit que personne.[36]

In his influential book *Young Turks in Opposition*, Hanioğlu disputes any connection other than strategic between the religious establishment and the Young Turk movement because of the latter's conception of religion "as an obstacle to progress," and recalls that some religious exponents had sided with the opposition to the Sultan "even before the overt activities of the CUP had begun."[37] However, in his memoir, Temo described Abdullah Cevdet as being "at the time [1889] very devout."[38] Moreover, Rıza's writings,[39] and Halil Ganem's first-hand historiographic work,[40] provide grounds for reconciling the two pictures of the relationship between Young Turks and members of the religious establishment – one identifying a real convergence between the two, the other assuming the convergence to be only strategic. This is because "there was also something of a religious revival in the Young Turk period, which found expression in a number of influential magazines and books;"[41] Rıza, for instance, would make clear that his criticism of the religious establishment was limited to the ulema, who, acting as "une corporation de théologiens généralement ignorants, paresseux et réactionnaires,"[42] and, representing a corrupted version of Islam, had colluded with the Sultan and consolidated his power while receiving his gratitude and protection in exchange.

As for the Sufi orders, the struggle for power between Young Turks and the Sultan, combined with the latter's treatment of Sufism and his attempts to introducing Pan-Islamism,[43] had split them in two groups: the orthodox orders, often under Arab leaders, supported the Sultan, while the heterodox orders sided with the opposition movement. However, even within each order, some sided with the Young Turk movement, some others with the Sultan. Among the heterodox orders were the Melamis and Bektaşi; some from the Bektaşi dervishes, influenced by Voltaire's writings, had reached a position nearing "a definitely materialistic atheism,"[44] and, therefore, were not put off by the religiously reformed approach that many Young Turks advocated; furthermore, many of them had become freemasons, as many Young Turks had done.[45] However, given that the Bektaşi order was ambitious and power-seeking,[46] it is possible that support for the Young Turk cause was, at least in part, inspired by the desire to join the winning side in the power struggle that raged through the Empire:

The Bektashi undoubtedly aimed at an ultimate religious supremacy in the countries touched by their propaganda. At the time of the Turkish revolution they had still hopes of a Bektashi state in Albania. Such a religious supremacy could hope to hold its own if supported by a sympathetic civil power.[47]

Exile as a necessity

As it will be discussed in detail further on, exile in Europe was both practical and formative for figures such as Rıza and Sabahattin: it provided political links with either Western government or civil society, and, at the same time, contacts with the European intelligentsia, which heavily influenced the intellectual development of the members of the organisation. This dynamic is not unique to Ottoman intellectuals but needs to be seen in the wider context of the attempts of Muslim intellectuals to reconcile technology, science and the idea modernity with religious and cultural realities. In this sense, the efforts of Rıza and Sabahattin can be seen as part of an intellectual wave consisting of a variety of actors. In 1826, Rifa`a Badawi Rafi al-Tahtawi (1801–1873) went to Paris and came back with a fully articulated argument about the compatibility between science and Islam.[48] In his writings, al-Tahtawi underlined the importance of justice and the protection of the poor from abuse – both from the French constitutional charter of 1814 – and admired the fairness of the French tax system. Moreover, he also argued that these principles can be found in Islam and that the goal of people should be,

> … adhering to shari`a; promoting science and knowledge; advancing agriculture, commerce and industry; and discovering the countries that can help achieve all this, inventing machines and equipment that facilitate the path to civilisation by providing the ways and means. Printing houses, for example, assisted education and learning, which are among the pillars of civilisation.[49]

Al-Tahtawi is not the only example of the trend to reconcile Islam with science and modern political ideas. In 1870, after having left the *Tercüme Odası* and having been in Europe for some time – where he published the journal *Hürriyet* (Freedom) and admired some aspects of progress,[50] Namık Kemal returned to the Ottoman Empire. Once back, he started advocating the importance of constitutionalism, the principles of which, according to him, were to be found in Islam. The powers of the ruler, he argued, resulted from the authorisation to rule granted to him by the umma and the justice of the state could only be maintained by consultation. Within this framework, everyone should have the right to scrutinise and criticise the government, both verbally and in writing, "given that sovereignty belongs to the people."[51] Moreover, the idea of consultation itself was to provide the maintenance of the cultural and religious heterogeneity of the Ottoman Empire, by creating and upholding the existence of provincial councils which were to deal with community affairs.

Similarly to what Namık Kemal was arguing, Jamal ad-Din al-Afghani (1838–1897), while speaking in Istanbul, in front of the *Darülfünun*, highlighted the necessity for education to be revived and sciences learned[52] as well as for the Muslim world to follow the example of the West on modernisation: "[M]y brothers, are we not going to take an example from the civilized nations? Let us cast a glance at the achievements of others. By effort they have achieved the final degree of knowledge and the peak of elevation."[53] It was acceptable, in al-Afghani's eyes, to take inspiration from the West in terms of scientific discoveries and knowledge as science itself, he remarked, does not belong to one civilisation: "… this true ruler, which is science, is continually changing capitals. Sometimes it has moved from East to West, and other times from West to East."[54] However, his remarks did not end at the appreciation of science but extended to the pivotal role that philosophy would play for the development of a modern society, in his case Islamic philosophy, as well as the necessity to expand and reform industry, commerce and agriculture.

All in all, Rıza and Sabahattin's discussion sounded very similar to those of al-Tahtawi, al-Afghani and Kemal: the idea of looking at the West as an example of technological society, the upholding of the importance of constitutionalism, expressed in the West but found also in Ottoman and Islamic precedents, and the utmost emphasis that should be given to the development of agriculture, commerce and industry were among the foundations of Young Turk ideology. Therefore, the development of Rıza and Sabahattin's ideas are to be seen as an integral part of a broader process whereby different actors were aspiring to transform the make-up of Muslim societies and, specifically in their case, attempting to answer the haunting question 'How can the state be saved?' In the case of Rıza and Sabahattin, voluntary, long-term exile was chosen as the means to be able to observe, discuss and synthesise all of the above. Exile, moreover, provided the chance to articulate a different version of Ottomanism, as proto-nationalism, to that of the *Tanzimat* period. The Ottomanism of the Young Turk in exile, precisely because formulated abroad, had the advantage of first-hand experience and deeper contact with the outside world, compared to the Ottomanism of the men of the *Tanzimat*. In this, too, Young Turk experience is not without comparison. Similarly, both Armenian and Algerian exiles, by the fact of being abroad and through the publication of journals, occupied a space that was instrumental in developing a new idea of Armenia and Algeria, respectively. Closer to the workings of the Young Turk émigrés, Armenians in exile, from the 1890s, contributed to turning a discourse of nationalism that "at first was no more than nostalgia for the country of their origins and the certainty that it existed,"[55] to an idea of the nation and its people, and this was the result of the development of the thought of intellectuals brought up in contact with the West. Central to the ideas of the Armenian organisations in exile in Europe, moreover, was the belief in equality among individuals and among nations,[56] a familiar thought of positivism, which so deeply inspired Rıza. In the case of the Algerian groups in exile at the beginning of the twentieth century, in France, two striking similarities emerge with the Young Turk experience. First was the idea of elitism, according to which the masses were not capable of understanding their predicament and needed to be awakened by an enlightened elite.[57] Second, and equally unfortunate for Algerians and Young Turks, was the fact that the attempts of both groups were short-lived and unsuccessful. However, both experiences represent a watershed in the sense that, as in the Young Turk case, the Algerian one constituted a "new, modernist and reformist expression of Islam and the nation. And, despite their apparent failure, they constitute a link across the century."[58]

In the case of the Young Turk movement, by 1895, the CUP had established its central branch in Istanbul and two external branches, one in Paris, one in Cairo. The following year, a wave of arrests led many Young Turk members to choose voluntary exile, altering the composition of the Istanbul branch from consisting mainly of students, to being controlled by high-ranking bureaucrats from various ministries, the military, and some ulema, all of whom were men of action. Following the change in leadership in the Istanbul branch, the Paris branch, which, under Rıza's leadership had become a meeting point of intellectuals, became the target of severe criticism, accused of being bent towards theoretical elaboration of little or no practical impact, and too involved with the positivist circle.[59] Its mouthpiece, *Mechveret*, until then regarded as the official organ of the Young Turk movement abroad, came to be challenged by *Mizan* (Balance), the weekly paper launched by Murat Bey in 1895.[60] In a reaction to the 'idle' stance of the Paris branch, in the summer of 1896, the Istanbul branch started working on a plan to assassinate Sultan Abdülhamit II. *Mizan* endorsed the plan, even if it required help and involvement from foreign countries to succeed, while the Paris branch opposed it in principle, due to Rıza's and Ganem's common position against the use of violence for political aims.[61] To resolve the impasse, a meeting was organised in mid-November 1896, which resulted in Rıza being demoted from being the head of the Paris branch, and *Mizan* replacing *Mechveret* as the mouthpiece of the CUP:

> Ahmed Rıza, who entered the meeting as leader of the movement, departed as editor of *Mechveret Supplément Français* on the condition that each issue be subject to the review and control of a board ... then it was determined that only *Mizan* would represent the CUP as its central organ.[62]

The planned coup went ahead and, in late 1896, it was about to be executed. Using his strong network of spies and secret police, the Sultan discovered it, as well as the recent foundation of two committees at the Military School of Pangaltı, the 'Committee Hüseyin Avni' and the 'Committee Süleyman

Paşa'.[63] A wave of arrests followed, which left the Istanbul branch in tatters, and spread demoralisation among the movement's sympathisers. Having realised the prominence Murat had reached in the movement, in August 1897, the Sultan came up with a coup de théâtre: the promise made to Murat through one of his representatives to go ahead with reform and grant full amnesty to Young Turks in jail, and safe return to those in exile, in exchange for the cessation of hostility in the Empire, and of the negative propaganda abroad. The Sultan's move was clever, in that, if his requests had been met, his position would be strengthened internally, and pressure from foreign governments and public opinion would be alleviated. It also proved to be a successful one: the Cairo branch, inspired by *Mizancı* Murat's articles, blindly drove itself into Abdülhamit II's hands:

> [t]he most devastating blow of all fell without warning: the Young Turks of Europe, with one or two notable exceptions, suddenly gave up the struggle against Abdul Hamid. Some of them, led by the idol of the society, Murat Bey, even trooped back to the shores of the Bosphorus to kiss the feet of the man for whom their vocabularies of vilification had only the day before been stretched to the utmost.[64]

Those who returned to the Empire met with different fortunes: some were received as heroes and offered important jobs,[65] while others were imprisoned or sent to confinement in remote locations. Allegedly, the different treatments received by Young Turks who gave themselves up after the amnesty related exclusively to their willingness (and capacity) to provide the Palace with useful information:

> Tous les Jeunes Turcs qui rentreront à Constantinople seront conduits au Palais dans le fameux cabinet du chambellan Tahir-bey. Celui-ci sommera les Jeunes Turcs de faire des révélations sur les affaires du Comité central. Ceux qui consentirons à trahir leurs frères seront immédiatement présentés à S. M. le sultan et seront comblés de grâces. Quant à ces qui n'auront aucune indication précieuse à donner, ceux-là seront envoyés de mission en mission jusqu'aux bagnes tripolitains. Cette décision a été prise officiellement par le grand-vizir, et a été communiquée par circulaire confidentielle à tous les gouverneurs des provinces. Voici les procédés Turc. Nous conseillons aux jeunes turcs de réfléchir avant de s'embarquer.[66]

With the Istanbul and Cairo branches reduced to almost nothing, the Paris one appeared on the verge of dissolution, with Rıza torn between dedicating himself to philosophy, or staying, as he put it, "sur le champ de bataille, à la tête de la lutte;"[67] the Sultan seemed to have come out of the struggle with the CUP the winner.

In 1899, however, the flight to Paris of *Damat* Mahmut Paşa (1853–1903)[68] with his two sons Mehmet Sabahattin and Lutfullah, changed matters. Being an influential figure of the establishment, his defection was a considerable blow to the Sultan and strengthened the Young Turk movement in the eyes of European governments. The arrival of Mahmut Paşa and his sons gave the Paris branch a new lease on life, making it look as if the much sought-after unity in the movement was, at last, within reach; influential figures, who had kept at a distance, or had lost hope that the movement would achieve tangible results – among them, Ali Haydar Mithat, the son of Mithat Paşa, and İsmail Kemal (1844–1919), then governor of Tripoli in Lebanon – joined the organisation.

The Ottoman press

Among the scientific and technological achievements of the late twentieth century, the introduction of the printing press played a major role in influencing developments in the Empire. The circulation of newspapers, magazines, and journals, facilitated by the creation of a postal system in the Empire in the 1830s, created a community of interested readers and gave them new opportunities to form an opinion in relation to events occurring in the public and political spheres. In this way, the audience for the confrontation between the ruling powers and their opponents was vastly enlarged, enabling dissenting voices to turn issues the establishment presented as marginal and individualistic into communal, and in some cases transnational, conversations.[69]

The first newspaper in Ottoman and Arabic was published in Egypt in 1828; its editor was Mehmet Ali Paşa (1769–1849), the *vali* since 1805. His initiative "encouraged [Sultan] Mahmud to undertake a similar project,"[70] the *Takvim-i Vekayi* (Calendar of Events), the Ottoman edition of the first official Ottoman paper, *Le Moniteur Ottoman* published in Izmir in French, began publication in 1831. Its goal was the promotion of the reforms undertaken in the Empire under the modernising sway of the *Bâb-ı Ali*; it remained the only paper in Ottoman until 1840. By 1851, upon the government's encouragement, a number of official newspapers and journals in different languages had been launched throughout the Empire: two were in Ottoman, four in French, four in Italian, and one, respectively, in Greek, Armenian, and Bulgarian.[71] Three years later, the annual circulation of these papers was estimated to be between 100,000 and 150,000 copies.[72] The impetus to publish continued under Abdülaziz's reign (1861–1876); it was under him, in the 1860s, that İbrahim Şinasi's *Tercüman-ı Ahval*,[73] the "first newspaper of opinion in the real sense,"[74] started publication. From then on, the output of the Ottoman press increased exponentially: in the provinces, newspapers were published in Ottoman and in the local languages; some became privately owned and featured criticism of the Sultan's policies and governance. *İbret*, the newspaper Namık Kemal founded in Istanbul in 1872, deserves special mention as the most influential of the time, and as the most outspoken critic of the *Tanzimat* reforms, under Kemal's short-lived editorship.[75] Other influential papers were *Tercüman-ı Hakikat* (the Interpreter of Truth), *İkdam* (Effort), *Sabah*

(Morning), and *Muhbir* (Informer) edited by Ali Suavi Efendi, published first in Istanbul, then in London. *İkdam*, founded in 1894 by Ahmet Cevdet (who would later become editor of the *Sabah*),[76] soon became the most popular newspaper in Istanbul with a circulation of 15,000.[77]

The spreading of the press in the 1860s and early 1870s contributed significantly to the emergence of an intellectual life throughout the Empire that was open to Western influences but in line with of Ottoman values; interestingly, it combined together culture and politics, attributing intellectuals the task of enlightening the people. Accordingly, the Ottoman press relentlessly insisted that government officials owed their loyalty to the people, not to their ruler, and that the promulgation of a constitution would resolve most of the Empire's problems, engaging its readers in discussions concerning citizens' obligations and rights, which could not arbitrarily be taken away.

By the time of Abdülhamit II's accession to the throne, in 1876, the Sultan found a press that felt entitled and empowered enough to articulate a harsh political critique:

> The *Vakit* (Time) stated on every occasion that the real sovereignty rested with the people and that they could depose their Sultan whenever they chose to do so. The *Istikbal* (Future) reminded the people again and again that the constitution was not a gift of the sovereign, but was obtained by a group of patriots after a hard struggle.[78]

In early 1876, there were at least forty-three papers in various languages published in Istanbul alone; four were in French, one in German, one in Italian, and one in English. When Abdülhamit came to power, the number of newspapers published in Istanbul had increased to forty-seven; of those, thirteen were in Ottoman, one in Arabic, nine in Greek, three in Bulgarian, nine in Armenian, two in Hebrew, two in French and English, and one in German.[79]

Exile as an opportunity

The press

The first two years of Abdülhamit II's reign gave the press some leniency; however, in 1878, Parliament was closed, the Constitution indefinitely prorogued, and a tough regime of censorship imposed, allegedly to "educate writers to write in the proper way,"[80] in reality, to stifle criticism. The Interior Ministry, under the supervision of the Ministry of Public Instruction, issued a list of regulations with which periodicals and books in all languages, but especially in Ottoman, should comply; everything, down to the smallest detail, was closely overviewed and censored:

La liberté de la presse a subi une atrophie progressive par suite d'une oppression de plus en plus intense et enfin elle est aujourd'hui réduite presque à zéro ... Les brochures et les livres à imprimer doivent être présentés en deux exemplaires qui sont revus et scrupuleusement censurés et pour ainsi dire, analysés par deux conseils de censure différents; la plupart de ces manuscrits sont refusés et les autres sont grossièrement tronqués. Cette vigueur de censure a pour but de tarir toutes les sources de réforme et de pensées nouvelles.[81]

According to the censorship regulations introduced, priority in the news was to be given to reports on the Sultan's health, the outcome of the harvest, and progress in the commercial and industrial sectors, and no news at all could be published without prior official approval. Gradually, a ban on the use of words like constitution, revolution, freedom, anarchy, tyranny, peoples' rights, equality, fraternity, fatherland, youth, dynamo, dynamite, nation, internationalism, hereditary prince, republic, deputies, senators, bombs, reforms, Mithat Paşa, and Armenia, was introduced.[82] Any infringement of press bans and regulations was harshly punished:

A quoi devons-nous attribuer la mort soudaine de dindessian elias [sic], maître de musique et imprimeur, dans la prison de la police centrale, arrêté, pour avoir imprimé, il y a plusieurs années, une poésie, qui par exemple excite les esprits arméniens?[83]

Soon the prohibition was extended to cover most domains of public interest, and included mentioning historical, political and geographical names and terms, and even words that may be somewhat connected to the figure of the Sultan. A word such as *burun* – nose – was to be avoided, "because it was perceived as an implied reference to Abdülhamid's particularly large nose ... [but] ... since burun also meant the geographic term cape in Turkish,"[84] it was to be replaced with a synonym in geographical descriptions. In a scientific article, the equation $AH=0$ was not permitted because it could be taken to mean Abdülhamit (initials AH) is a zero.[85] This circumscription of the domain of matters that could be discussed in the press led to a race for the publication of semi-scientific articles and treaties which had nothing to do with the political situation of the time. Titles such as "Travel in Air or Under the Sea," "The Intelligence of Cats," "Myopia among Students in Germany," give an idea of the kind of articles published at the time.

Notably, censorship was not limited to internal news but extended to foreign affairs, particularly in the case of the mention of assassinations, or attempted assassinations, of rulers, to prevent inspiration and emulation. For instance, in 1894, the Istanbul official press reported the assassination of Marie François-Sadie Carnot by an Italian anarchist as follows: "nous avons le vif regret d'annoncer à nos estimables lecteurs que Carnot, l'honorable président de la République française, qui était souffrant depuis quelques jours, vient de mourir hier à minuit."[86] Similarly, the Istanbul press initially did not mention at all the assassination of Nasreddin (1831–1896),[87] Shah of Iran; when, a few months later, reference to the news appeared, it, like the one referring to Carnot, was completely distorted, as the 'Young Turkish' press noted: "L'assassinat du Schah de Perse Nasreddin par Moulla-Riza, était, comme on s'en rappelle, transformé par la presse turque en une mort plausible et douce! Chargé d'ans et de gloires, le roi des rois avait rejoint ses augustes ancêtres dans la tombe!"[88]

In less than a year, censorship had reduced a free, opinionated, and vigorous press to a tool in the hands of the Sultan. By the beginning of 1900, things had deteriorated to such an extent that Paul Fesch went as far as declaring that:

> [d]epuis trente ans, la presse n'existe plus en Turquie. Il y a bien des journaux, même assez nombreux; mais les ciseaux de la censure les taillent, les mutilent de si émasculante manière qu'ils n'ont plus aucune puissance. Si j'osais, je dirais que le sont des journaux hongres, ou mieux, pour rester dans la couleur locale, des eunuques.[89]

The introduction of press censorship on Abdülhamit's part had a two-fold effect, one intentional and anticipated the other unintentional and surprising. The first one was the disappearance of independent papers: as soon as one would treat subjects that might challenge the Sultan's position – as in the case of praising works of individuals directly or indirectly related with the First Constitutional Period – it would be closed down, its editors and contributors imprisoned or exiled. The introduction of a high stamp tax for newspapers forced a considerable number of publishing houses out of business; those that managed to stay open, were soon coerced to close down through bribes and the offer of honorary titles to their editors. A case apart was that of publications that aimed exclusively to blackmail the Sultan:

> In 1898 and the following years, it was, in fact, the usual practice for ambitious functionaries without strong palace protection, to make a European trip as Young Turks, to publish, or to make an attempt to publish, mutinous literature, and then to sell their silence for a superior position in the government service.[90]

The unanticipated consequence of the introduction of censorship was the gradual migration abroad, during the 1890s, of many a Young Turk, who had reached the conclusion that political debate within the borders of the Empire was blocked altogether, and that it was necessary to re-settle in countries where the press was free, such as France and Switzerland, or where the opposition to the Sultan was viewed positively, as in partly autonomous ones like Egypt and Greece:

> La réaction de cette oppression fit fonder à la jeune génération pleine d'énergie et d'espoir, des organes indépendants publiés dans les villes libres comme Paris, Genève, Le Caire, Bucarest, Bruxelles, etc. Les publications sont introduites clandestinement en Turquie. Le nombre des journaux paraissant à l'étranger en différentes langues est supérieur à celui qui se publie actuellement à Constantinople.[91]

From their new places of residence, Young Turk émigrés launched a good number of publications: *Mizan*, published first in Cairo then in Geneva, *Mechveret*, published in Paris, Geneva and Brussels, *Osmanlı*, published in Geneva, London and Folkestone, and *Vatan* (Fatherland), published in Athens, were particularly influential. Notably, much to the Sultan's dismay, the CUP would manage to smuggle and circulate in the Empire *Mechveret*, *Mizan* and other opposition papers published abroad, leading to a narrowing of the influence of the home press: from 1891 to 1896, the number of Ottoman daily newspapers fell from six to three. But genuine difficulties were involved in publishing abroad. Publishing was a non-profit business; journals and newspapers were often distributed for free, and any returns they would bring would come from voluntary contributions on the part of committed, and affluent, readers. Those returns were meant not just to cover publication costs, but also to fund meetings and trips through which members of the Young Turk movement would liaise with each other, and with potential allies.

Another way to raise funds for the opposition was the organisation of banquets, where sympathetic donors could get together and become acquainted with Young Turk émigrés who would relate the socio-political situation of the Empire. On 23rd December 1896, to celebrate the twentieth anniversary of the promulgation of the constitution, *Mechveret* organised one such banquet, the 'Banquet de la Jeune Turquie', attended by some of the most *en-vogue* intellectuals of the time: "M. Pierre Laffitte, le chef vénéré des Positivistes et professeur au collège de France,"[92] and Pierre Quillard,[93] as well as journalists from *Le Figaro, La Paix*, and foreign newspapers. The banquet ended with the wish for the next anniversary of the Constitution to be held on the shores of the Bosporus. The freedom of movement enjoyed by Young Turk émigrés allowed journals' and newspapers' editors and contributors to tour Europe to try and broker loans and donations from sympathetic governments, political parties, and influential interest groups. For the launch of *Mechveret*, Rıza organised a meeting of Ottoman students and émigrés in Paris through which enough money to jumpstart publication was raised; according to Rıza himself, the initial sum, which paid for the printing equipment (press and characters), was 100 francs.[94]

Prince Sabahattin was also involved in fundraising attempts, following his arrival to Paris, where he, his father and brother were lodging at the Grand Hotel under close watch from the French Police. One of the daily *Rapports* of the French Police gives evidence of a trip to London the two brothers took on the 3rd of January 1900, ten days after their arrival in France: Lutfullah was said to return five, Sabahattin nine, days later. According to the *Rapport*, the scope of the trip was to try and broker a loan of 629,000 francs, but nothing came of it; so, in March the same year, the two went to Geneva, for the same purpose, and to the same effect. Somehow, towards the end of the year, they managed to get sponsored: on the 6th of November, returning to Paris from yet another trip abroad, the brothers left the hotel and settled down in an apartment for which they paid an advance sum of 25,000 francs and a fee of 4,500 as *loyer annuel*.[95] The new accommodation must have taken up most of the money raised if, according to the same police *Rapport*, their father, Mahmut Paşa, requested a loan of 300,000 francs, probably from a banking institution; his request, however, was turned down because his assets in the Empire, which he offered as guarantees, had been recently confiscated by the government.

The Parisian intellectual milieu

Among the various cities that hosted Young Turk émigrés (Paris, Cairo, Geneva, London, Folkestone, Naples, Brussels, Bucharest, etc.), Paris was the most popular because many Young Ottomans had made it their home in the 1860s and 1890s, and since French had for long been the language of the Ottoman elite. According to police sources, by the late 1870s, the Ottoman diasporic community in Paris included, ranked according to size, Jews, Armenians, Syrians, Greeks, Lebanese, and a small number of Turks, localised mainly in and around the 11ème arrondissement (near the Père Lachaise Cemetery, which had a Muslim section), Rue de la Roquette, Rue Sedaine, and Rue St. Ambroise, and the *8ème arrondissement*, mainly around the Boulevard des Malesherbes. At the end of the nineteenth century, according to Ottoman ambassador to France Naum Paşa, the Ottoman presence in Paris amounted to around 20,000 people, while the *Service des Étrangers* and the *Ministère du Travail* put the number at a maximum of 15,000.[96]

Another reason why Paris was particularly appealing to Young Turk émigrés related to the influence of its press, which, ever since the nineteenth century, had taken the lead in organising and stirring political dissent while under state censorship: "[Victor] Hugo compared the dramatic censorship to the Inquisition, terming it 'detestable' and a 'prison' for writers, which 'like the other Holy Office', had its 'secret judges, its masked executioners, its tortures and mutilations and its death penalty.'"[97] Therefore, members of the Young Turk organisation were convinced that the liberal section of the French public that had fought strongly against censorship in the past would be ready to support the Young Turk struggle in case of need. Paris was, therefore, the ideal place to learn techniques to bypass censorship, and strategies to succeed in influencing public opinion. Among those strategies, the use of caricatures or other ironic images of politicians was frequently used:

French authorities were even more afraid of the potential impact of visual, as contrasted with written expression of dissent, such as might be offered by caricature and the theatre. This was because a large percentage of the especially-feared 'dark masses' were illiterate and thus 'immune' to the written word, but they were not blind and thus perceived as highly susceptible to subversive imagery.[98]

Following in the footsteps of the French press, the Young Turk press used caricatures in newspapers and plays to promote political and social satirical discourse: *Mechveret* published a series called *Scènes Hamidiennes*, which came out in instalments written either by foreigners,[99] or by Ottomans who wished to remain anonymous.[100] The participation and involvement of non-Ottomans, and especially Europeans, to the opposition's journals was especially important. The Ottoman masses might not have been regular readers but they surely must have been impressed by the news of an intellectual co-operation between what was perceived as the modern intelligentsia of Europe and the Ottoman one, in this case treated as equal by its European partner.

All in all, it is fair to say that the rupture between the Istanbul and Cairo branches of the CUP on one side, and the Paris branch on the other at the time of the first attempted coup, was a key event in that the distance it created between the Paris émigrés and the central leadership was instrumental in offering the mental freedom that enabled those émigrés and their fellow exiles in other countries to actively collaborate with Europeans interested in political and social change in the Empire, and, thus, sharpen and refine the movement's intellectual output. Far from being irrelevant to developments within the Empire, the intellectual debates that engaged the exiles spread through the press that they managed to smuggle across the border; accordingly, "in spite of these repressions [of the late 1890s], the Young Turk movement continued to grow alarmingly, and the Sultan, feeling that the main impulse came from the exiles abroad, tried a new approach."[101] The full immersion into European culture together with the good reception of the ideas and goals of the Young Turk émigrés led most of them to thinking of themselves as the natural and legitimate heirs of the Young Ottomans endowed with the capacity, which had escaped their predecessors, to educate the citizens of the Empire on social and political issues, galvanise them into action, and bring about change. Accordingly, the intellectual phase of the movement was characterised by a deeply elitist conception of political activism:

> Ce que nous appelons nous l'Élite, c'est l'Élite intelligente et pensante, l'Élite qui demande à la foi ses hautes inspirations, à la raison ses lumières, à la science ses expériences les plus concluantes et ses brillantes découvertes. L'Élite pour nous, c'est la glorieuse phalange des hommes qui ont souffert pour les propres convictions et de ceux qui ont combattu pour la liberté et la justice. L'Élite pour nous, ce sont les hommes qui ont

du [sic] et de la fermeté, les courageux, les vaillants, les incorruptibles, ceux qui osent penser haut et élever la voix en faveur de la vérité.[102]

As the quote above shows, among the qualities that the members of the political elite should possess to be recognised as CUP leaders, courage, honesty and endurance had maximum prominence,[103] qualities that were essential also to the development of patriotism, an essential part of Ottomanism.[104]

Evidence that the Young Turk press, published in various European cities, and distributed through clandestine channels in the Empire, was effective in widening support for the movement comes from Abdülhamit's perception of it as a serious threat which lay behind his efforts to persuade first the French then the Belgian authorities of the need to launch a prolonged attack against *Mechveret* and its editor, Ahmet Rıza, as discussed in Chapter 3.

Notes

1 The date of the first meeting is in a letter Temo wrote to Karl Süssheim, a German Orientalist, who, during his visits to the Ottoman Empire, befriended a number of Young Turks and published essays on their struggle against Sultan Abdülhamit II. Colin Heywood, "Review of The Diary of Karl Süssheim (1878–1947): Orientalist between Munich and Istanbul, by Barbara Flemming and Jan Schmidt," *The Journal of the Royal Asiatic Society* 13, no. 2 (2003): 247–248. Interestingly, the Young Turk movement was from the start so diversified ethnically and religiously that it appeared to be more 'Ottomanist' in composition than the Young Ottomans had been in spirit.
2 İbrahim Temo, *İbrahim Temo'nun İttihad ve Terakki Anıları* (Istanbul: Arba, 1987), 13–15.
3 Ibid., 16–17.
4 Paul Fesch, *Constantinople aux derniers jours d'Abdul-Hamid*, 2nd edn (New York: Burt Franklin, 1971), 341.
5 Prior to the establishment of the Translation Office, every diplomatic transaction between the Ottoman and foreign governments had been carried out between the dragomans (translators) of the embassies and the official translator of the Imperial *Divan* (Council), who, until 1821, had been members of minorities, often of the Phanariote Greek families. The Phanariote Greeks were part of the Istanbul Greeks who, during the seventeenth and eighteenth centuries, acquired important positions within the civil bureaucracy, for instance, as official translators, or became influential bankers and wealthy merchants, often having links with the Patriarchate. For this reason, they were looked at with suspicion by the Greeks of Peloponnesus, who, eventually, organised a rebellion against their fellow countrymen in Istanbul. With the onset of the Greek War of Independence (1821–1831), Ottoman statesmen grew wary of appointing Greeks to such important posts: "[t]his left the Ottoman government with a serious communications problem at a time when diplomatic contacts were becoming more and more important to the survival of the Empire. Between 1821 and 1833 the business of translation was conducted through makeshift arrangements." Zürcher, *Turkey, A Modern History*, 46.
6 Findley, *Bureaucratic Reform*, 204.
7 Kemal Karpat, "The Transformation of the Ottoman State, 1789–1908," 255. Given that part of the training entailed being posted abroad, those working at

the Translation Office had the opportunity to become aware of some misconceptions regarding the West, as they could witness *prima facie* the dichotomy between Western Countries' theory of government, and their actions, especially as regards foreign policy.
8   In his novel T*urfanda mı yoksa Turfa mı, Mizancı* (so called as editor of the journal *Mizan*) Murat wrote an account of his service in the Translation Office, in the form of a parody.
9   Findley, "The Advent of Ideology," 156.
10 Ahmet Rıza, "Une Explication," *Mechveret Supplément Français* 1, no. 10 (May 1896), 1.
11 "La visite de S.A. la princesse Nazli au Comité," *Mechveret Supplément Français* 1, no. 20 (October 1896), 1.
12 Born Ahmet Şefik, was then known as *Mithat* (the Laudable, for his achievements) Paşa. For his memoir, see Ali Haydar Mithat, *Midhat Paşa'nın hatırları* (Istanbul: Temel Yayınları, 1997).
13 Roderic Davison, *Reform in the Ottoman Empire, 1856–1876* (Princeton, NJ: Princeton University Press, 1963), 144–145.
14 "Contemporaries generally acclaimed him successful, although grudgingly in many cases and not without admixture of criticism. What impressed travellers and residents in Bulgaria first was the program of public works, vigorously pushed and much of it completed, an achievement unheard of in other parts of the Empire. Paved roads, bridges, street lights, public buildings, schools, steamer service on the Danube, model farms with agricultural machinery imported from Europe ... [o]f greater importance for the prosperity of the ordinary farmers were the agricultural credit cooperatives ... Midhat is still acclaimed in Turkey as the father of the agricultural bank, and in Bulgaria today as the founder of the best-developed credit cooperatives in the Balkans." Davison, *Reform in the Ottoman Empire*, 152.
15 For an in-depth discussion of the First Constitutional Period, see Robert Devereux, *The First Ottoman Constitutional Period – A Study of the Midhat Constitution and Parliament* (Baltimore, MD: The John Hopkins Press, 1963).
16 Davison, *Reform in the Ottoman Empire*, 145.
17 "Midhat Pacha," *Mechveret Supplément Français* 8, no. 135 (December 1902), 4; "Midhat Pacha," *Mechveret Supplément Français* 8, no. 136 (January 1903), 4.
18 "England and Turkey," *English Supplement to the Osmanlı* 1 (July 1898), 17.
19 "The Blot on Turkey,," *English Supplement to the Osmanlı* 1 (July 1898), 24–31.
20 Accordingly, Lewis described it as "organised liberty." Lewis, "The Impact of the French Revolution," 106.
21 Notably, liberty, equality, nationality, freedom and justice came to be denoted as 'human rights'. The influence of positivism here is evident.
22 See, for instance, Thierry Zarcone, *Secret et sociétés secrètes en Islam* (Milan: Archè, 2002) and Paul Dumont, "Freemasonry in Turkey: A By-product of Western Penetration," *European Review* 13, no. 3 (2005), 481–493. It was through the lodge Italia Risorta that Young Turks became acquainted with the views of Italian patriots such as Giuseppe Mazzini and Giuseppe Garibaldi.
23 "Rapports divers sur le sujets ottomans pendant la guerre de 1914," *Préfecture de Police de Paris* – BA 1.169 Mahmoud Pacha (beau-frère du Sultan de Constantinople; and Rıza, *Ahmed Rıza Bey'in Anıları*.
24 Tunçay, "In Lieu of a Conclusion," 167.
25 Lewis, *Emergence*, 172–173.
26 Cléanthi Scalieri, A*ppel a la justice internationale des grandes puissances par rapport au grand process de Constantinople par suite de la mort du feu Sultan Aziz* (Athens: Imprimerie l'Union, 1881), 17.

27 Identified as the seed from which the Young Turk movement would emanate, Hanioğlu, *Young Turks in Opposition*, 36–37.
28 Dumont, "Freemasonry in Turkey," 485.
29 Ibid., 482.
30 Fesch, *Constantinople aux derniers jours d'Abdul-Hamid*.
31 "[A] number of the Young Turks were Freemasons, notably Ahmet Rıza Bey," Dumont, "Freemasonry in Turkey," 489.
32 Şükrü Hanioğlu, "Notes on the Young Turks and the Freemasons, 1875–1908," *Middle Eastern Studies* 25, no. 2 (April 1989), 193.
33 Dumont, "Freemasonry in Turkey," 489.
34 The close relationship between Young Turks and Freemasons would extend well into the twentieth century: many a Freemason welcomed the 1908 Revolution, and described Young Turks' actions as imbued with Masonic values, forging an alliance with the new Unionist regime. Here is David Cohen, from the lodge *Veritas* of Salonika, Secretary General of the *Grand Orient de France*, commenting on the revolution: "Après l'heureux événement qui vient de se produire en Turquie et auquel, je suis heureux de le dire, la propagande de nos idées, a pris une assez large part, il était de mon devoir de penser à la fondation d'une Loge à Constantinople sous la dépendance de notre GRAND ORIENT." Quoted in Eric Anduze, *La Franc-Maçonnerie de la Turquie Ottomane 1908–1924* (Paris: L'Harmattan, 2005), 9.
35 Ali Haydar Mithat, *The Life of Midhat Pasha* (London: John Murray, 1903), 119–120.
36 Mourat Bey, *Le Palais de Yildiz et la Sublime Porte – Le Véritable Mal d'Orient* (Paris: Imprimerie Chaix, 1895), 9.
37 Hanioğlu, *Young Turks in Opposition*, 49, 50.
38 Temo, *İttihad ve Terakki Anıları*, 15. The figure of Cevdet is both interesting and exemplifying of Young Turk changes throughout the years. Very devout at the beginning of the Young Turk movement, he went through a drastic change culminating in a strict adherence to materialism and had a central role in the founding of the group known as *Garbcılar* (Westernisers). In his later writings, it is difficult to understand how much he genuinely believed that science and Islam could be reconciled or used Islam as a tool to slowly substitute religion with materialism. Cevdet's trajectory is important as it represents very well the path of many Young Turks at the time: shifting, throughout their lives, from one stance to the other, in reaction to different political and social situations. It is important to highlight that Ottomans changed their viewpoint, that ideas were in constant evolution, and that precisely because of the formative nature of the intellectual period, these changes take place as Young Turk history evolves. For more on Cevdet, see: Şükrü Hanioğlu, "Garbcılar: Their Attitudes toward Religion and Their Impact on the Official Ideology of the Turkish Republic," *Studia Islamica* 86 (1997), 133–158, and Necati Alkan, "The Eternal Enemy of Islam: Abdullah Cevdet and the Baha'i Religion," *BSOAS* 68, no. 1 (2005), 1–20.
39 Ahmet Rıza, "Une nouvelle tactique," *Mechveret Supplément Français* 1, no. 13 (June 1896), 3; Ahmet Rıza, *Tolérance Musulmane* (Paris: Clamaron-Graff, 1897), 20; Ahmet Rıza, "Vitalité de la Jeune Turquie," *Mechveret Supplément Français* 2, no. 45 (October 1897), 3.
40 Halil Ganem, *Les Sultans Ottomans*, vols 1 & 2 (Paris: Chevalier-Marescq, 1901–02).
41 Lewis, *Emergence*, 397.
42 Rıza, *La Faillite morale de la politique occidentale*, 138.
43 Octave Depont and Xavier Cappolani, *Les Confréries Religieuses Musulmanes* (Algiers: Adolphe Jourdan, 1897), 261–262.

44 Ernest E. Ramsaur, "The Bektashi Dervishes and the Young Turks," *The Moslem World* 1, no. 32 (January 1942), 8.
45 George Young, *Constantinople* (London: Methuen & Co. Ltd., 1926), 197–198.
46 Because of their power-hungry nature, some among the Bektaşis, on the other hand, are reported to have been very close to the Palace in the Hamidian era, and enjoyed special privileges: "Pour être Bectachi, il faut être musulman de naissance et recommandé au Palais par un mullah stipendié. Sitôt élu, le Bectachi doit partir pour la Mecque et faire le voyage traditionnel pout acquérir le titre de pèlerin. La nation lui doit à son retour, le respect, la vénération et il est alors, par ordre du sultan, en dehors de la loi." Fehmi, *Tablettes*, 15. According to the same source, members of the Bektaşi order would regularly take part in the interrogation of suspects: "C'est encore à ces moines hamidiens qu'est livré le Turc révolutionnaire pour lequel aucun consul des puissances ne peut et ne veut réclamer. Quand ces bandits tiennent un Turc qui ne pense pas comme le Maître, ils ne le lâchent jamais." Fehmi, *Tablettes*, 18.
47 Frederick W. Hansluck, *Christianity and Islam under the Sultans*, vol. 2 (Oxford: Clarendon Press, 1929), 438; Hansluck based his assessment of the Bektaşi plan "on good Bektashi authority," Hansluck, *Christianity and Islam*, 438, n. 4.
48 John Esposito and John Donohue (eds), *Islam in Transition – Muslim Perspectives* (New York: Oxford University Press, 2007).
49 Charles Kurzman (ed.), *Modernist Islam, 1840–1940: A Sourcebook* (New York: Oxford University Press, 2002), 36.
50 In 1872, Kemal wrote an article, *Terakki* (Progress), in the journal *İbret* (Lesson), on his journey in London. The article recounts his astonishment at what he considered as impressive infrastructural progress in the city, hoping that the Empire would embark on a similar path of reconstruction. Robert Landen, "The Young Ottoman: Namık Kemal's 'Progress', 1872," in Camron Amin, Benjamin Fortna, Elizabeth Frierson, *The Modern Middle East: A Sourcebook for History* (New York: Oxford University Press, 2006), 406–410.
51 Kurzman, *Modernist Islam*, 145.
52 Nikkie Keddie, *Sayyid Jamāl ad-Din 'al-Afghāni' – A Political Biography* (Berkeley and Los Angeles: University of California Press, 1972), 63.
53 Ibid., 64.
54 Kurzman, *Modernist Islam*, 104.
55 Anaide Ter Minassian, *Nationalism and Socialism in the Armenian Revolutionary Movement, 1887–1912* (Cambridge, MA: The Zoryan Institute, 1984), vi.
56 Ibid., 7.
57 McDougall, *History and the Culture of Nationalism in Algeria*, 29.
58 Ibid., 35.
59 Fesch, *Constantinople aux derniers jours d'Abdul-Hamid*, 338.
60 Given his close association with the journal, Murat Bey came to be known as *Mizancı* Murat. He became "the leading figure in the press of the time ... the idol of the intellectual classes." Ahmet Emin, *The Development of Modern Turkey as Measured by its Press* (New York: Longmans, 1914), 65.
61 Rıza is reported as having "horror of concessions obtained by violence," Ramsaur, *The Young Turks*, 25, and Ganem would express the conviction that "[i]l serait inutile, sinon dangereux, de recourir de nouveau aux révolutions de palais qui n'ont jamais donné à la nation que des résultats négatifs." Ganem, *Les Sultans Ottomans*, 298.
62 Hanioğlu, *Young Turks in Opposition*, 84.
63 Fesch, *Constantinople aux derniers jours d'Abdul-Hamid*, 344.
64 Ramsaur, *The Young Turks*, 46.
65 Murat became a member of the State Council, and İshak Sükûti and Abdullah Cevdet, who returned a couple of years later, were appointed to prestigious

diplomatic positions. Notably, Cevdet, who had moved to Geneva in 1896, had started publication of a journal, the *Osmanlı* (Ottoman), destined to become highly influential under Sabahattin's influence.

66 Youssouf Fehmi, "L'Amnistie et les Jeunes Turcs," *La Petite Republique*, 8873, 31 Juillet, (1900), 1.
67 Fesch, *Constantinople aux derniers jours d'Abdul-Hamid*, 344.
68 Damat Mahmut Paşa was the son of Admiral Halil Paşa and Seniha Sultan, daughter of Sultan Abdülmecit and sister of Abdülhamit II. Before his flight to Paris, Mahmut had been state counsellor and Minister of Justice.
69 For the role of the invention of the printing press as one of the key instruments in the production of nationalist ideologies in Europe and elsewhere, see Benedict Anderson, *Imagined Communities*, 2nd edn (New York: Verso, 1991).
70 Berkes, *The Development of Secularism*, 126.
71 Fesch, *Constantinople aux derniers jours d'Abdul-Hamid*, 32.
72 Orhan Koloğlu, "La formation des intellectuels à la culture journalistique dans l'Empire Ottoman et l'influence de la presse étrangère," *Varia Turcica* XXIII (Istanbul: The Isis Press, 1992), 123–141.
73 Şinasi "[n]ot only established a new style of prose that was grammatically revolutionary, but also a new mode of thinking, and new words to express it, such as citizens' rights, freedom of expression, public opinion, liberal ideas, national consciousness, constitutional government, liberty, natural rights of the people, etc." Berkes, *The Development of Secularism*, 197–198.
74 Berkes, *The Development of Secularism*, 197.
75 Less than a year after starting *İbret*, Kemal was forced to emigrate again; he went to Cyprus.
76 The *İkdam* and the *Sabah* survived the 1908 Revolution, and remained influential under the following régimes.
77 Fesch, *Constantinople aux derniers jours d'Abdul-Hamid*, 63.
78 Ahmet Emin, *The Development of Modern Turkey*, 52.
79 Fesch, *Constantinople aux derniers jours d'Abdul-Hamid*, 35–36.
80 Berkes, *The Development of Secularism*, 260.
81 "La Presse en Turquie," *Osmanlı Supplément Français* 1, no. 6 (May 1898), 2–3.
82 See Ebru Boyar, "The Press and the Palace: The Two-way Relationship between Abdüalhamid II and the Press, 1876–1908," *Bulletin of SOAS* 69, no. 3 (October 2006), 417–43; Fesch, *Constantinople aux derniers jours d'Abdul-Hamid*; Scalieri, *Appel à la justice internationale*.
83 Scalieri, *Appel a la justice internationale*, 110.
84 Boyar, "The Press and the Palace," 420.
85 Fesch, *Constantinople aux derniers jours d'Abdul-Hamid*, 58.
86 "La Nullité de la Presse en Turquie," *Osmanlı Supplément Français* 1, no. 9 (October 1898), 4.
87 "La Presse en Turquie," 2.
88 "La Nullité de la Presse en Turquie," 4.
89 Fesch, *Constantinople aux derniers jours d'Abdul-Hamid*, 50.
90 Emin, *The Development of Modern Turkey*, 69.
91 "La Presse en Turquie," 3.
92 "Banquet de la Jeune Turquie," *Mechveret Supplément Français* 2, no. 26 (January 1897), 4.
93 Pierre Quillard (1864–1912) was the founder of the review *La Pléiade* (1884). He was a poet, a political activist with anarchist leanings, the translator of classical Greek works, a defender of Dreyfus and an opponent of the Hamidian regime, which he held responsible for the massacre of Armenians between 1894 and 1896. Quillard lived in Istanbul between 1893 and 1897 and, in 1900, founded

the journal *Pro Armenia*, founded by the Dashnaks and supported by many French democratic/socialist leaders.
94 Ahmet Rıza, "L'Inaction des Jeunes Turcs," *La Revue Occidentale* 2, no. 115 (1903), 91.
95 "Rapports divers sur le sujets ottomans pendant la guerre de 1914," *Préfecture de Police de Paris* – BA 1.169 Mahmoud Pacha (beau-frère du sultan de Constantinople).
96 "Rapports divers sur le sujets ottomans pendant la guerre de 1914," *Préfecture de Police de Paris* – BA/1653–109.700–2-A. The figures related to the Ottoman presence in Paris are important in that they give an idea of the potential readership of the Young Turk press.
97 Robert Justin Goldstein, "Fighting French Censorship, 1815–1881," *The French Review* 71, no. 5 (April 1998), 788; see also Hanioğlu, *Preparation for a Revolution*, 309.
98 Goldstein, "Fighting French Censorship," 785.
99 Nicolas Bafouillard, "Scènes Hamidiennes," *Mechveret Supplément Français* 3, no. 62 (September 1898), 3.
100 "Scènes Hamidiennes – La politique de Karakeuz," *Mechveret Supplément Français* 3, no. 52 (February 1898), 2.
101 Lewis, Emergence, 195.
102 Halil Ganem, "L'Élite," *Mechveret Supplément Français* 3, no. 52 (1February 1898), 1.
103 There is a clear analogy between Ganem's characterisation of elitism and political activism and that of social scientist and psychologist Gustave Le Bon (1841–1931). In his most important book, *La Psychologie des foules* published in 1895, Le Bon explained why the capacity for change could not rest with ordinary people, making an elitist conception of political activism a necessity: '[t]he part of the people has been the same in all revolutions. It is never the people that neither conceives them nor directs them. Its activity is released by means of leaders ... new ideas penetrate the people very slowly indeed. Generally, it accepts a revolution without knowing why, and when by chance it does succeed in understanding why, the revolution is over long ago.' Le Bon, *The Psychology of Revolution*, www.gutenberg.org/cache/epub/448/pg448.html, 30.
104 Hanioğlu gives a rather negative evaluation of Young Turk elitism: "A single persistent strain running through Young Turk publications was their elitist perception of the masses as despicable ... Le Bon's antipathy toward revolutions, especially the French revolution, became intrinsic to the Young Turk Weltanschauung, which viewed 'the people' as a 'foule'." Hanioğlu, *Young Turks in Opposition*, 206.

3 Ahmet Rıza and *Mechveret*

Introducing Ahmet Rıza

Events following the first wave of arrests of Young Turks on the part of Abdülhamit II in and around Istanbul in 1896 and 1897, when an attempted coup against the Sultan was discovered and foiled, led those Young Turk members who had a chance to emigrate to do so, and many of them made Paris their new home. Upon arrival, they would be greeted by the head of the local branch of the movement, Ahmet Rıza, who had settled there back in June 1889, following the example of prominent Young Ottomans who had chosen exile back in the 1860s and 1870s,[1] appreciating the opportunities that exile offered to political activists, particularly in terms of shaping a solid framework for the reformed Empire and garnering support for it, whether among Ottomans or Europeans. This chapter illustrates Rıza's thinking on a number of salient points making up that framework (the relationship the Young Turk movement was to have with the West, with the Sultan, and with Ottoman minorities, and the role of religion in the state),[2] and assesses it as a contribution to shaping the Ottoman identity of the reformed Empire.

Ahmet Rıza was born in Istanbul in 1858. His father, Ali Rıza Bey, was nicknamed *İngiliz* Ali (the Englishman) for his admiration for Great Britain, for his mastery of the language and for having had tight links with England during the Crimean War (1853–1856). During his life, Ali Rıza held a number of important official posts in the Ministry of Foreign Affairs, at the Ottoman Embassy in Vienna (at the time one of the three most important posts in Europe, after London and Paris), and had been appointed member of the first Ottoman senate.[3] Ahmet Rıza's mother, Fraulein Turban, of Hungarian origins, was born in Munich and then moved to Vienna where she met Rıza's father.[4] When they married, she converted to Islam,[5] and became Naile Sabıka *Hanım*. Educated at the *Mekteb-i Sultani*,[6] in the early 1880s, Rıza took up a position at the *Bab-ı Âli Tercüme Odası*, which gave him a first taste of the intellectual attractions of the West. In 1884, he moved to France to attend the Institut National Agronomique of Paris-Grignon. He stayed there for two years and was immediately mesmerized by France; in a letter to his sister, he wrote that: "[à] Marseille j'étais stupéfié, à Paris j'ai complètement perdu la tête."[7] Upon returning to the Empire, he was appointed Principal of the Bursa High School and director of the Education Department of the Bursa province, the *vilayet* of Hudavendigâr. Even though this was an important post, as Hudavendigâr was one of the most advanced provinces in terms of agricultural development, Rıza was deeply disappointed with the job, and the overall situation the Empire was in:

> My father sent me to Paris for agricultural studies. Three years later, while passing my exams, I received a notification about his death. I was looking for a job as I returned to Istanbul. But I was neither hired, nor was I provided with money to open a farm. Finally, although I did not want this, I had to take a state job. Arab Hakki Paşa was the agriculture minister. He told me that there was no job at the ministry. In France, there is a big agriculture university and three agriculture academies; over 100 students graduate from there each year, and all of them find jobs. Although nothing has been done about agriculture in our country and there are many things to do, a man who studied [abroad] with his own money and came back [to the Empire] is told 'there is no job'. I applied to the Education Ministry. I was offered a job as a chemistry teacher and high school manager in Bursa with a 2,400 kuruş salary. I accepted. The Bursa education director was a turbaned man called Veli Efendi. Being satisfied with my efforts, Education Minister Munif Pasa [soon] appointed me as Bursa Education Director with a 3,000 kurus salary ... I observed the working of the state for a year and a half. I understood that everything was so messed up that it was impossible to serve either at the ministry or at any other similar place. I decided to go to Paris to express my concerns from there.[8]

Initially, Rıza motivated his request to absent himself from his job to visit Paris with a desire to see the *Exposition Universelle*;[9] his request, however, met with a cold reaction:

> After the exams were over, I asked permission to leave for holidays. I came to Istanbul. 'If you allow me to have a month off, I will dedicate my holiday to an exhibition in Paris. There is no obstacle to that.' I said to Münir Pasha. 'That is wrong! You are appointed by a ferman, you need permission from the palace. Who else was planning on going there? The Palace is concerned that the exposition coincides with the anniversary of the Revolution.[10]

Having nonetheless gone to Paris, Rıza submitted to the Sultan an application for funds towards some publishing projects he had in mind:

> After I visited the Industry Exhibition in Paris in 1889, I started to arrange all the necessities to publish a collection, a book and a

newspaper. While trying to sustain my life, I was also trying to publish the collection. I was going to the library every morning and attending conferences every evening. Soon after, I presented my first project to the Padishah.[11]

His application met with a rather unexpected, and bewildering, reply:

The project was taken into consideration and a verdict was issued that as an output of my education, I should not present the project to the Padishah's office and not publish anything. They sent me a 2,000 lira award as well. I did not accept it. The reply followed that 'the money bestowed [upon you] cannot be refused. It has to be taken'. I refused it again.[12]

Bonding with the Parisian Milieu

Once again in Paris, Rıza found accommodation in a small apartment on the last floor, at 48 rue Monge, in the Latin Quarter[13] and spent his time studying, working and planning how to create a forum for dissent against the Ottoman state of affairs. His arrival there was a turning point in his life as the French capital held a number of important meanings: it represented technological advancement as opposed to the stagnation of the Ottoman Empire, and was the capital of the Revolution – incidentally the *Exposition Universelle* was taking place at its centenary. Having severed his ties with the establishment, Rıza started to look for local collaborators for his publishing plans. He became acquainted with Halil Ganem, a Syrian Maronite Christian born in Beirut in 1846, who had begun his career in 1862 as member of the commercial court in his native city. Initially appointed dragoman of the Beirut *mutasarrifiye*, and subsequently of the *vilayet* of Syria, Ganem went on to hold the same post at the Ministry of Foreign Affairs. During the Constitutional period, he became the Syrian delegate to the first Ottoman Parliament, until he fled to Paris following Sultan Abdülhamit II's suspension of the Constitution in 1878. There, he began an active publishing career as editor of a couple of Paris-based journals, *La Jeune Turquie* and *al-Bāsir* (Foresight), and of a Geneva-based one, *Hilāl* (The Crescent), as well as contributor to the *Journal des Débats* and *Le Figaro*, and, later on, author of a two-volume historical monograph, *Les Sultans Ottomans*.[14] Ganem personified the ideal partner for Rıza: he was ready to actively oppose Sultan Abdülhamit II, was well positioned within the French intellectual circles, and had profound Ottomanist leanings, contrary to other Ottomans from minorities who, while residing in Europe, contributed to publications that were sympathetic to minorities. The two men forged a long-lasting cooperation and friendship. In 1895, Rıza founded the new journal, in Ottoman, *Meşveret* with a supplement in French, *Mechveret Supplément Français* and was almost immediately joined by Ganem. The journal attracted "prominent men, Christian and Muslim,"[15] Young Turk émigrés, but also French intellectuals,[16] prompted by a genuine desire to see the Ottoman Empire modernised and reformed in a liberal fashion. Rıza and Ganem hegemonised it, while the other contributors dithered between association and dissociation.[17] Determining the identity of all those who contributed to *Mechveret* has proven an elusive task: information from primary sources and the secondary literature is vague and somewhat contradictory, perhaps reflecting the fact that some Young Turks contributed to the journal only for short periods, or supported it but preferred to remain anonymous.

Soon, Rıza had succeeded in making friends with influential, well-established, figures among whom Georges Clémenceau (1841–1929), Pierre Laffitte (1823–1903),[18] Edmond Demolins (1852–1907) and Gustave Le Bon by participating in the weekly Wednesday lunches, *les déjeuners du mercredi*, and, thus, positioning himself as a protagonist on the Parisian intellectual stage. He became a regular contributor to European journals such as *La Revue Occidentale*, and *The Positivist Review*, and the newspaper *La Paix* where he wrote on Armenian affairs. His achievements met with public recognition, as the French newspaper *La Dépêche* indicates, describing Rıza's intellectual 'folder' as containing:

> de la philosophie, de l'histoire, de la politique, de la métaphysique; [inside it] Confucius et Zoroastre s'y rencontrent avec Luther et Voltaire, les pères de l'Eglise y heurtent l'Encyclopédie, Mahomet y coudoie M.J.B. Say et Michelet. Mais celui qui domine de toute sa grandeur, c'est Auguste Comte.[19]

He was invited to give talks on a number of occasions, at important venues, to distinguished audiences: at the *College libre des sciences sociales*,[20] at a conference on "Les Institutions sociales en Turquie,"[21] at the meeting of the *Société Positiviste de Paris*,[22] and at the "Hommage international à Auguste Comte" organised by *La Revue Occidentale* on 18th May 1902.[23]

With reference to the last, all important, occasion, *La Revue Occidentale* described Rıza in warm terms:

> Quand on fait les honneurs à des hôtes de passage, on néglige les amis de tous les jours, ceux de la plus grande intimité; aussi nous tairons-nous sur le succès qu'ont obtenu M. Simon, parlant au nom des positivistes du Brésil, et M. Ahmet Riza, directeur du *Mechveret*.[24]

To explain the reference to Comte in the above quote, it is important to mention an episode that would have a massive impact on Rıza's political and philosophical thinking. One day, having a browse in a bookshop, he picked up a reader on positivism:[25] it was the beginning of a fascination and a life-long commitment, which would be subsumed in the editorial line of *Mechveret*, and reverberate on the Young Turk movement. Many aspects of positivism squared well with Rıza's social and political persuasion: in particular, the belief in a harmonious evolution of human societies towards the development of interpersonal relations grounded on benevolence and mutual solidarity rather than on competition,[26] and the amelioration of health and living conditions thanks to a scientific appreciation of natural phenomena based on careful observation.[27] It is possible that the penetration of socialist ideas in the Empire in the second half of the nineteenth century had prepared Rıza to receive Comte's message,[28] which has many points in common with socialism, especially in terms of valuing the collective against the individual.[29] Rıza must also have found a number of other aspects of positivism as appealing. Positivism was both appreciative of Islam as well as not rigid and, thus, adaptable to the Ottoman Empire allowing the space for religion as a cultural component and point of reference. Comte himself had regarded Constantinople as a key place for his definition of a global positivist politics, after Athens, Rome and Paris.[30] Lastly, Rıza, as expressed also in the pages of *Mechveret*, appreciated the impartiality of positivist principles, and its notion of friendship and equality among people.[31]

Mechveret: *layout and content*

The reference to Comte's positivism was evident in *Mechveret*: its first thirty two issues had the motto 'Ordre et Progrès' emblazoned on the front page. Furthermore, the dating system of the journal followed the Comtean calendar, which started in 1789 – the date of the French Revolution – and named the months (13) according to historical figures who had contributed the most to the advancement of mankind.[32] The first issue of *Mechveret*, dated 27th Frédéric 107, spelled out the Young Turk programme:

> Nous voulons travailler non pas à renverser la dynastie régnante que nous considérons comme nécessaire au maintien du bon ordre, mais à propager la notion du progrès dont nous désirons le triomphe pacifique. Notre devise étant 'Ordre et Progrès', nous avons horreur des concessions obtenues par la violence. Nous demandons des réformes, non pas spécialement pour telle ou telle province, mais pour l'Empire tout entier; non pas en faveur d'une seule nationalité, mais en faveur de tous les Ottomans, qu'ils soient Juifs, Chrétiens ou Musulmans. Nous voulons avancer dans la voie de la civilisation mais nous le déclarons hautement, nous ne voulons avancer qu'en fortifiant l'élément ottoman ... Nous tenons à garder l'originalité de notre civilisation orientale et, pour cela, n'emprunter à l'Occident que les résultats généraux de son évolution scientifique, seuls vraiment assimilables et nécessaires pour éclairer un people dans sa marche vers la liberté ... Nous nous opposons à la substitution de l'intervention directe des puissances étrangères à l'autorité ottomane.[33]

The content of *Mechveret* was not strictly political,[34] and on top of putting "les lecteurs étrangers au courant des tendances et des vœux du parti de le

Jeune Turquie,"[35] featured articles and translations on all sorts of scientific, philosophical and literary topics.[36] Moreover, the *Supplément* was created with the aim of allowing exchange between all the groups in the Empire[37] and of becoming the symbol of Ottomanism. The *Supplément* re-iterated the connection between *Mechveret* and the CUP, presenting it as the 'Organ of the Young Turkey' (*Organe de la Jeune Turquie*), and its faithful mouthpiece: "tout ce qui émane de notre Comité est intégralement publié dans le Mechveret."[38] An interesting question is why Rıza decided to establish such a close connection between the Young Turk movement and *Mechveret*, going as far as to claim that the latter represented the voice of all Young Turks. Did he think *Mechveret*, as the mouthpiece of the Paris faction, represented, in the late 1890s, the 'real' Young Turk movement, or was he trying to use *Mechveret* as a tool to assemble in a coherent, unified, entity as many Young Turks as possible, irrespective of their allegiance to one, or another, faction? The question does not have a definitive, unequivocal answer as, in the light of the dismantling of the Istanbul branch, and of the fact that Sabahattin had not yet appeared to challenge his leadership, Rıza may well have genuinely thought that the position expressed in *Mechveret* represented, at the time, the voice of the whole Young Turk movement. On the other hand, though, taking at face value the name he chose for it, *Mechveret* meaning consultation, one may be inclined to think that the connection Rıza established between it and the movement aimed at making the former a forum for discussion, to reach a consensual strategy that would result in unity of action.[39]

On the West

Rıza greatly admired the philosophical and scientific achievements of the West but criticised it for succumbing to vices that, in his eyes, had undermined those very achievements; he was incensed at the aggressive and colonialist foreign policies that some European countries had deployed throughout the nineteenth century, which resulted in numerous military interventions. He thought that, with those, the West had de facto halted the advancement of civilisation, becoming immoral towards other peoples and other cultures:

> [J]'aime ma Patrie, mais j'aime aussi, et d'un même amour, l'humanité et la vérité. Autant la politique barbare de l'Occident me révolte, autant ses progrès intellectuels, ses découvertes scientifiques et leurs prodigieuses applications m'inspirent d'admiration et de respect.[40]

Criticising the military intervention of Western powers in other countries presented as motivated by a disinterested desire to 'help', Rıza praised the value of human solidarity among peoples which he regarded as an antidote to ethnic and religious prejudices, and a means to fighting ignorance and parochial interests, and attaining the 'positive truth' to which Comte's philosophy aspired.[41] Rıza denounced offers of involvement in matters internal to the Empire from the Great Powers (Europe and Russia) as politically and economically motivated, and, therefore, inspired by self-interest and the hope to destabilise the Empire by adding more elements of friction to an already fragile social equilibrium. Accordingly, he denounced the requests to reform the Empire advanced by the Great Powers as nothing but a pretext for intervention, wishing the latter's involvement to be limited to: "un appui moral. Nous nous opposons à la substitution de l'intervention directe des puissances étrangères à l'autorité ottomane."[42] Historical evidence suggests Rıza had a point there: earlier examples, as already mentioned, ranged from Russia's attempts to stir up revolts in Greece during the temporary occupation of Morea in 1770, to Bonaparte's France's pushing his generals to foster ideas of independence throughout the Ionian Islands in 1797, to Russia's stirring disturbances in Bosnia, Herzegovina and Bulgaria,[43] which ended up with the latter gaining autonomous status and Bulgaria being brought under Russian protection.[44] The self-interested nature of foreign countries' attitudes to the Empire was exemplified by the Tsar of Russia. Having taken a direct interest in developments in Armenia, the Tsar sided with the Sultan, and presented the latter's military intervention in the province to the other European powers as conciliatory and well-intended.[45] As to Britain, the benevolent, protective, attitude to the Empire had started in 1833, following the Treaty of Hünkâr İskelesi, which had seen the influence of Russia greatly increased, making the self-interest behind it manifest. After allying with the Empire against Mehmet Ali Paşa in 1839, and, later on, endeavouring to block the way to Russia's attempts at making territorial gains by supporting the Balkan Slavs, a superiority complex had spread through Britain whereby anyone else was deemed inferior,[46] a perception that opened the door to involvement, even military intervention, dressed as a civilising mission.[47] Further evidence of the self-interested nature of the Great Powers' involvement in internal matters of the Empire was offered by the increased number of missionaries sent to Ottoman lands – primarily from France and Russia – allegedly, to "sauvegarder les chrétiens contre les Softas qu'on accuse de vouloir l'extermination des infidels."[48] In fact, Rıza noted, the missionaries' actions often broke international law in using religion as a means to stir up nationalist feelings among non-Muslim minorities, thus reviving old wounds:

> [P]uisque la France et la Russie, ces deux puissances chrétiennes par excellence, défendent aux missionnaires protestants de faire de la propagande ... de quel droit ces missionnaires veulent-ils que nous leur permettions de venir chez nous raviver les haines des âges passés?[49]

On religion

An interesting point in the historiography of the Young Turk movement relates to its relationship with religion, against which the movement's secularist approach has often been quoted as a stumbling block.[50] In Rıza's specific case, his commitment to positivism has appeared irreconcilable with an appreciation of religion;[51] this, however, was not the case in Rıza's own eyes:

> L'islamisme n'est nullement hostile à la République; au contraire, il ne connait, en principe, comme chef que celui qui est élu par la décision de l'assemblée nationale ... c'est la dictature le mieux organisée et la plus rapprochée de la République.[52]

Not to be taken by surprise at Rıza's respect for religion in the light of his positivist leanings, it should be recalled that Comte himself admired the Catholic Church for rescuing the Greek heritage from possible destruction, and fostering a questioning interest in nature throughout the Middle-Ages, when monks had copied the texts of the great masters (Plato and Aristotle in particular), and experimented with herbs and medicinal plants. It should also be recalled that Comte insisted on the need to sharply demarcate science from religion, and denounced atheism as a stumbling block to scientific advancements. This is because, on his account, atheism would:

> [E]extend the metaphysical stage indefinitely, by continuing to seek for new solutions of Theological problems, instead of setting aside all inaccessible researches on the ground of their utter inanity. The true Positive spirit consists in substituting the study of the invariable Laws of phenomena for that of their so-called Causes, whether proximate or primary – in a word, in studying the *How* instead of the *Why*.[53]

Echoing Comte, Rıza highlighted the fact that, before becoming a tool in the hands of the Hamidian regime, Islam had for centuries encouraged the advancement of scientific knowledge and the study of philosophy,[54] and, therefore, had represented an element of 'regeneration' and 'progress' for Ottoman society:

> Comment une doctrine qui fut un élément si puissant de régénération et de progrès est-elle devenue aujourd'hui entre les mains de quelques fanatiques ignorants, hypocrites et malveillants, un instrument d'intolérable tyrannie? Question redoutable sur laquelle j'appelle l'attention du khalife actuel et dont la solution contribuerait plus que toute autre réforme au relèvement du monde musulman. N'est-ce pas un signe de décadence profonde que de voir des gens mal renseignés ou mal intentionnés qui se disent pourtant musulmans, s'opposer à toute critique des croyances religieuses et interdire de les soumettre aux lumières de la philosophie et de la raison?[55]

What he had problems with was the turn taken of late by some sectors of the religious establishment, which, greedy for power, to keep their privileges, had sided with Abdülhamit II, helping him perpetuate his dictatorial regime, leaving people in ignorance, and turning Islam from an example of religious tolerance into a fanatic force[56] guilty of unleashing "une sorte de terreur jésuitique qui épaissit les ténèbres de l'ignorance et fit perdre à l'Islam son perfectionnement moral."[57] Rıza thought that, in reforming the Empire, Islamic values[58] and customs would provide a shield against the temptation to succumb to a process of Westernisation, and help hold together a multi-ethnic empire according to the Ottomanist project.[59] Most importantly, never did Rıza blame Islam for the decline of the Empire: "[l]a vérité m'oblige à dire de suite que si le Koran avait contribué en partie à la grandeur [de l'Empire], ce n'est pas lui qui a fait la décadence."[60] For Rıza religion was a private matter, and all religious beliefs deserved the same respect: "nous avons le respect de toutes les croyances;"[61] accordingly, the Young Turk movement was characterised by multi-confessionalism: "[l]a Jeune Turquie se compose de membres appartenant à toutes les confessions, qui ont pris pour règle de s'unir en leurs communs intérêts pour la sauvegarde et la défense de leurs idées et de leurs Patrie."[62]

He explicitly asserted the separation between the domain of religious beliefs and that of politics: "[l]a religion doit toujours rester dans le domaine privé; elle ne doit jamais servir de base à un mouvement social et politique,"[63] and went to great lengths to assure that the victory of the Young Turk movement against the Sultan would result in a multi-confessional empire: "la Jeune Turquie, quels que soient les changements qu'elle pourra introduire dans l'état actuel des choses, maintiendra intacts ces privilèges" [namely, the right of Christians to keep their language, schools and church].[64]

And that whatever rights had already been granted to any religious minority, they would not be taken away: "La Chambre [of Parliament] ne touchera ... ni aux autres privilèges accordés aux sujets israélites et chrétiens de l'Empire."[65] Rıza thought that, with such reassurances in place, the Ottomanist project would become within reach, as Albanians, Armenians, Macedonians and all other minorities could regard themselves first and foremost as Ottomans, and place their particular identity on a less prevalent plane. Interestingly, in Europe, Rıza was seen as a religious man: French journalist Philippe Dubois, for example, described him as "un des rares musulmans de la Jeune Turquie qui aient conservé intact leur patriotisme et leur religion."[66] In the Empire, in fact, he was branded as an atheist, due to Sultan Abdülhamit II's counter-propaganda aimed at discrediting the opposition, and to the animosity that affected sections of the Young Turk movement where the fight for leadership was felt more intensely.[67]

On the problems of the Empire

As a reformer, Rıza was deeply interested in identifying the causes of the problems affecting the Ottoman Empire, which he saw as a multi-faceted affair.[68] He began his analysis tracing the first attempts at reform back to the reign of Sultan Selim III, which, though ineffective, set an example for the next two sultans, Mahmut II and Abdülmecit. The latter, according to Rıza, inaugurated a time of genuine reform with the introduction of the *Hatt-ı Şerif* of Gülhane, "le décret de réorganisation de l'empire dans le sens d'un rapprochement entre toutes les confessions,"[69] brought about by a group of men "qui ont pris pour règle de s'unir en leurs communs intérêts pour la sauvegarde et la défense de leurs idées et de leur Patrie."[70] On Rıza's account, Abdülmecit's reign was a time of slow but steady progress, marked by moderate and conciliatory domestic and foreign policies, accompanied and supported by the development of the educational infrastructure and military apparatus.[71] But he pointed his finger at Abdülhamit II for making a u-turn with respect to Abdülmecit's policies, and deeply endangering the well-being of the Empire with a selection process for the members of the establishment based on nepotism, whereby influential positions (advisory councils and high bureaucrats) were traded for the promise of loyalty to the palace in a structure of mutual dependency.[72] Far from understanding the sacred mission bestowed on them by the high offices they occupied, many members of the establishment "n'ont songé qu'à fonder leur fortune personnelle sur les bonnes grâces de leur souverain."[73] As a result of the Sultan's selection process described above, Rıza detected degeneration in morality, and a lack of technical competence among the ruling elites. Moreover, Abdülhamit II and other sultans before him had busied themselves with wars in the attempt to keep a tight hold on power, neglecting the modernisation of a class, the bourgeoisie, that Rıza identified as the engine for progress and, above all, the custodian of critical moral values:[74]

> Elle [la bourgeoisie] dirigeait le peuple, lui servait d'exemple; elle constituait une autorité intermédiaire entre le souverain et la nation; elle tempérait, mitigeait l'omnipotence de l'un et les exigences de l'autre; aux heures de crise, elle les relevait et leur donnait l'élan. Leur maison était le refuge des talents, le foyer commun de l'hospitalité, les archives vivantes des traditions et de la constitution morale de la nation.[75]

Rıza identified the malfunctioning of the educational system as yet another cause of the problems affecting the Empire. In an article in *Mechveret*, signed by the person behind the pen-name of Fuad, the writer denounced that what little reform had been implemented was mainly cosmetic, resting, in essence, on "l'apparence – brillante assurément – des édifices, des institutions."[76] At the same time, however, the *Mechveret* group credited Abdülhamit for having aspired to reform the system, especially at the beginning of his reign. The founding of the School of Civil officials, the School of Law, School of Foreign Languages, and the School and Museum of Fine Arts, anticipated that suitable civil servants and bureaucrats would be trained there. But the problem resided in three factors. The first, more structural, factor had to do with the lack of instructors with a modern education and training. The second involved government spies. These managed to deceive the Sultan into believing that a large number of turbulent students had turned the schools into a venue for the propagation of liberal ideas and revolutionary politics. This had important consequences, leading to the third factor. People were either encouraged to stay away from schools or decided to leave the Empire, which resulted in a brain drain. According to the writer, the Sultan had opted for breeding an uneducated youth, or one moulded at schools according to his specific interpretation of Ottomanism[77] in order to keep it under the yoke of the state. The Sultan had in fact engaged in strong school censorship, going as far as censoring textbooks that mentioned terms such as 'fatherland' or 'revolution'.[78]

On Sultan Abdülhamit II

Rıza's, and *Mechveret*'s, attitude towards Abdülhamit II's rule changed over time, reflecting the effects of unfolding events: roughly speaking, three phases may be identified. The first one, from early 1895 to mid-1896, aimed at establishing some sort of co-operation between the movement and the Sultan; accordingly, the tone used in addressing Abdülhamit II was conciliatory: "tout le monde sait que Votre Majesté, depuis qu'Elle dirige les destinées de l'Etat, a toujours été animée des meilleurs sentiments."[79] By contrast, Rıza identified civil servants and bureaucrats as responsible for the malfunctioning of the state apparatus and accused them of betraying the Sultan's trust:

> [d]evenus flatteurs en devenant vos serviteurs, au lieu d'être le trait d'union qui rattache un souverain à ses peuples et les interprètes des sujets dans les conseils de Votre Majesté, ils ont élevé entre eux et Vous une barrière afin d'étouffer la voix du peuple qui s'élevait pour les condamner et pour déposer jusqu'aux pieds de Votre Trône les doléances auxquelles votre âme est si sensible.[80]

A second, very short, phase may be identified around May to June 1896; it focussed on requests to the Sultan to restore the Constitution, offering the movement's co-operation in exchange:

> Notre campagne contre le Sultan cessera aussitôt que ce dernier aura mis à exécution la Constitution qu'il a solennellement promulguée et dont il a proclamé lui-même les bienfaits et l'indispensable utilité dans un Hatt demeuré célèbre, et que, du reste, il n'a jamais rapporté. Nous ne lui demandons que d'assurer l'ordre et le progrès ... Que le Sultan se mette à l'œuvre et il trouvera en nous de sincères auxiliaires.[81]

Still, the co-operation with the Sultan Rıza called for was impossible to achieve in light of the different, irreconcilable, paths to reform respectively envisaged. This is because Rıza perfected his idea of the Empire as a 'fatherland', descending directly from the Young Ottomans' experience during the First Constitutional Period, making patriotism a frequently discussed theme: "les Jeunes Turcs [sont] ... animés d'un profond amour pour leur pays."[82] Rıza's patriotism was subservient to the Ottomanist project of reshaping state power and citizens' rights so as to create a situation in which all segments and strata of society would be equally represented in the Empire, which would be felt as an asset, a legacy, a heritage for all to enjoy: "Nous demandons des réformes, non pas spécialement pour telle ou telle province, mais pour l'Empire tout entier; non pas en faveur d'une seule nationalité, mais en faveur de tous le Ottomans, qu'ils soient Juifs, Chrétiens ou Musulmans."[83]

This view was in sharp contrast with Abdülhamit II's, who, obsessed with fear that the Western powers intended to bring down the Ottoman Empire, especially after the humiliating defeat in the Russian war of 1877–1878, had long abandoned the idea of equal rights for all, and concentrated on attempts to strengthen the central power to the detriment of general liberties.

The third phase started in the second half of 1896, prompted by the Sultans' military campaign in South-eastern Anatolia, which Rıza condemned without hesitation: "[D]éplorables événements ... [sont] les récents massacres d'Arménie. Ils sont le résultat propre du gouvernement du Sultan, qui sème dans son empire la division et la discorde et qui est impuissant à en réprimer les terribles conséquences."[84]

Still, Rıza refrained from advocating violent means to achieve regime change, and so did Ganem; accordingly, the position of *Mechveret* on the use of violence for political aims was that a revolution would be disastrous as it would bring about the collapse of the Empire and open the door to foreign military intervention on the pretext of safeguarding ethnic and religious minorities. Even if foreign military intervention was not to follow a revolution, this would put the various ethno-religious components of the Empire against each other, bringing chaos and shattering hopes in an Ottomanist society; for Rıza, Ganem and their followers, good thinking, not violence, would be the winning weapon: "ce ne sont point les massacres qui ont fait la Révolution française, ce sont le grands penseurs du XVIII siècle."[85] Nonetheless, the verdict against Abdülhamit II was a harsh one:

> L'autorité du Sultan est donc légitime tant qu'elle procure le bien-être. L'islamisme défend d'obéir à un chef dont les actes ne sont pas conformes aux principes de l'Islam; il oblige même la nation de déposer ou de punir de mort, le souverain qui, par ses crimes et sa tyrannie, rend son peuple malheureux.[86]

There was also the matter of the heightened tension between the Young Turk movement and the Sultan, with the factual surrender of the Cairo branch, whose members had been lured back to Istanbul by Abdülhamit's deceptive promise of pardon and amnesty, followed by the wave of arrests that ensued from the failed coup. Accordingly, from early 1897 onwards, *Mechveret* started featuring a series of combined attacks against Abdülhamit II, which attributed to him the entire responsibility for the lamentable state the Empire was in. This related to territorial losses amounting to one half of the Empire's domains (the Balkan states, Tunisia, and, to a certain extent, Egypt);[87] financial and economic disaster,[88] with the agricultural, industrial, and commercial sectors in tatters;[89] social grievances, relating, in particular, to the malfunctioning of the postal and telegraphic services;[90] and geopolitical complaints relating to the fact that the Empire had lost international standing even with respect to the already diminished position it had occupied at the beginning of the nineteenth century.[91] Reminding his readers that, according to Islamic principles, the Sultan was chosen to safeguard society and ensure its wellbeing, and in the face of the mess just described, Rıza went as far as stating that the Sultan had put himself above the law of men, and the law of God.[92] The next step was to call the Sultan illegitimate:

> [L]e souverain qui viole toutes les lois de son pays et toutes les traditions de sa maison, qui a été cause de catastrophes sans précédent, qui a alimenté les passions religieuses, énervé l'armée, détruit la marine, ruiné les finances, perdu un quart de l'Empire, humilié la dignité nationale, fomenté les plus terribles représailles, oblitéré les sens moral des fonctionnaires, créé partout le chaos et l'anarchie – un tel souverain est un danger public et un usurpateur.[93]

What Rıza achieved, was to legitimise his accusation towards the specific person of Sultan Abdülhamit, but avoid a direct attack on the sultanate:

> Ahmed Rıza opérait une dissociation entre le corps éternel du sultan de la dynastie ottoman et le corps corrompu d'Abdülhamid. Cela permettait d'atténuer la tension inhérente à sa politique d'opposition au système hamidien, en critiquant Abdülhamid mais insistant en même temps sur la sacralité du sultanat.[94]

Mechveret levelled more accusations at the Sultan to do with the poverty that beset the country,[95] the increased difficulty at reforming it,[96] and the illegitimate character of his rule as un-Islamic despot.[97] Given his refusal to give in to advocating violent means to achieve political aims, Rıza cited examples of how the matter of the ruler's legitimacy had been dealt with in the past through binding *fetvas* (legal opinions). One example he mentioned related to the election of the first of the *Rashidun* Caliphs Abu-Bakr (Caliph from 632 to 634):

> Demande – Lorsque la présence d'un chef de croyants au siège du Khalifat cesse d'avoir l'approbation des Musulmans ou seulement d'une

> grande partie d'entre eux, le chef des croyants peut-il continuer à se maintenir à son poste contre le gré de ses coreligionnaires?
> Réponse – Non, il doit se rendre à leurs désirs et abandonner sa fonction.
> (On sait qu'Abou-Beker, après la cérémonie de la soumission monta sur l'estrade en criant: 'S'il y a une partie mécontent de mon élection, je suis prêt à me retirer').[98]

The other example was a more recent one, dating to the recent reign of Sultan Abdülaziz:

> Demande – Si le commandeur des croyants tient une conduite insensée et s'il n'a pas les connaissances politiques exigées pour gouverner, s'il fait des dépenses personnelles que l'Empire ne peut supporter, si son maintien sur le trône doit avoir des conséquences funestes, faut-il, oui ou non, le déposer?
> Réponse – La loi du Chéri dit: Oui.
> Si l'on compare le règne d'Abdul Aziz à celui d'Abdul Hamid, on n'hésiterait pas à reconnaître, que ce dernier a mérité cent fois plus que son prédécesseur d'être frappé par un des fetwas ci-dessus.[99]

Combined together, the two examples showed that legal decisions relating to the impeachment of the Sultan had a solid base in Islamic and Ottoman history, and might be successfully used to remove Abdülhamit II, also in the eyes of those Ottomans closer to a religious reading of the position of the Sultan-Caliph. The conclusion was that: "une pacification durable à l'intérieur de notre pays est impossible avec le régime gouvernemental actuel."[100]

On the relationship with minorities

The relationship between the central power and minorities became a serious issue for the Sultan in the last decades of the nineteenth century, as the massacres in south-eastern Anatolia testify; but the policies he deployed to deal with any grievance that the minorities might raise became a concern for the European governments, as well as for the Young Turks. On the 23rd December 1896, a banquet was organised in Paris under the auspices of *Mechveret* to celebrate the twentieth anniversary of the promulgation of the Ottoman Constitution in 1876; this was attended by Young Turks of all ethnic groups and religious confessions, and by French intellectuals sympathetic to their cause. On that occasion, Rıza spoke forcefully in favour of Ottomanism and denounced the Sultan's treatment of minorities:

> A ce banquet des Grecs, des Arméniens, des Arabes et des Turcs, tous enfants de la même patrie, se trouvaient réunis. Une seule pensée de paix et de concorde unissait tous les cœurs: c'était une protestation contre le

> despotisme du Sultan et les scènes d'horreur dont la Turquie a été le théâtre dans ces deux dernières années. Puisse l'union cordiale et sincère qui a caractérisé cette soirée être engagé de la fraternité qui régnera un jour dans l'Empire, lorsque, délivré de la tyrannie qui l'opprime, il prendra son essor vers la liberté.[101]

In an article in *Mechveret*, Rıza quoted the position expressed by an Armenian member of the CUP:[102]

> Cette lutte [against the regime of Abdülhamit], pour la continuer, pour la mener à bien, il faut que les Arméniens s'unissent aux Turcs … Les Turcs – du moins les Turcs dont nous entendons parler, et ils sont légion – ont les mêmes aspirations que nous, souffrent des mêmes iniquités, visent au but où nous visons. Un rapprochement s'offre de soi-même, la cause commune s'impose. C'est un devoir. C'est plus: c'est une inéluctable nécessité. Inéluctable par la nature de nos mœurs, le genre de notre prime éducation, le caractère de nos rapports. L'identification est là, claire et nette … La main dans la main, avec les Turcs libéraux, nous sommes une force. Abandonnés à nous-mêmes nous ne représentons plus qu'un principe qu'aucun effectif n'étaie. A cette caduque règle machiavélique: Diviser pour régner, dont le Sultan s'est fait une loi, opposons cette autre vieillerie toujours neuve: L'union fait la force.[103]

Similar to what was expressed in the last few lines of the quotation above, Rıza had precise guidelines as to what was needed to withstand the fight against the regime of Sultan Abdülhamit II:

> … isoler les différents partis les uns des autres, diviser les membres d'un même parti, tel est le dernier dessein de la politique du Sultan. Les massacres des Arméniens et la guerre turco-grecque ont malheureusement servi cette politique néfaste en contribuant à accentuer l'antagonisme entre musulmans et chrétiens. … Nous prions donc nos compatriotes Arméniens, comme nous en avons prié dernièrement les Hellènes, de ne pas se prêter à cette politique astucieuse d'Abdul-Hamid, en se livrant, par quelques-uns de leurs organes, à des critiques contre l'islamisme, critique qui ne peuvent qu'éloigner de nous autres, libéraux, les croyants fanatiques, et qui, en somme, servent au Sultan de prétexte pour soulever contre les Arméniens et les Jeunes-Turcs des haines religieuses. La religion doit toujours rester dans le domaine privé; elle ne doit jamais servir de base à un mouvement social et politique.[104]

Certainly, a total convergence of intent between the various Young Turk organisations could only have been possible through a substantial restructuring of specific areas of governance and politics. As explained earlier, pivotal in this reconfiguration of the multiple components of the Empire would be a new position for religion and a revival of an egalitarian national Ottoman sentiment. According to the *Mechveret* group, the proto-national ideology upon which the Ottoman Empire was to rest, at least until 1902, was the specific version of Ottomanism that is being reconstructed and analysed throughout this chapter. This implied two reforms: first, as discussed earlier on in the chapter, religion would not be part of the state and of its policies, but would be relegated to the private sphere. In the words of Rıza himself, "[l]a question religieuse étant pour nous affaire d'ordre absolument privé, … Il n'entre pas dans notre programme de mêler la religion à la politique; nous avons le respect de toutes les croyances."[105] The second reform, dependent on the first, would consist in the full inclusion of ethnic and religious minorities within the state's representative branches – that would be resuscitated with the revival of the 1876 Constitution – and within its legal system. The *Mechveret* group did not want to change the ethno-religious balance of the Empire but to uphold it. The will for inclusion was confirmed to the journal's European readers through the pages of *Mechveret*: "La Chambre [referring to the chamber of parliament formed after the establishment of the constitution] ne touchera … ni aux autres privilèges accordés aux sujets israélites et chrétiens de l'Empire."[106] In the view of the *Mechveret* group, the application of existing laws and regulations would suffice to create equal citizenship rights and obligations for all components of the Ottoman population. Sure enough, this attitude entailed the negation of rights, reforms and privileges granted to any single group. This meant that Macedonians, Armenians and Albanians had to regard themselves as Ottoman first and foremost and only assert their particular sub-identity within this framework. Rıza and his group ostracised from the Young Turk umbrella movement any group that worked for the acquisition of independence, or special status of a minority, as individualistic attitudes.[107] Such factions would not be partners in the struggle against the Sultan but, on the contrary, their actions would result in the destabilisation of governance and end up being of help to the Sultan's oppressive measures. Therefore, the constitution of activist groups based on ethnic affiliation, as shown by the Armenians in the previous years, was considered to be counterproductive to the interests of their compatriots, and dangerous because it aimed at constituting a national league (of Albanians in the north and Macedonians) that would harm the idea of the *Mechveret*-style Ottomanism. The specific interests of some of these committees had contributed to the consolidation of sentiments of hostility towards Muslims, and had drawn the Christian population of the Empire closer to Europe, forging for themselves the appearance of religious martyrs. This had been made clear when, referring to certain revolutionary committees, Rıza wrote:

> Avant de parler des comités révolutionnaires je tiens à maudire la détestable administration du Sultan qui leur à donné naissance. Les comités ou ligues politiques sont toujours, dans un Etat, un signe de désordre et de faiblesse. L'Empire ottoman est devenu un champ de

rivalités, où chaque parti sème des haines et ne récolte souvent que la mort. ... C'est dans cette anarchie que l'égoïsme d'Abdul-Hamid trouve complète satisfaction. Il est donc de son intérêt de laisser se créer, se développer des parties révolutionnaires, qui, par leur propagande séparatiste, divisent le peuple ottoman et l'empêchent de travailler, de concert avec ces différents comités, contre le tyran commun.[108]

What emerges from the above is that the plan of the *Mechveret* group for the future Ottoman Empire was unconditionally based on a unitary national entity that nonetheless preserved pluralism, understood here as the equal status of all ethnicities, with their respective particularities and religions being allocated to the private domain. This idea of Ottoman citizenship, if reflected in country-wide institutions, would strengthen the cohesion of a newly emerging state but would simultaneously relegate ethnicity to a marginal place: the common good, seen by *Mechveret* as the ideology behind Ottomanism, was in no way to be endangered by any type of other sentiment of belonging or affiliation.

In formulating the above approach, however, Rıza did not consider a number of issues. The fact that he regarded the existing laws as sufficient, if properly applied, to uphold a real equality between different ethnic and religious groups does not entail that the minorities were of the same opinion. Moreover, as will emerge from the Conclusion, there were undoubtedly sections of the minorities which believed in the Ottomanist plan but they did so either because they thought the alternative would position them in a worse situation, or because they opted for the federalist plan of Sabahattin which, in their eyes, gave them more assurance of the real possibility of equality and self-administration than that of the *Mechveret* group. It seems evident, therefore, that Rıza misread the intention of those members of the minorities within the Young Turk organisation as these would at first work together with the *Mechveret* group in order to get rid of Abdülhamit, only to move on to a more autonomous plan of action in a later stage, unless sufficiently satisfied with further changes. Here, the tension in Rıza's ideology rested in the fact that he did not consider that his plan had been formed from a dominant position and was not wholly appreciative of the 'next' necessary step that the *Mechveret* was to develop if the minorities were to be incorporated in the group he headed.

The trial against Mechveret

The warm welcome given to Young Turk émigrés in Paris had initially fostered in them the hope that the French government would support their cause:

> [N]ous ne demandons pas à la France ou aux autres puissances d'intervenir *manu militari* en faveur de la liberté pour soutenir la nation contre

> la tyrannie exorbitante du sultan et pour rétablir la Constitution. Nous sommes les adversaires décidés de toute intervention matérielle. Mais l'intervention morale et puissante de la presse en faveur de la noble cause de la Constitution, nous l'avons toujours désirée et provoquée.[109]

That this would not happen became crystal clear on 11th April 1896, when the French Interior Ministry, giving in to pressure from the Ottoman Ambassador Münir Bey,[110] charged the *Préfecture* (represented by Monsieur Antoine Puybaraud)[111] to ban the publication of *Mechveret*,[112] and invite Rıza to promptly leave the country. The exchange between the two men went as follows:

> Vous combattez la politique du Sultan, dit M. Puybaraud à Ahmed-Riza. Or le gouvernement veut être agréable au Sultan. Je suis chargé par M. le ministre de l'intérieur de vous inviter à quitter Paris dans le plus bref délai possible. Partez, on vous paiera les frais du voyage. Mais n'essayez pas de vous soustraire à cette expulsion officieuse, sinon le gouvernement se verrait réduit à prendre contre vous une mesure de rigueur.[113]

Given that the French government had no valid reason to act as it did, since all the articles published in *Mechveret* had been respectful of the law,[114] Rıza asked Puybaraud: "Why do you expel me, does an honest man not have the right to reside in Paris? [Puybaraud replied], This is about politics."[115]

Much as the measures the French government had undertaken against *Mechveret* and Rıza must have aroused disappointment and cause for serious concern in him, they also testified to the threat the Sultan felt as coming from the Young Turks émigrés' intellectual activism, and its potential for creating a united front between the opposition and the European governments. The news of the ban on *Mechveret* spread instantly, and French press reacted vehemently to what it regarded as an attack on the freedom of expression of a man who was fighting for justice and freedom in his native country:

> Pauvre France! Longtemps elle fut le refuge de la pensée libre, qui n'a rien de commun avec ce que de grotesques suppôts de loges ont baptisé libre-pensée; pendant des siècles les révolutionnaires – flétris de l'épithète de révolutionnaires pour les besoins de la cause des jouisseurs – y trouvèrent un véritable asile contre la persécution, toujours odieuse d'où qu'elle vienne et qui qu'elle vise ...[116]

Practically all influential newspapers – *L'Evénement, Le Jour, La Paix, La Libre Parole, L'Autorité, L'Echo de Paris, La Justice*, and *La Dépêche* – attacked the ban, and even more the request for Rıza to leave France describing it as an "odieuse attitude," a "lamentable mesure," and "une Expulsion sournoise;"[117] journalist Philippe Dubois, who covered the *Mechveret* trial for *L'Intransigeant*, described Rıza as "nullement un révolutionnaire ... simplement un libéral."[118] It was also noted in the press that other countries, on similar occasions, had acted differently, and protected freedom of thought and speech; as in the case of the refusal of the English government to hand over to France, or either expel, the refugees of the *Commune*, and of Abbas, the Khedive of Egypt to expel Murat Bey. The subservient attitude of the French government to the Sultan's wishes was all the more hard to understand, given that the Sultan had spurred the killing of fifty thousand Christians in the Armenian *vilayets*, whom France, a Catholic Country, was expected to protect.[119] French public opinion followed the press in what came to be known as *L'affaire Ahmet Rıza* siding with *Mechveret*; so much so, that "Rıza acknowledged that the trial had promoted the Young Turk cause more than one year of publication of *Mechveret*."[120]

The Sultan was clearly not happy with this turn of events, and renewed pressure on the French government, which, giving in once more, launched a court case against *Mechveret*; this ended on 4th of August 1897 with a reprimand and a mild pecuniary conviction for the editors, Rıza and Ganem, though the ban against the journal remained in place.[121] In publicity terms, the whole '*affaire*' was a success for Rıza: not long after the trial ended, publisher Chevalier-Marescq came forward with an interest in the booklet *Procès contre le Mechveret et La Jeune Turquie*, and in Ganem's manuscript *Les Sultans Ottomans* that would be published later on.[122] Still Rıza had to find another place to publish *Mechveret*; initially, he opted for Geneva, but, though he was granted residency there, he could not set up a printing office because of lack of funds. When a modest donation was offered from Brussels, he started publishing *Mechveret* in Ottoman from there, though only for a few weeks, until the end of September 1897 when the Belgian government banned the journal on account of publishing articles deemed 'unfit', and took steps to arrest Rıza with a view to expelling him.[123] A stratagem was found to by-pass the ban against *Mechveret*: handing over editorial responsibilities to Belgian MP Georges Lorand, albeit only officially.

All in all, publication of Mechveret from Geneva and Brussels was erratic, and it was not until sometime later that it resumed regularly, and that the journal could circulate in various cities in Europe and beyond: Paris, Christiana, Copenhagen, Berlin, Hamburg, Cologne, Brussels, Geneva, Athens, and Cairo.[124]

The ban against *Mechveret* in France and Belgium, and the attempts at expelling Rıza from both countries contributed significantly to focussing attention on the question of the relationship between the Young Turk movement and the European governments. Rıza relinquished his initial optimism and lost all hope that the West would express moral support for the Young Turk cause, accusing it, in fact, of hypocrisy[125] in overtly exhorting the Sultan to move on with reform while covertly supporting him and, in actual facts, stabilising his position: "Le Sultan actuel étant soutenu par le Tzar et par l'empereur d'Allemagne ... c'est elle [*i.e.* Europe] qui a fortifié l'omnipotence du Sultan et l'a rendu indomptable."[126] To make his position all the more clear, Rıza wrote an open letter to the French parliament, repeating the accusation to France, and other European governments and to Russia of cooperating with the Sultan's oppressive regime, while, bestowing their protection on some minorities (Christian ones), and requesting reforms to the latter's exclusive advantage, fomenting divisions within the Empire. Exhibiting once more his positivistic beliefs, Rıza urged reform that would be inspired by the principles of "égalité, la sécurité de la vie, de l'honneur et des biens, enfin les garanties et le contrôle auxquels toute agglomération d'êtres humains a droit en ce siècle."[127] Joining forces with Rıza, Ganem published an article in *Mechveret*, also in the form of an open letter to the French parliament, which mixed praise for the impact of French liberal ideas on the aspirations for progress of the Ottoman population with accusations directed at the French government for being, in reality, an accomplice of Sultan Abdülhamit II's in exacting vengeance on the citizens of the Empire.[128]

Rıza and the Ottomanist plan

Rıza had moved to Paris in self-imposed exile full of enthusiasm, persuaded that France offered a great potential for personal and political development. He worked hard at establishing himself among Parisian intellectuals, and earned their respect and a degree of popularity. But through the trial against *Mechveret* and his host government's attempt to expel him, Rıza experienced first-hand the hypocrisy of the French authorities which gave in to the Sultan's request to silence the journal and ostracise him while pretending to uphold freedom as an absolute value.

His personal difficulties must have contributed to making the question of the relationship the Young Turk movement should entertain with the West a cornerstone of his thinking; so much so that he would devote an entire book, *La Faillite morale de la politique occidentale en Orient*, written upon years of experience of European politics, to properly discuss it. Its opening reveals a sharp approach to the question:

> Le titre que je donne à cet ouvrage n'est pas tout à fait juste, car la politique de l'Europe à l'égard de la Turquie n'a jamais été subordonnée à la morale. Le succès était le seul but, la force seule créait le droit. De tout temps, l'intérêt religieux et l'intérêt matériel ont été les mobiles essentiels de cette politique.[129]

On Rıza's account, the intellectual achievements and the scientific advancements of the West had translated in economic not 'humanistic' and positive terms, and, therefore, had not improved society: "[l]a civilisation n'a pas supprimé la barbarie, elle l'a tout simplement raffinée."[130] It appears from what was just quoted that he was not affected by an envy of the West, and was in no mood to concede defeat before it, although his attitude was not one of principle mistrust: hence he could not be described as an advocate of

"Westernisation against the West."[131] Rıza's stance on the question of the West–East relationship may have been influenced, alongside positivism and personal difficulties he had to endure, by the work of Gustave Le Bon, whom he met and befriended at the *déjeuners du mercredi*.[132]

With his forceful and passionate defence of religious tolerance, accompanied by the denunciation of the corruption of sectors of the religious establishment and the political use of religion of Abdülhamit II's pan-Islamism, Rıza expressed a genuine affirmation of Ottomanism which, though connected with the desire to prevent the disintegration of the Empire, does not appear to have been strategically subordinated to it. In conclusion, combining Comte's concept of progress (as, mainly, a moral achievement) with Le Bon's analysis of the relationship between Western and Eastern cultures, Rıza came to the conclusion that, in reforming the Empire, it would be best to allow the Ottoman aspect to keep its hegemony:

> Désirant garder à notre civilisation orientale son caractère propre et ses traditions, nous n'avons voulu emprunter à l'Occident que 'les résultats généraux de son évolution scientifique, seuls vraiment assimilables et nécessaires pour éclairer un peuple dans sa marche vers la liberté et le progrès'.[133]

Overall, Rıza carried out a work of synthesis, that was to be central in the conceptualisation of Ottomanism, between positivism and Islam which proved that the Empire could retain its particular heritage and Muslim background and fuse this with ideas, inspired by the Western experience, of a society organised and functioning according to the demands of modernity. In Rıza's scheme, religion was to be tailored a new role but, nonetheless, an important one from the perspective of the individual. Positivism was to serve as the vehicle through which all this could actually be attained: it was a philosophical approach that did not oppose religions, it gave the Ottomans a sense of equality both in the internal composition of society as well as on the international scene, and provided a framework that encapsulated the greatness of the Muslim civilisation of the past.

In the actualisation of this specific blend of Ottomanism, violence was to be, as discussed earlier, totally rejected. This came out of the idea that such a process would strain the already difficult relationship among ethnic and religious groups and would invite Europe to interfere and possibly occupy the Empire. Armed revolution was also counter to the peaceful attitude of positivism. Tightly connected to this non-violent vision is the role that the West would be expected to play in the process of reform. According to the *Mechveret* group, no European government would provide disinterested help to the cause of reform, and, consequently, the only constructive support was the ideological co-operation of the European liberal civil society. The idea of moral help becomes central when considering the importance of Rıza's plan to build a national sentiment based on multi-confessionalism and ethnic plurality as the basis of the future Empire. This plan envisaged a particular blend of Ottomanism in which utmost importance was given to the indivisibility of the Empire without a consideration of other alternatives, such as the federalist option of the group headed by Sabahattin, as discussed in the next chapter. Whoever would push for reform or achievements that would benefit only one ethnic or religious part of Ottoman society could consider himself as an enemy of the reform and type of Ottomanism the *Mechveret* group supported.

Notes

1. As discussed in the previous chapter.
2. The sources on which Rıza's thinking has been reconstructed come primarily from *Mechveret*, the journal he founded with Halil Ganem, and other publications of the time; the same applies to the question of the relationship the Young Turk movement should entertain with the West, which Rıza further elaborated in his monograph, *La Faillite morale de la politique occidentale*, published in 1922. As already mentioned, even though the book was published later than the events discussed here, Rıza's position on the topics discussed throughout this chapter did not change. The content of the various articles that featured during the period 1895 to 1902, in fact, is substantially reiterated by Rıza in the book *La Faillite morale de la politique occidentale*. This can be concretely seen in Rıza's view of the masses, expressed in the same terms on p. 206 of the book and earlier in his article "L'Inaction des Jeunes Turcs," 91. Equally, his negative view of practical support from the West features as the leitmotiv of his entire book but also as one of the main points of the programme of Rıza's circle as expressed on the first issue of *Mechveret*, La Rédaction, "Notre Programme," *Mechveret Supplément Français* 1, no. 1 (December 1895), 1. Lastly, the idea that European powers operate solely out of their own gains is clearly stated in Rıza's book but also voiced earlier on, both in 1902 and 1903: "Avrupa Matbu'atı Niçin Türkler Aleyhindedir ve Bulgarlar Leyhindedir?" *Şûra-yı Ümmet* 35 (August 1902) and "Question de Macedoine," 211–212.
3. Erdal Kaynar, "Ahmed Rıza (1858–1930) Histoire d'un vieux jeune turc," PhD diss. (Paris: École des Hautes Études en Sciences Sociales, 2011), 56.
4. Ibid., 57.
5. Lewis, *Emergence*, 193.
6. The *Mekteb-i Sultani* was the most important one in the country.
7. Kaynar, "Ahmed Rıza," 139.
8. Rıza, *Ahmed Rıza Bey'in Anıları*, 9.
9. For discussion of how the *Exposition Universelle* and similar events were viewed at the time, see, Zeynep Çelik, *Displaying the Orient. Architecture of Islam at Nineteenth Century World's Fairs* (Berkeley: University of California Press, 1992); and Zeynep Çelik and Leila Kinney, "Ethnography and Exhibitionism at the Expositions Universelles," *Assemblage* 13 (December 1990): 34–59.
10. Rıza, *Ahmed Rıza Bey'in Anıları*, 10. Sure enough, the opening of the 1889 Paris Exposition on the centenary of the French revolution Revolution was something of an embarrassment for the powers still ruled by monarchies. The Ottoman statesman in Paris, Esad Paşa, somewhat anxious as to the appropriate course of action, telegrammed that the British, Austrian, Russian and German ambassadors had made it clear to him that they would absent themselves from Paris on the occasion. This would mean that he would be the "only ambassador of a

11 Rıza, *Ahmed Rıza Bey'in Anıları*, 10–11.
12 Ibid.
13 Kaynar, "Ahmed Rıza," 191.
14 Ganem, *Les Sultans Ottomans*.
15 Hanioğlu, *Young Turks in Opposition*, 39.
16 Charles Kurzman, *Democracy Denied, 1905–1915 – Intellectuals and the Fate of Democracy* (Cambridge, MA: Harvard University Press, 2008), 41.
17 Ramsaur, *The Young Turks*.
18 Kurzman, *Democracy Denied*, 41.
19 "Une expulsion sournoise," *La Justice* (April 1896), *Mechveret Supplément Français* 1, no. 9 (April 1896), 6.
20 His talk, entitled "La politique sociale de la Turquie," *La Revue Occidentale* 2, no. 111 (1899), 84.
21 Held on Sunday 5th of March 1899, *La Revue Occidentale* 2, no. 111, 366.
22 Held on 18th January 1901; his talk, entitled "La Religion islamique," *La Revue Occidentale* 2, no. 113 (1901), 43 – extracts of the speech are on pp. 54–57.
23 *La Revue Occidentale* 2, no. 114 (1902), 124–126.
24 Ibid., 28.
25 Personal communication from Professor François Georgeon at SOAS on 11 March, 2009. Rıza had already read on positivism in Istanbul when, in 1887, he discovered a book by Dr. Jean-François Robinet, an old collaborator of Auguste Comte. However, the turning point towards positivism came when Rıza befriended Pierre Laffitte, whom he met in Paris, in 1890. Kaynar, "Ahmed Rıza," 193.
26 Auguste Comte, *Système de politique positive* (Paris: L. Mathias, 1851–1854).
27 Auguste Comte, *Cours de philosophie positive* (Paris: Ballieres et Fils, 1864).
28 Although no socialist theorist appeared among the Young Turks, "the social radicalism of the non-Muslim socialists appealed to the Young Turks, liberal and unionist alike. They shared the ideas and the ideals of the French Revolution as the inspiration for their movement." Feroz Ahmad, "Some Thoughts on the Role of Ethnic and Religious Minorities in the Genesis and Development of the Socialist Movement in Turkey: 1876–192," in Tunçay and Zürcher, *Socialism and Nationalism in the Ottoman Empire*, 18.
29 Notably, it was the ethnic minorities that had developed a bourgeoisie and an intelligentsia (Greek, Bulgarian, Armenian and Jewish of Thessalonica) that were mainly responsible for the introduction of socialist ideas into the Empire, Ahmad, "Some Thoughts on the Role of Ethnic and Religious Minorities in the Genesis and Development of the Socialist Movement in Turkey: 1876–1923," 13.
30 Kaynar, "Ahmed Rıza," 198.
31 Ibid., 200.
32 The complete list of months in the Calendar was as follows: Moses, Homer, Aristotle, Archimedes, Caesar, Saint Paul, Dante, Gutenberg, Shakespeare, Descartes, Frederick II, Bichat.
33 La Rédaction, "Notre Programme," 1.
34 Here is how *The Times* described the new publication: "The Young Turkey party has started a fortnightly paper in French and Arabic, which is to be the organ of the Turco-Syrian committee of reforms presided over by [sic] Hali Ganem Effendi ... The object of this committee is the restoration of the Constitution and reforms." *The Times*, 16th December 1895.
35 La Rédaction, "Notre Programme," 1.
36 Perhaps, on account of that, the *Supplément Français* sold better than *Meşveret* itself.

Ahmet Rıza and Mechveret 75

37 Among the various non-Muslim participants worthy of mention were Armenian Pierre Anmeghian (signing his articles as Ottomanus), Jew Albert Fua (signing Un Ami de la Turquie) and Greek Aristidi Efendi (signing G. Umid). Kaynar, "Ahmed Rıza," 385.
38 Le Comité, "Déclaration," *Mechveret Supplément Français* 1, no. 19 (September 1896), 1.
39 Whatever Rıza's intention, his leadership of the Paris branch and editorship of *Mechveret* were the object of intense and renewed criticism, which led to almost constant skirmishes, Hanioğlu, *Young Turks in Opposition*, 95–6, 128.
40 Rıza, *La Faillite morale de la politique occidentale*, 14. Notably, Rıza did not extend his criticism of European rulers to European citizens, acknowledging their honesty and moral principles.
41 Comte, *Cours de philosophie positive*.
42 La Rédaction, 'Notre Programme', 1.
43 Léouzon Le Duc, *La Turquie est-elle incapable de réformes?*, 7.
44 Kuran, "The Impact of the Turkish Elite in the Nineteenth Century," 109.
45 Ahmet Rıza, "Une Explication," 1–2.
46 Rıza never changed his mind and, even in the 1920s, was still convinced of the same, as he reiterated through the pages of his book. Rıza, *La Faillite morale de la politique occidentale*, 34.
47 There was a further, subtle, reason for Rıza's firm opposition to any foreign involvement with matters internal to the Empire: since, in the past, all foreign interventions had had extremely negative effects, the very idea had become very unpopular in the population's eyes. The Sultan presented all suggestions for reform coming from foreign powers as an infringement of sovereignty, and used public aversion to it to resist any such reform. From the point of view of the opposition, denouncing foreign intervention as unacceptable was a way to deprive the Sultan of his rhetorical stratagem.
48 Ahmet Rıza, "Les Missionnaires en Turquie," *Mechveret Supplément Français* 1, no. 3 (January 1896), 2. Rıza also lamented that the governments that sent missionaries to the Empire went as far as requesting the Ottoman population, Muslim or otherwise, to indemnify those missionaries who claimed experiencing material damage during their mission.
49 Ibid., 2.
50 "Büchner's battle against religion [was] a mainstay for the Young Turk ideology at the outset of the movement," Hanioğlu, *Young Turks in Opposition*, 22.
51 Ramsaur, *The Young Turks*.
52 Ahmet Rıza, "Le positivisme et l'Islamisme," *La Revue Occidentale* 2, no. 103 (1891), 116.
53 www.marxists.org/reference/subject/philosophy/index.htm.
54 Ahmet Rıza, "Le calife et ses devoirs," *La Revue Occidentale* 2, no. 108 (1896): 93–98.
55 Rıza, *Tolérance Musulmane*, 20.
56 Elsewhere Rıza would highlight the tolerant attitude of Islam towards dissent and criticism, calling the latter "une des essences de l'islamisme," Rıza, "Vitalité de la Jeune Turquie," 3.
57 Rıza, *Tolérance Musulmane*, 139.
58 There might have been a hint of positioning in Rıza's attempt to preserve the sensitive balance between Islam, as the main religion of the empire, and other faiths present in it, which was constantly threatened by the Sultan's centralised despotism, and by the West's request for selective reform for minorities. This is because, as many small, but strategically important, opposition groups were emerging, especially in the Balkans and Armenia, Rıza's stance might have been

partly inspired by a desire to please, and contain, the minorities' individualistic requests.
59 There is a similarity here between Rıza's position and Ziya Gökalp's. *Turkish Nationalism and Western Civilisation – Selected Essays of Ziya Gökalp*, translated and edited by Niyazi Berkes (London: Allen and Unwin, 1959), 284–289. See, also the following passage: "European civilisation will have a beneficial effect on us, not only with its science and technology, but also in matters of taste and morality. But this influence is permissible only to the extent that it helps to dismantle the Persian one. The moment it attempts to supplant what it destroys, it has itself become harmful and should be resisted." Ziya Gökalp, *Hars ve Medeniyet* (Istanbul: Toker Yayınları, 1995), 15.
60 Rıza, *Tolérance Musulmane*, 140.
61 Rıza, "Une nouvelle tactique," 3.
62 Ahmet Rıza, "La Russie et la Jeune Turquie," *Mechveret Supplément Français* 1, no. 10 (May 1896), 4.
63 Ahmet Rıza, "Aux Arméniens," *Mechveret Supplément Français* 3, no. 57 (June 1898), 7.
64 Ahmet Rıza, "Chrétien, Musulman et Humanité," *Mechveret Supplément Français* 1, no. 11 (May 1896), 3.
65 Ahmet Rıza, "Pourquoi l'Europe ne réclame pas le Rétablissement de la Constitution en Turquie," *Mechveret Supplément Français* 1, no. 21 (October 1896), 4.
66 Philippe Dubois, "Expulsion de M. Ahmed-Riza," *L'Intransigeant* (April 1896), reproduced in *Mechveret Supplément Français* 1, no. 9 (April 1896), 5.
67 Hanioğlu, *Young Turks in Opposition*.
68 It may be interesting to recall, at this junction, Ganem's position on the causes of problems for the Empire, which he identified in a combination between despotism and fanaticism: "voilà les deux principales causes de la décadence de l'empire ottoman et de la dégénérescence, de plus marquée, de la dynastie." Ganem, *Les Sultans Ottomans*, xi. On Ganem's account, despotism was the manifestation of a dying entity, the ultima ratio with which the Sultan would try and hold on to power, and fanaticism the twist impressed to Islam by corrupted ulema that had become subservient to the Sultan to preserve their own privileges.
69 Ahmed Rıza, "La Russie et la Jeune Turquie," 4.
70 Ibid.
71 Ahmed Rıza "Appel aux cabinets européens," *Mechveret Supplément Français* 1, no. 16 (August 1896): 1–2.
72 Antecedents of Rıza's criticism, brought forth, for instance, by Lutfi Paşa and Koçu Bey, are discussed in Lewis, "Ottoman Observers of Ottoman Decline," 71. Comparing what Ahmet Rıza considered the causes of decline of the Empire to what Lutfi Paşa, the Grand Vizier of Sultan Süleyman, and Koçu Bey, advisor of Sultan Murat IV, respectively wrote 300 and 250 years earlier, gives an idea about how Rıza envisaged change. Regardless of the difference in times, it is worth noticing that the general negative features are common to all three; this helps position the efforts of Rıza within a longer and broader discourse around religious and political reform in the Ottoman Empire.
73 Ahmet Rıza, "Sixième Lettre Ouverte," *Mechveret Supplément Français* 2, no. 24 (December 1896), 2. A letter by Abdullah Cevdet published in *Mechveret* made similar accusations using very crude language: "Les hauts personnages et la plupart des agents de la Préfecture, se recrutent dans les rangs des vulgaires criminels condamnés à perpétuité, mais qui sont graciés par décret spécial de leur Auguste collègue, le Sultan, violateur de lois." Abdullah Cevdet, "Les prisonniers politiques en Turquie," *Mechveret Supplément Français* 3, no. 56 (May 1898), 5.

74 Here is another similarity with Ganem's position that, to improve the worsening situation, the elitist Ottoman intellectual circle had to propagate the modern and progressive ideals, as "[l]a prospérité d'une nation dépend de la culture intellectuelle de ses chefs." Ganem, *Les Sultans Ottomans*, 298.
75 Rıza, *La Faillite morale de la politique occidentale*, 135.
76 Fuad, "L'Instruction Publique en Turquie," *Mechveret Supplément Français* 1, no. 3 (January 1896), 1.
77 Fortna, *Imperial Classroom*.
78 On the particular issue of censorship and for a comprehensive list of the banned words, refer to Chapter 2.
79 Un Ami de la Turquie, "Lettre Ouverte," *Mechveret Supplément Français* 1, no. 1 (December 1895), 2.
80 Ibid.
81 Rıza, "Une Explication," 1.
82 Fuad, "Deuxième Lettre Ouverte," *Mechveret Supplément Français* 1, no. 10 (May 1896), 2.
83 La Rédaction, "Notre Programme," 1.
84 Rıza, "Chrétien, Musulman et Humanité," 3.
85 Le Comité, "Déclaration," 1.
86 "Soumission ou Déposition," *Mechveret Supplément Français* 1, no. 14 (July 1896), 4.
87 G. Umid, "Au feu!" *Mechveret Supplément Français* 2, no. 29 (February 1897), 2.
88 The Empire had gone bankrupt in 1875.
89 Umid, "Au feu!" 2.
90 "Banquet de la Jeune Turquie," 4.
91 Ahmet Rıza, "Mechveret & Sultan," *Mechveret Supplément Français* 2, no. 36 (June 1897), 5, and G. Umid, "La Situation en Orient," *Mechveret Supplément Français* 2, no. 37 (June 1897), 1.
92 Rıza, "Mechveret & Sultan," 5–6.
93 "Soumission ou Déposition," 1.
94 Kaynar, "Ahmed Rıza," 75.
95 See, among others, Fuad & Rechid, "Responsabalité du Sultan," *Mechveret Supplément Français* 1, no. 19 (January 1898): 2–4. Halil Ganem, "Causerie Politique," *Mechveret Supplément Français* 3, no. 50 (December 1896): 1–2.
96 G. Umid, "Anarchie morale & matérielle," *Mechveret Supplément Français* 2, no. 25 (December 1896), 2. Rıza, "Mechveret & Sultan," 5.
97 Ahmet Rıza, "Anniversaire d'Abdul-Hamid," *Mechveret Supplément Français* 3 n. 62, (September 1898), 3–4.
98 Ahmet Rıza, "Le Sultan Illégitime," *Mechveret Supplément Français* 2, no. 37 (July 1897), 4. To mark the change of attitude, Rıza recalled that, five years earlier, the movement would address any request to him as a plea: "[l]orsque, il y a cinq ans, nous avons pour la première fois, soumis au Sultan notre rapport sur la nécessité des réformes, nous avons usé à son égard de toutes les formes de la prière." Rıza, "Mechveret & Sultan," 5. I explain and translate the term soumission used by Ahmed Rıza, as the *bay'a* of the Caliph.
99 Rıza, "Le Sultan Illégitime," 4.
100 Rıza, "Mémoire," 1.
101 "Banquet de la Jeune Turquie," 3.
102 Probably, *Mechveret* contributor Pierre Anmeghian.
103 Ahmet Rıza, "Turcs et Arméniens," *Mechveret Supplément Français* 3, no. 63 (September 1898), 2.
104 Rıza, "Aux Arméniens," 7.
105 Rıza, "Une nouvelle tactique," 3.

78 *Ahmet Rıza and Mechveret*

106 Rıza, "Pourquoi l'Europe ne réclame pas le Rétablissement de la Constitution en Turquie," 4.
107 Ibid., 3–4.
108 Ahmet Rıza, "Les Comités Révolutionnaires," *Mechveret Supplément Français* 4, no. 74 (April 1899), 1–2.
109 Fuad, "La Constitution Ottomane," *Mechveret Supplément Français* 1, no. 7 (March 1896), 2.
110 Georges Clémenceau, "Pour faire plaisir au Sultan," *La Dépêche* (April 1896), reproduced in *Mechveret Supplément Français* 1, no. 9 (April 1896), 7–8.
111 M. Puybaraud was branded in the press as the "grand eunuque blanc de la police républicaine," Clémenceau, "Pour faire plaisir au Sultan," 7.
112 Interestingly, and revealingly in terms of who had interest in the ban, this did not apply to *Mechveret Supplément Français*.
113 Philippe Ciais, "L'Expulsion d'Ahmed-Riza," *L'Echo de Paris* (April 1896), reproduced in *Mechveret Supplément Français* 1, no. 9 (April 1896), 5.
114 As Rıza would say at the trial: "Les principes dont s'inspire le Mechveret sont bien connus: nous ne faisons pas de distinction entre races et religions, nous défendons l'égalité et la justice. Ces principes se retrouvent tous dans la législation religieuse et civile de l'Empire ottoman, et nous n'avons qu'y obéir en citoyens respectueux de toute institution établie et équitable." *Procès contre le Mechveret et La Jeune Turquie* (Paris, Chevalier-Marescq, 1897), 2.
115 Rıza, *Ahmed Rıza Bey'in Anıları*, 15.
116 Georges Barbezieux, "Odieuse Attitude," *La Paix* (April 1896), reproduced in *Mechveret Supplément Français* 1, no. 9 (April 1896), 3.
117 A collection of articles on the affair is in the Archives of the Paris Police, "Mahmoud Pacha (beau-frère du sultan de Constantinople)," *Préfecture de Police de Paris* – BA1.169.
118 Dubois, "Expulsion de M. Ahmed-Riza," 6.
119 Clémenceau, "Pour faire plaisir au Sultan," 8.
120 Kaynar, "Ahmed Rıza."
121 For a comprehensive and detailed account of the trial, see *Procès contre le Mechveret et La Jeune Turquie* (Paris: Chevalier-Marescq, 1897), 92. The verdict reads: "Condamne ... Ahmed-Riza-Bey et Halil-Ganem à 16 fr. d'amende et, à raison des considérations ci-dessus relevées, leur fait application de loi Bérenger." This law allowed for the suspension of the sentence for first-time offenders like Rıza and Ganem.
122 Halil Ganem, *Les Sultans Ottomans*.
123 Ahmed Rıza, "Le Mechveret Turc en Belgique," *Mechveret Supplément Français* 3, no. 49 (December 1897): 5.
124 It was also sold in Algerian town of Bougie, at the house of an Ahmed Ben Derrah. *Mechveret Supplément Français* 4, no. 83 (October 1899), 3.
125 Interestingly, the same accusation that Rıza was to wage against the West in his book, published in 1922.
126 Ahmet Rıza, "Le Sultan Illégitime," 4.
127 Ahmet Rıza, "Lettre au Parlement Français," *Mechveret Supplément Français* 2, no. 47 (November 1897), 1.
128 Halil Ganem, "Notre Requête au Parlement," *Mechveret Supplément Français* 3, no. 57 (July 1898): 1–3.
129 Rıza, *La Faillite morale de la politique occidentale*, 5.
130 Ibid., 11.
131 Orhan Koçak, "'Westernisation against the West': Cultural Politics in the Early Turkish Republic," in Celia Kerslake, Kerem Öktem and Philip Robins (eds), *Turkey's Engagement with Modernity – Conflict and Change in the Twentieth Century* (New York: Palgrave, 2010), 305–22.

132 In his monumental work *La Civilisation des Arabes* (Paris: Fermin-Didot, 1884), Le Bon addressed the question of the relationship between cultures, challenging the received view that it is always the dominant – in political and military terms – culture that supplants the less powerful one, arguing that this one-way narrative wrongly omitted from discussion examples of cultural cross-fertilisations as nothing more than exceptional instances. Instead, Le Bon suggested that cultures go from a dominant position to a marginal one in an almost cyclical way, de-mythologising the idea of cultural superiority, which had always accompanied, and biased, discussion of the West–East relationship. On the subject of cultural and intellectual development, Le Bon was struck by the enthusiasm with which Arabs through the centuries had cultivated and fostered knowledge: "L'ardeur qu'ils [Arabs] apportèrent dans l'étude est véritablement frappant," *Le Bon, La Civilisation des Arabes*. Book V, 38. He reached the conclusion that "l'action exercée par les Arabes sur l'Occident fut également considérable, et que c'est à eux qu'est due la civilisation de l'Europe." Le Bon, *La Civilisation des Arabes*. Book V, 152. He described the Arab philosophical school as the natural heir of the Greek one, praising the establishment of universities throughout the Arab world and beyond – in Baghdad, Cairo, Toledo and Cordoba – which, equipped with up-to-date laboratories, observatories, and libraries, had promoted remarkable advancements in mathematics, algebra and geometry, in astronomy, physics, and mechanics, and in chemistry, with specific mention of discoveries related to the synthesis of alcohol, sulphuric and nitric acid, and the invention of the distillation technique.

133 "L'intervention des étrangers," *Mechveret Supplément Français* 6, no. 107 (December 1900), 1.

4 Mehmet Sabahattin and social science

Introducing Mehmet Sabahattin

Mehmet Sabahattin was born in Istanbul in 1879 into a very influential family, one that took a deep interest in political matters, especially concerning the reform of the Empire. His father, *Damat* Mahmut Celalettin Paşa (Mahmut Paşa from now on), the son of the late Minister of the Navy, Bahriye Gürcü Halil Rifat Paşa, served at the Sublime Porte, and acted briefly as Minister of Justice before being appointed to the Ottoman Embassy in Paris; Sabahattin's mother, Seniha Sultan, daughter of Sultan Abdülmecit I,[1] was politically minded and in many ways a woman ahead of her time. In line with the family background, Sabahattin received a modern and eclectic education, during which he bonded with three of his tutors, Şemsettin Sami Bey (Frashëri), who worked at the Translation Office,[2] the Swiss men Barchille Bertradot and a Monsieur Charlier.[3]

An important event in the family life was Mahmut's falling out with Abdülhamit II. Initially, Mahmut, had been a close confidant and aide to the Sultan. When, however, he started criticising some of Abdülhamit's policies and exhorted him to do more, especially in the realm of civil liberties,[4] he fell out of the royal grace. Being convinced that liberal reform was the only method to modernise and revitalise the Empire, and seeing no way of this happening under Abdülhamit, Mahmut and his two sons Sabahattin and Lutfullah planned to move to France in self-imposed exile. Upon their arrival, they were to join forces with members of the Young Turk movement already there, gather enough support from the Great Powers to persuade the Sultan to revise his policies, or step down in favour of an enlightened ruler, which the majority of the Young Turk movement believed to be the former Sultan, Murat V.[5] Sabahattin is said to have been the motor behind the planned flight, as Demetra Vaka[6] reveals in her study of the prince:

> We must carry our fight into the open, my father. We must join those Ottomans who in France, in Switzerland, in Belgium are trying to help our people realize the possibility of rising and demanding a better government. My uncle maintains that these men abroad are adventurers,

vilifying his beneficent rule in order to induce him to buy them off. When the people of Turkey hear that the Sultan's brother-in-law and the Sultan's sister's two sons are joining these men, they will give less credence to this calumny. Therefore, my father, since whatever usefulness you had in this country you have no longer, we must leave.[7]

Once the decision had been taken, and the three men had discussed with Seniha Sultan and Sabahattin's pregnant wife their intention and received approval, the problem to face was a logistic one, and the first thing to do was assemble enough cash to pay for the journey and the accommodation to be found in Paris. To this aim, Mahmut's assets had to be sold, and in a discrete manner not to arouse the Sultan and his circle's suspicion. Initially, he approached an English Jew – one of the family's business advisors – who suggested the family assets should be transferred to a friend of his who would sell them, deposit the money in a foreign bank in his name and, when the fugitives would have reached Paris, transfer the money to them.[8] When, following repeated requests from the man for large sums of money, allegedly necessary to cover the cost of the journey, Sabahattin became suspicious, he went for help and advice to a Swiss man of his own household, probably the Monsieur Charlier mentioned earlier, and the English Jew was exposed as one of Abdülhamit's spies.

In order not to raise suspicion of a change of plans, and also because the prince was "... enjoying the pitting of ... [his] wits against those of the spy,"[9] Sabahattin did not cut off ties with the English Jew but, at the same time, entrusted his Swiss tutor to organise his departure for the day before the one organised by the spy. On the re-scheduled day, the three men boarded another steamer, disguised as stokers and pretended to work on it until the boat passed the Dardanelles. The steamship was the French boat *Géorgie*, bound for Marseille; they boarded on it either the 14th or 16th December 1899[10] in the dark of the night, after having left a letter to Seniha Sultan.[11] In the meantime, the news of their flight had reached the Palace; the three men were thought to be on another boat, the *Congo*, which was stopped and searched from 3 a.m. to 7 p.m. while the *Géorgie* was left to pass undisturbed.[12] A frantic search for the fugitives was launched: a regiment was sent to Adrianople to inspect the trains bound for Europe, a plea addressed to the prince of Bulgaria requesting to check everyone passing through his domains, all boats leaving for Europe thoroughly combed. Furthermore, all Ottoman embassies in Europe were instructed to inform their host governments that the son-in-law of the Sultan had left the Empire after having abducted his two sons, stolen his wife's jewellery, and killed a servant of the harem, a "young and handsome slave girl."[13] The dispatch sent from Istanbul to all the embassies and representatives of the Ottoman Empire abroad read as follows:

> Mahmud Pasha, who of late has shown signs of insanity, has left Turkey without authorisation, kidnapping the two minor sons of Her Highness

Seniheh Sultan, his wife. Since, according to our laws, sons of the imperial household are under immediate and absolute direction of our august master and since, moreover, Her Highness, the Princess, [is] insisting upon regaining her minor sons, I beg you to take whatever measures you consider efficacious and to search for them minutely. In case Mahmud Pasha should be in the country to which you are accredited, immediately call upon the authorities and demand that the insane man, as well as the two children he has stolen, be extradited and returned to Constantinople under surveillance. By imperial order you are to telegraph the result of your efforts at once.[14]

Needless to say, all accusations were fabricated to discredit Mahmut in the eyes of the Europeans, and, in case he had been apprehended, obtain his extradition. The propaganda against him did not stop there: the Porte informed the French government that he had converted to Christianity,[15] and was planning to 'sell his services' to Great Britain.[16] When the *Géorgie* reached Marseilles, the three fugitives were met by the Ottoman Consul General who pleaded with the French police officers not to let the three disembark; much to his disappointment, having questioned the fugitives, and established that the father had no mental illness, and that the two sons had left the Empire of their own will, the authorities officially welcomed them on French soil. This must have happened on 19 December 1899, as *Le Figaro* reported their arrival on 20th December: "Le paquebot *Géorgie* de la Compagnie Paquet ... est arrivé ce soir à Marseille ... ayant à son bord Mahmoud-pacha ... et ses deux fils Sabaheddin, âgé de vingt-trois ans, et Lout Falah [Lutfullah], âgé de ... [vingt[17]]-deux ans."[18]

Settling in Paris

Having arrived in Paris on 22nd December, Mahmut and his sons established their residence at the Grand Hôtel on Boulevard des Capucines.[19] They were eager to meet Rıza, and Rıza was eager to welcome them into the Paris branch of the CUP, as an exchange of letters published in *Mechveret* shows. Mahmut Paşa praised Rıza's activism and anticipated fruitful collaboration with him;[20] Rıza's replied thanking "un des plus éminent personnages de mon pays"[21] and welcoming his participation in the movement:

Notre parti se sent déjà trop heureux de voir un membre, le plus en vue, de la famille impériale lui tendre sa main puissante pour travailler avec lui à la délivrance de la patrie. Ce qui fait le plus de plaisir à mes compagnons de lutte et à moi, c'est que ce témoignage de sympathie vient d'une personne instruite, d'un ancien ministre aux idées larges et libérales ... Si un personnage aussi haut placé que le beau-frère du monarque ne se trouve plus en sécurité dans son pays, quel est donc le sort réservé aux simple citoyens?[22]

Rıza used Mahmut's standing in the Ottoman society to show the all-pervasive character of the opposition to the Sultan: "[d]es plus bas échelons de la société jusqu'aux rangs les plus élevés, tout le monde le [Abdülhamit II] déteste et le flétrit."[23] A month later, in an open letter to Sultan Abdülhamit published in *Mechveret*,[24] Mahmut Paşa explained the reasons for his and sons' flight:

> ... certain que je ne saurais plus vous faire entendre la vérité tant que je serais à Constantinople, j'ai pensé: puisque le Sultan est incapable et se refuse à écouter et à comprendre, il faut que j'éclaire la nation, que je lui expose les dangers du régime actuel et la nécessité de le transformer. C'est afin de remplir ce devoir et de dégager ma conscience de toute responsabilité que je suis venu en Europe. Je suis Musulman et Turc; je désire servir ma patrie sans distinction de race et de religion: mes deux fils ont les mêmes intentions; ils sont venus ici uniquement pour m'aider à remplir ce devoir sacré.[25]

One of the main problems the CUP faced at the time concerned funding; to try and remedy the situation, the three men started conducting exploratory missions in Geneva, London, Cairo, Corfu, and Brussels.[26] They met with M. Kaiserlian, director of the French company *L'Union*, in order to receive a loan of 629,000 francs, they were turned down on a loan of 300,000 francs; while London was, for example, the address of a letter in which *Damat* Mahmut promised to give back a substantial amount if granted a loan of 12,000 pounds.[27] Although they were unsuccessful in their attempts to raise funds, travelling and networking across Europe gave them visibility, reflected in Mahmut's several pleas for help towards the Young Turk cause addressed to the French Prime Minister, the French President, the Russian and German Emperors, and the King of Belgium. Mahmut and his sons attracted attention also from the press, especially in France, England and Switzerland, and were in direct contact with M. Guillard and M. Vaughan, respectively editor and director of *L'Aurore*, with M. Nadaud of *La Paix*, M. Verlez editor of a financial paper, and Countess Mathilda Colonna de Cesari, director of *La Revue d'Europe*.[28] French publicist, historian and poet Pierre Quillard interviewed Mahmut for *L'Aurore*;[29] other interviews appeared in *Le Matin*,[30] and *La Libre Parole*.[31]

The more publicity Mahmut Paşa and his sons attracted, the more embarrassing their flight to Paris became for *Yıldız* palace, particularly in light of their insiders' knowledge of the Sultan's plans, as well as of his weaknesses and fears. In an attempt to lure them back to Istanbul, the Ottoman Ambassador to France, Münir Bey, repeatedly visited them, offering the Sultan's pardon, and large sums of money,[32] but to no avail:

> Pour le faire fléchir, tout fut employé; tout échoua. Plus de vingt émissaires que je pourrais nommer – des officiers, des ministres, des

ambassadeurs étrangers, le Khédive lui-même – lui [*Damad* Mahmud] furent envoyés à lui et à son fils, le prince Sabaheddine, la bouche pleine de promesses ou de menaces, en France, en Suisse, en Égypte, à Corfou, en Belgique.[33]

This was because, as Mahmut himself stated:

Je ne veux rien, ni pour mes fils, ni pour moi. Je veux que le Sultan gouverne honnêtement ... Qu'il change, qu'il donne à son peuple les garanties que celui-ci est en droit d'attendre et nous ne mettrons pas d'autres conditions à notre retour.[34]

Rıza was among those who had anticipated the Sultan's attempted bribery of Mahmut Paşa:

Placé entre un passé noble et honnête, et un nom illustre à se créer dans l'avenir, Mahmoud pacha voudra certainement rester fidèle à la tâche qu'il vient de s'imposer; il ne se laissera pas tromper par les promesses fallacieuses d'Abdul-Hamid, il ne rentrera pas en Turquie avant d'avoir obtenu quelques réformes sérieuses et palpables au profit d'un peuple qui a tant de respect et d'estime pour lui.[35]

The French authorities – the *Ministère de L'Intérieur et des Cultes* (the Ministry of Home Affairs and Religion), the *Direction de la Sûreté Générale* (Directorate of General Security) and the Paris *Préfet de Police* (Police Prefect) – closely followed the three men, and Ottoman spies did the same.[36] Sabahattin complained to the French Prime Minister, Pierre Waldeck-Rousseau, about the latter's involvement:

Vous n'ignorez pas Monsieur le Président du Conseil que par un abus inconcevable, qui a été justement dénoncé à la tribune de la Chambre des députés, par la droite comme par la gauche, l'espionnage du Sultan Abdul Hamid II aurait organisé à Paris, une police pour traquer comme des criminels des Ottomans coupables de vouloir, pour leur patrie, des réformes que l'Europe entière a souvent projeté d'imposer au gouvernement actuel. Si nous ne nous trompons, Monsieur le Président du Conseil, vous avez solennellement promis que le scandale dénoncé ne se reproduirait plus. Vous ignorez donc, certainement, que, sans tenir aucun compte de votre déclaration à la tribune et, au mépris des manifestations unanimes de l'opinion, l'espionnage du Sultan s'est réorganisé en France, à Paris, comme naguère; son audace semblerait, si c'était possible, avoir encore grandi. Et pas plus tard qu'hier, deux agents de l'ambassadeur du Sultan sont venus faire subir à notre concierge un interrogateur minutieux sur nos personnes, les visites que nous recevons, etc.[37]

Life in Paris had become really difficult for the three exiles, especially for Mahmut Paşa, once the French authorities had informed him that "his presence was an embarrassment to them."[38] He started moving from place to place (from Geneva to Cairo, and from Cairo to Corfu) and when his health showed unequivocal signs of serious deterioration, Sabahattin settled him in a villa near Brussels, where Mahmut would die in 1903 aged 48.[39] The two brothers managed to remain in Paris, albeit semi-incognito, in rented rooms in suburban Suresnes. However, Lutfullah appeared not to have a true penchant for politics. A contemporary observer wrote, for example, that "Prince Lûtfullah ... likes to make merry and is always short of money."[40] According to a brochure written by one of the confidants and friends of Sabahattin, Joseph Denais, Lutfullah was back in Istanbul by 1906.

Sabahattin's encounter with Edmond Demolins' *Science sociale*

A medical student at *La Sorbonne*, Sabahattin had added to his interest in politics a passion for the social sciences that he came to regard as key in solving political issues. He became acquainted with thinkers such as Frédéric Le Play,[41] Henri De Tourville[42] and, above all, Edmond Demolins.[43] His first encounter with Demolins' writings was a chance event, as was the case for Rıza's first encounter with positivism.

> One day, both materially and mentally exhausted, sadly wandering through a famous street in Paris, Edmond Demolins' renowned work ... caught my eye in a shop window. I immediately went in and acquired the book. That night, I tackled the book and read it from beginning to end. Until that time, I had never come across answers in any other sociological publication like that of the author to what are the reasons for the superiority of the Anglo-Saxons ... The next day I went to the same bookshop and purchased all of Edmond Demolins works ... At this time, I was honoured with the great thinker's friendship [and had] adhered to the organisation of La Science Sociale and further became honoured by the opportunity to befriend other honourable members of the organisation and work with them. I read the works of the founders [of the school], Frédéric Le Play, Henri De Tourville and all works by the thinkers that became a part of that trend with such eternal passion and gratitude. I thought that with these methods an analysis of the social structure of the Ottoman Empire could be possible and that the opportunity to prepare a necessary reform program had made itself available.[44]

The book Sabahattin referred to in the above passage is Demolins' *A quoi tient la supériorité des Anglo-Saxons?* published in 1897.[45] Sabahattin's almost magical encounter with the text and its repercussion on the prince's thought has been described by Hamit Bozarslan in the following manner: "'[u]n jour j'ai lu un livre, et ma vie a changé.' Cette toute première phrase du roman *La vie nouvelle* d'Orhan Pamuk résume parfaitement la trajectoire du Prince Sabahaddin ... *A quoi tient la supériorité des Anglo-Saxons* de Demolins changea en effet son itinéraire intellectuelle, ou mieux, lui en offrit un."[46]

As the title of the book itself indicates, the author was fully persuaded that Great Britain occupied a 'superior' position among nations in relation to its economic success, in turn due to trade and the industrial revolution having started and being better established there than anywhere else. The book was based on observations Demolins made during a long stay in Great Britain upon invitation from various schools to inspect and assess their syllabi. During his stay, Demolins had a good chance to discuss educational matters with university professors and schoolteachers, as well as the make-up of the Anglo-Saxon society with sociologists and people from various walks of life. He would summarise his findings by way of a comparison between the French and British societal arrangements, reaching the conclusion that the two stood at the antipodes, with the British organisation being far superior. The emphasis on personal initiative that Anglo-Saxons developed since their first years of schooling accounted, in his view, for their eventual political and economic success. Therefore, Demolins stressed both the importance of private initiative in already-formed individuals and, at the same time, highlighted the necessity to structure the education system around the principle of fostering this attitude within the forthcoming generations. Coming before the school, however, was another formative structure with a pivotal role in shaping the individual: the family. Similarly to that which he observed and admired of the Anglo-Saxon education system, Demolins appreciated the Anglo-Saxon family environment, where, contrary to the French habit, children were pushed to rely on their own capacities and impulses instead of relying on the family for the provision of sustenance and work opportunity.

According to Demolins, societies and their different manifestations can be divided in three types. Every type depends on the role of the family in the rearing of children, and of the role of the state as provider of employment and of the framework for more individualist development:

1   Societies of a *communistic* [47] *family formation* are characterised by the grouping of several couples into one household ... the children do not rely on themselves for their establishment, but on the family community.
2   In societies of a *communistic state formation*, the large public community takes the place of the dissolved family community; here, the young people rely principally on the State for their establishment in life, through the many appointments that the State distributes in the army or the different civil services.
3   [In] *societies of an individualistic formation* [48] ... the individual relies for his establishment neither on the family nor on the state, which disposes few appointments, because public powers are not much centralised and do not employ a very large number of officials. Here, the individual relies

principally on his own energy and resources to succeed in an independent career.[49]

Based on the above, the French and Anglo-Saxon social realities stood on two opposites. Demolins viewed France as a society of communitarian formation, "characterized by a tendency to rely, not on the self, but on the community, on the group, family, tribe, clan, public powers, etc."[50] Instead, according to him, '*societies of an individualistic formation* [of which England was one of the best expressions] are characterised by a tendency to rely, not on the community, not on the group, but on the self. Amongst them, the private man (*le 'particulier'*) triumphs over the public man.'[51] The nature of society is then mostly reflected in, or born out of, the education system, which prepares the new generations to lead their respective countries into the future. According to Demolins, the English education system continuously adapted to new realities and challenges, and, because it prepared individuals for practical work, it possessed "a really social character."[52] Parallel to the more conventional didactical and theoretical teachings, schools in England emphasised practical and physical work that prepared pupils for life outside schools. This latter aspect would help them develop their interests in business according to an entrepreneurial mind-set and strengthen their capacity to adapt to the challenges of life. The end result would be a general sense of fulfilment for the individual, who, by producing for himself, would in turn contribute to the improvement and growth of his or her country. In this way, Demolins explained England's overwhelming commercial power. In France, on the contrary, Demolins thought that the system formed men for a society that was stagnant: "the actual necessity is that men should be adapted to the new conditions of the world – which call on individuals to take care of their own welfare. The old social framework, on which men formerly depended, is either broken or insufficient."[53] Additionally, because the French system was still based on old requirements and necessities and did not adapt to the more modern challenges, it had fallen behind the Anglo-Saxon one.

As mentioned earlier, the school was not the only place where new generations were moulded. The family constituted a pivotal training ground for adult life and had to be seen as the first foundational step before modern schooling. According to Demolins, in this field, too, the difference between the two countries was striking. In individualist societies, the family is centred on parental bonds that are geared towards the development of an independent individual, as children's emancipation is the major task of parents. This way, children are made aware that their parents will not be responsible for their situation in life, and they will also have to develop their own entrepreneurial spirit and initiative. On the other hand, in societies of communitarian formation, the family tends to create the reality that the schools replicate and, more generally, of the education system. The new generations feel secure that the state will employ them as civil servants (a profession that occupies most of the working force in communitarian societies), suffocating, in this way, any prospect for the emergence of private initiative. The children are made to enjoy the fruits of their parents' achievements and are reassured that the family or tribe nucleus will be an asset for the future. Relying on these expectations, no appeal for private endeavours is likely to emerge. This tendency will lead towards decadence, according to Demolins, because it pushes the individual to abandon independent enterprise such as agriculture, industry, and commerce. This type of family attitude will also result in a passive generation, more geared towards accepting its status, especially at the national level, rather than actively seeking avenues to progress.

After family and school, it is around the three sectors of agriculture, industry and commerce that the Anglo-Saxon, as an individualist society, has built its superiority vis-à-vis the communitarian counterpart. It is precisely around these three sectors that societies must focus their attention in order to adapt and benefit from new realities. Demolins provides, in a nutshell, his point of view on the nature of the two systems, communitarian and individualist, and their application on the ground:

> [a]nd if one single example can give an idea, ... of the difference between men formed by the new methods and men formed by the old ..., look at what they have made of Northern America, and then look at what the other race has made of Southern America ... On the one side, a forward motion of Society, and the greatest known development of agriculture, commerce and industry; on the other, Society thrown backwards, and plunged to grovel in a morass of idle, unproductive town life, and given up to officialism and political revolutions. In the North, we have the rising of the future; in the South, the crumbling and decaying past.[54]

All this must have sounded very familiar to Sabahattin, who found that a communitarian society fitted perfectly with the reality of the Ottoman Empire. As the pillars of Demolins ideal society were family, education and private initiative, these became not only the basis of Sabahattin's thought but, to some extent, also his obsession. What Sabahattin found specifically instructive in explaining the state of the Empire as a society of communitarian formation can be summed up in two main aspects that characterised the last 40 years of the Empire. One aspect was the exponential expansion of the bureaucracy that had hampered the entry of the younger generations into fields such as commerce, industry and agriculture, which needed development if the Empire wanted to prosper. The second factor was the promise of a state that would absorb the entire workforce that had rendered the population passive and reluctant to ask for changes, fearing they would upset a status-quo that safeguarded their economic well-being and that of their offspring. Sabahattin also became an unconditional admirer of Great Britain;[55] accordingly, the strategies to reform the Empire in view of its present decadence, which he would present in his book *Türkiye nasıl kurtarılabilir? (How Can Turkey Be Saved?)*

published in Istanbul in 1918, relied heavily on Ottoman society being re-shaped according to the Anglo-Saxon model.

How can Turkey be saved?

The final aim of Mehmet Sabahattin was to switch from a communitarian to an individualist society in the Ottoman Empire. The prerequisites for such a switch, were the following:

> Some important fundamentals that need careful consideration regarding the creation and organisation of this movement: 1. The educational institutions for girls and boys that are inspired by Social Science's close examination of individualist education and of educational conditions in English 'Public School' and new schools that will individually and separately materialise in the most suitable locations of the nation, and the procurement of worthy educators and educator-families from those schools. 2. To utilise the benefits of the sphere of Anglo-Saxon education in order to bring about individualist moral qualities in our youth, and for their private lives to benefit from its structure – such as family and farm. 3. The implementation of the necessary support that will illustrate to the youth that will be raised through these means to settle resolutely to the soil and to create their independence with their manual labour.[56]

Sabahattin's aim was to communicate his experiences and convictions both to the governing elite and the intellectuals of the Empire. This, however, seems to be simultaneously the strength of Sabahattin, as well as the greatest shortcoming of his political vision. It seems unlikely that a book on philosophy and sociology could have reached out to the members of the Young Turk organisation after 1908, bent on acquiring as much power as possible in their own hands, let alone to the masses. It appears that Sabahattin, probably due to his background, his exclusive education, and his role in the organisation of the Young Turks of Europe, could not understand how to bridge the intellectual and organisational gap that divided him from most of the realities of the Empire. Sabahattin was not able to provide a short-term plan but only a set of changes of a long-term character. However, the problem of representation extends to the whole Young Turk opposition especially during its intellectual phase (1895 to 1902). As discussed at length in other sections of this book, the elitist nature of the intellectuals who led the movement was undoubtedly a source of ideological eclecticism and richness, but equally one of the most fundamental reasons for the failure of the project.

Sabahattin shared not only the conclusions drawn by Demolins in his book, but also the method through which these considerations had been reached. What Sabahattin found both most fascinating and useful was the attempt to analyse a specific society from a new perspective, that of comparative sociology. In fact, the book's early section emphasises the fact that economics, law and ethics alone cannot be used to understand the social realities of a given country, as it had been done until the emergence of the *Science sociale*, conceived by Frédéric Le Play, Henri de Tourville, and Edmond Demolins. These disciplinary fields, according to the prince, could not wholly explain society precisely because they were directly the results of a given social structure. *Science sociale*, instead, deals directly with social issues, upholds observation as its primary tool, and merges the features of what today would be called the fields of social science, with a positivistic approach:

> *Thanks to this great social synthesis that is being continuously perfected, humankind, in both its public and private life, is recipient of the most necessary and the most valuable foundation of a central science, that will serve as its sole guide and thereby gather around itself all of the other sciences!* [57]

As we have seen, the family and the creation of an entrepreneurial mind are extremely important for Demolins and for Sabahattin. For the latter, these need to be coupled with decentralisation, and private initiative, which become the prerequisite for any other consequent change.

Sabahattin found striking similarities between Demolins' characterisation of communitarian societies and the Ottoman one, accusing the Hamidian regime of having done nothing more than perpetuating a crisis that was rooted back in the past, that the Sultan had made more severe through his despotism, nepotism, favouritism, which had blocked any hope of dynamism. Hence, on Sabahattin's account, the dire situation the Empire was in was only on the surface the making of Abdülhamit, and had, in fact, begun during the *Tanzimat* period, which, through the reforms of the bureaucracy and schooling system had preserved the communitarian societal system, which hampered economic development:

> [W]hat has been occurring since the promulgation of the Gülhane Charter is the conviction that we have entered the path of efficiency and progress. Yet, when analysed, it becomes clear that the method laid down by the Tanzimat was to collect into a *public treasury* the revenues that had, until then, been the subsistence of those governing in the nation, and, thence, to keep officials of public life, who are obliged to survive on the payments made from this treasury, docile and at the command of the *centre* that holds the management of the treasury in its hands. ... It is our knowledge that the public life of progressive and strong individualist societies is not organised in this way. Perhaps, it is in complete opposition to this: the public powers are, unequivocally, not in the hands of a civil servant organisation. This means that the Tanzimat is not able to engender motion in the direction of individualism for our public life ... because *the order that was desired to be given to public life with the Tanzimat was not the outcome of progress that had occurred in private life* – private life

is in its former state. It is for this reason that the essence of the Tanzimat consists of binding those functionaries of government, who are sustained by private life, to the centre.[58]

He criticised in particular the enlargement of the bureaucracy during the *Tanzimat*, which, keeping a centralised structure of power, had helped perpetuate the communitarian nature of Ottoman society: "The essence of the *Tanzimat*, as the future will demonstrate, consists of the creation of a large assembly for public life, meaning, a body of bureaucrats that fall into the framework or a central administrative structure, whilst having gathered income to the centre."[59] As to the re-organisation of the educational system, Sabahattin condemned it as being aimed at providing abstract, sometimes even cumbersome, knowledge, and failing to attract qualified teachers in sufficient numbers:

> With the Tanzimat, also, begins the foundation of our monumental schools: the need for men, who, on one hand, will work the newly assembled machine, and, who, on the other hand, will assemble and repair the imperfect machine with the strength of intellect, is evident. It is indispensable for a foundation that has materialised under these conditions to be based upon a *barrack lifestyle in 'discipline', and reason and books in 'education;'* it deserves particular attention that physical conditioning, however, is utterly neglected![60]

His evaluation was based on the consideration that, in communitarian societies such as the Ottoman one, education would be an aim in itself, while in individualistic societies it would be a means to achieve personal success:[61]

> It is seen that with us, like higher education, primary education, too, takes on an administrative and political shape. And for this reason, by the strength of government, securing for teachers a position superior to family patriarchs, and, beyond the instruction of children, entrusting them with the great responsibility of becoming intellectual and political guides … Children, in general, to earn their living whilst remaining with their families, *rely upon their familial community, not their* [own] *initiative*. By this means, they are left completely deprived of the incentive that brings about an expansion of knowledge in individualist youths.[62]

His judgement of the reforms, which Rıza (Ganem, and many more Young Turk exponents) so heavily praised, was equally harsh, those reforms had all failed to produce the desired outcome because they had failed to identify the causes of the problem:

> In fact, our reformists, who have been proliferating since the era of the Tanzimat, nurtured a sincere aspiration for renewal; alas they were utterly

unable to discover the manner in which these aspirations could materialise. Only, as conditions for progress, liberty, constitutionalism, education, morality, and, finally, the necessity to Westernize, were – and are presently – advocated perpetually! All of these claims, however, have neither been able to bring the society, nor the mentality labouring to reform it, a single inch further; because, these diverse manifestations we invoke, do not give birth to social structure, on the contrary, whether positively or negatively, these are born from social structure.[63]

Another cause of the ineffectiveness of the *Tanzimat* and Young Ottoman reformers, related to their reliance on the effects of the promulgation of a constitution; following Demolins' argument, Sabahattin maintained that the political arrangement in itself would not contribute to the standing of a country among the others, or to the modernisation of a social system:

For example, constitutional methods of rule exist in Spain and in England! America's North is governed by republicanism, as is its Centre and its South! That being granted, the differences between these societies are beyond comparison! Naturally, the astounding differences do not originate from the sameness of their forms of government but, rather, from the distinctness of their social structures ... *In communitarian formations that bestow to public life the role of adjudicator of private life*, whatever the form of rule may be, whether absolutism, constitutionalism, or republicanism, the result is always the same: political defeat and social poverty! ... It is on account of this that, years before constitutionalism, we began revealing that we would be unable to manifest genuine independence solely by means of changing our form of government and laws.[64]

On his account, it would be the transition from a communitarian to an individualistic society that would bring about the necessary change: "Genuine progress in public life comes into existence neither from constitutionalism, nor parliamentarianism, and neither does it come from republicanism! It might be from *private initiative* that bestows strength and order to private life!"[65] Following on from that line of reasoning, Sabahattin noted a difference in the social composition of the British and French Parliaments in the year 1895; of the 583 delegates of the British Parliament, 62% came from occupations in which private initiative was a prerequisite – 17% dealt in commerce, 22% in industry, and 23% in agriculture – while the civil servants amounted to a meagre 8% of the total. Of the 633 members of the French Parliament, 21,5% came from commerce, industry, and agriculture – respectively providing 3,5%, 6,5%, and 11,5% – while the civil servants amounted to 15%, the remaining delegates having unspecified occupations. In other words, the sectors that provided the driving force of the economy – commerce, industry and agriculture – were under-represented in the French Parliament in comparison with the British one, and the same held for the Parliament of the

Ottoman Empire. This state of affairs had blocked social mobility, and produced stagnation, while, on Sabahattin's account, economic development was the key to progress:[66] "It is work, especially agriculture that is going to save us. Asia Minor is as big as France and richer than France in natural resources. Work, instead of warfare, will put us on par with the other progressive nations."[67] Sabahattin lamented that, in the Empire, positions as state functionaries and military personnel were occupied almost exclusively by the middle class. The desire to obtain and keep those positions, and the privileges that came with them, had made the middle class the victim, and the accomplice, of despotic Hamidian rule. Moreover, the sucking of the middle class into the bureaucratic and military occupations had left the three key sectors of the economy – agriculture, commerce and industry – to the lower class, which lacked the knowledge and the capital necessary to promote, and benefit from, those sectors, leaving them in constant stagnation.

Against the disastrous, and complex, scenario Sabahattin painted, the recipe he offered for the reform of the Empire was strikingly simple and straightforward: turn Ottoman society from a communitarian to an individualistic one, and wait for the effects of the change to mature. The process whereby the change would be achieved was the full adoption of the Anglo-Saxon social model, particularly in terms of the schooling system, family life, and orientation.

> My program is to send thousands of our young men and women to the different Anglo-Saxon countries, to those regions where the climate corresponds to ours, to receive practical agricultural education but also live in the homes of your [Anglo-Saxon] better middle class in order to bring back your spirit as well as your technical knowledge.[68]

Interestingly, Sabahattin did not appear to envisage that the adoption of the Anglo-Saxon way of life could engender negative consequences of any sort on the citizens of the Empire.

> While communitarians always expect to achieve their social welfare and freedom by public means, and are never able to meet their expectations anywhere, individualists succeed in securing their social welfare and freedom through their private initiative and their endeavours tailored to changing necessities – through that resolute social organisation of theirs which instils this means of subsistence and discipline into every premise. In an individualist formation, people acquire the knowledge the jobs they hold require through experience in their professional lives. And by this means, individualists who, at the onset, are proportionally poorer in terms of their general knowledge, with observation and experience, obtain the practical knowledge and truths that will secure the success of their jobs as they go forth in life, more thoroughly and intimately. For this reason, contemporary sciences that stem from observation and

experience, and tread the path of discovering evident universal truths, are product of the intellectual developments of individualist circles![69]

The quote above expresses the gist of Sabahattin's answer to the Ottoman identity question, and it was a radical one indeed: instead of being bogged down with pondering which elements of Western culture should be adopted, and which elements of Ottoman culture should be preserved, and how the two should be integrated, he suggested that the Anglo-Saxon social model should dislodge the Ottoman one in specific sectors:

> For the benefit of ourselves and the whole of humanity, the question of the perpetuation of our existence, for which we have been unable to find a solution by military or political means for centuries, and thus presently endure as a calamity that will meet a finale of categorical demise, can only be resolved in this manner.[70]

Sabahattin was perhaps too harsh, and certainly too abrupt, in his evaluation of the economic situation of the Empire, as major changes had occurred in its mode of production in the last quarter of the nineteenth century. Industry had started, mainly in the form of mining and manufacturing, helped by foreign capital invested in the exploitation of the Empire's natural resources; the commercialisation of desirable crops (cotton, poppies) led to the establishment of a nation-wide market in urban but also in rural areas.[71] The limits on trade imposed by the Capitulations, especially with respect to the textile industry, held back development, causing the Empire to import more than it exported. But, all in all, living conditions had improved for many, and this reflected in a sharp increase in the population.[72]

Decentralisation and private initiative

Sabahattin accompanied the emphasis on creating an entrepreneurial mindset in the new generations with the need for the state to shrink so as to allow for private initiative to emerge and flourish, and thought that starting a process of administrative decentralisation was a step in the right direction.[73] This is because he thought it would not be good enough to spur a sense of private initiative among the citizens without providing them with an environment conducive to develop it. Between 1900 and the years right after the Congress of Ottoman Liberals of 1902, this stance remained a political thought without a concrete organisation behind. However, in the year 1906, this emerged:

> C'est dans ce but que nous venons de former une Ligue de décentralisation pour éclairer la masse turque sur le fond et la nature des réformes qui nous paraissent indispensable. Bien entendu, cette transformation politique doit être accompagnée immédiatement de l'amélioration des

conditions économiques de l'Empire, afin qu'on puisse mettre en valeur ses ressources inépuisables, qui restent aujourd'hui encore inexploitées.[74]

Sabahattin believed that the introduction of a system of decentralisation would enable the local authorities to cater for the needs of the citizens of each specific area of the Empire, leading to a better management of resources. Accordingly, he urged replacing "migratory civil servants"[75] entrusted with the management of areas they would know very little about with local officials who would know people's needs and be accountable to them. He also thought that a decentralised empire would contribute to the pacification of the existing ethnic, religious and political tensions and that the state of peace, so obtained, would spur economic prosperity, and deter foreign powers from interfering on the pretext of safeguarding the rights of minorities:

> To bring about order in local government organisations, in a manner that will correspond to regional and occupational needs, current *vilayets* need to be separated into *territorial zones arranged by virtue of their natural and social conditions*. (By this means, a few *vilayets* can be incorporated into a single zone).[76]

In pursuing this, he thought that foreigners could at times be employed in high offices, marking one of the main differences between him and Ahmet Rıza.

> An assembly of order should be created for each zone: some personages amongst the English dignitaries who have i*n esse proven suitability* in the administration of places such as India and Egypt, and will be admitted into government services, should be positioned as chief officers of these assemblies, and thereby their *organisational skills* should be profited from.[77]

Sabahattin thought that the Christians in the Empire had fared better than the Muslims because, often out of necessity, the former had lived under some sort of decentralised power, while the latter had remained in the grip of the central one. As a result, the Greeks, Armenians, and Bulgarians had the freedom of choosing their patriarchs, and had developed local private initiative, fostering their personal entrepreneurial interests, while Muslims were hampered, if not paralysed, by the prospect of obtaining a job as state functionaries.

The matter of judiciary reform, which Sabahattin considered to be strategic, was the one and only occasion in which he expressed praise for the workings of the *Tanzimat* statesmen, who, through the *Hatt-ı Şerif* of Gülhane, had introduced the concept of the right to a fair trial for every citizen regardless of their ethnic or religious background.

> *The position of a judge is one that requires the highest sense of responsibility. As for sense of responsibility, it is the product of individual liberty!* ... It is clear that we confront the matter of structure even in the area of the judiciary: *the court system that brings about the preservation of rights in the most secure manner relies upon social men who, having attained a solid freedom of conscience with the privileged place they have achieved in their private lives, grant peace and security to their surroundings.*[78]

However, he added that decentralisation would improve also the legal system:

> Even today, there are some individuals in some regions of our nation who occupy a social position that is able to garner the esteem and trust of the people surrounding them, and who naturally undertake the role of being their arbiter. For the resolution of small and limited cases, these individuals can be appointed as 'justices of peace' by the government. By this means, we will have henceforth entered the path of benefiting from great men of private life for the easy and rapid local distribution of justice.[79]

Sabahattin raised another issue within the broader aspect of decentralisation that has to do with the distribution of public and private property. Because of the nature of ownership in the Ottoman Empire, he claimed that the revenues and ways to generate wealth are not used to their full potential:

> The social solution to the question of property is *to switch, with consistent efforts, from communal ownership to personal ownership. When it comes to the administrative assurance of ownership* under the present circumstances: 1. The proliferation and distribution of Imperial [Land] Register administrations in a manner that will provide the greatest ease to land and property owners; 2. Putting into execution a general census, of the variety that will secure the production of records and sound titles, which will be fundamental for ownership law and taxation; 3. It is necessary for the administration and formation of the assemblies that will conduct these transactions and create the census to be entrusted to an *assembly of order.*[80]

On religion and the relationship with minorities

One of the best sources of evidence of Sabahattin's stance on religion is in his reply to a speech on the revival of Pan-Islamism that Sir Edward Grey, British Minister for Foreign Affairs, gave in 1906.[81] In it, Sabahattin explained that Islam and fundamentalism were not synonymous; actually, he blamed influential Westerners, such as Edward Grey, for the misunderstanding of Islam, maintaining that Pan-Islamism was not a fundamentalist manifestation and that its re-emergence was a reaction to the aggressive and at times brutal policies of the West towards the Empire. Sabahattin attributed religion the capacity to play a role in sustaining feelings of community and shared belonging, and identified Islam as the glue that would hold together all the Muslims of the Empire. However, he also recognised that religion can become a political tool of oppression. What distances Rıza and Sabaheddin, though, is the manner in which this dynamic can be changed. As explained in the previous chapter, Rıza blamed the decay of religion on the corruption of the Sultan and the religious dignitaries and, hence, their removal could lead to a more positive role of religion. Rıza also saw in Islam one of the vehicles through which changes at the top could be pursued. For Sabahattin, instead, the communitarian or individualist character of society is what changes the role of religion. Following once more Demolins' approach, Sabahattin stated that:

> Protestantism, too, is such that it promotes despotism in communitarian settings and freedom in individualist settings! Religions, in this case, because they are abused in communitarian structures, deviate to the degree of becoming an intermediary arbitrator and in that way, with time, beget severe reactionary currents.[82]

Extending the argument to Islam, he claimed: "those who suppose the religion of Islam to be an obstacle to progress are completely deceived in this supposition of theirs. That which is an obstacle to progress is not our religion but our social structure."[83] Furthermore, Sabahattin was sensitive to the fact that some of the policies attached to what was claimed to be Pan-Islamism at that stage, were misleadingly inclusive. Abdülhamit II used a Pan-Islamic discourse as a political tool internally in order to rally support around his feeble position: "Mais nous savons qu'Abdul-Hamid II n'a jamais envisagé son Khalifat à la manière des vrais adeptes du panislamisme."[84] In reality, the Sultan deployed this discourse to counteract the section of Ottoman-Muslim society that was demanding some type of Western-style secularism; this would threaten the Sultan's theocratic status. Sabahattin equally underlined how the emerging intellectual Ottoman youth, because of its geographical proximity with Europe, had reached a level of synthesis between Ottoman and European thinking that turned them into products of modernity. If this class would, in the near future, lead the Empire, then a proper idea of Islam and Pan-Islamism would actually work towards reconciliation with the West. However, this will only work if the West itself changed its policy towards the Ottoman Empire. These assertions support the overall claim that the members of the Young Turk movement should not be considered to be non-believers. As in most communitarian societies, as Sabahattin would phrase it, religion has become the oppressive tool in the hands of the regime. This was, according to him, the case in the Ottoman Empire under Abdülhamit II first, and the Unionist government after 1908.

The perception of religion is intimately connected with the view of the ethnic minorities. Only by tailoring a new, more private role for religion, in fact, would it have been possible to include the religious and ethnic minorities in a reform plan that would appear feasible to them. The first step, similarly to what Rıza had formulated, was that any reform was to be applied to the whole population of the Empire regardless of religious affiliation. For instance, in the case of the Armenians, Sabahattin recognised the oppression that they had undergone since the late 1890s and, his father first and himself later, had both publicly declared this.[85] He denounced the brutality and harshness that they had been submitted to. However, he directly blamed Abdülhamit for them, while at the same time he discarded what others had called Turkish fanaticism. But Sabahattin also added that the situation did not constitute a separate issue but fell within the broader matter of the question of Ottoman minorities, involving other segments, such as the Kurds, the Albanians and the Arabs. According to Sabahattin, what the Great Powers referred to as the Eastern Question could and should have only been solved by the efforts of the Ottoman Empire. In the quest for a solution, because the Armenians were numerically not sufficient to constitute a nation *per se*, they should set aside their weapons and use ideas and ideals in their place.[86] In conclusion, the solution was to create a common federal homeland where Armenians would hold the same rights as the Turks. Even though, as time progressed, the viability of a multi-ethnic Empire was becoming faint, Sabahattin insisted that it was the best option even for those few non-Muslim components left; in the case of the Armenians, Sabahattin repeatedly called on the Young Turk movement to discuss, instead of oppose, their demands.

One of the major faults Sabahattin identifies in the organisations within the Young Turk movement was precisely that none of them could find a viable option to offer to the religious and ethnic minorities. In his view, the minorities were caught between two evils: on the one side, the absolutism and politically charged Islamism of the Sultan, on the other, the uncertainty and a lack of practical vision for their future on the part of the opposition. This explains, for example, how Sabahattin went from an ideology imbued with elitism and conservatism to one of revolution. However, revolution was not, for him, a technique to acquire power. Rather, revolution was, in his view, part of progress understood here as a gradual evolution. "Le passage à l'action révolutionnaire de Sabahaddin, synonyme de la mobilisation des populations urbaines, s'expliquait par l'urgence d'agir pour mettre fin à l'exile et à la passivité, marquer 'l'an zéro' de 'la réforme des hommes et des femmes', mais pas pour un changement d'ordre eschatologique."[87]

On the West

Sabahattin's evaluation of the implication of foreign countries in matters internal to the Empire oscillated over time:

[b]efore this period [the 1850s], they [the Turks] had preserved an Asiatic character; in the present day, they look to Europe for inspiration. Today they have established an army after European fashion and have endeavoured to improve their civil and political institutions. The Liberal movement under Murad V, however, was suffocated by the hostility of Russia, and the destruction of Constitutional Turkey has greatly facilitated the advance of the absolutism of Abdul Hamid II. The monarch who bears this name is not, strictly speaking, a national product; he is the product of Russian absolutist reaction ... and that is the explanation of Turkey's apparent slowness in adopting the European civilisation.[88]

He saw France and Great Britain as crucial allies of the Young Turk movement in bringing about a meaningful reform of the Empire, the former through the influence of its own great intellectuals, the latter through that of social structure. Interestingly, he refrained from advocating westernisation for the sake of it, or taking direct inspiration from any one country:

in the same way that by undertaking the imitation of any nation we will be unable to become that nation and that, essentially, our becoming is not even found to be desirable, also, neither can we gain anything more than that which we already are by only embracing our nationalism. Because, the result that will be attained with the social capability that the most active agricultural and economic development brings forth and the individualist education that progressively uncovers this capability can at no time be assured through feeling and desire. However, in our realm of ideas, the idea of Westernising is taken to mean equipping our nation with the material and immaterial means of the West. And we assume that if we were to create, also in Turkey, foundations such as perfect paved roads, railways, ports, canals, dreadnaughts, libraries and schools, banks ... et cetera, as in the most advanced countries, we are able to raise Turkey to the level of civilisation of the West![89]

What is surprising in Sabahattin's passage above is his failure to see that by suggesting a sociological mutation in the Ottoman society that would bring it to coincide with the British one, which he advocated throughout his analysis of the cause of the problems of the Empire, he had done exactly what the passage exposed as being wrong: suggesting that the Empire should 'impersonate' the West. It is possible that the criticism of adopting Westernised infrastructures – such as roads, railway lines, etc. – without adopting Westernised structures – family and schooling system – in the above passage was a way to mark his distance from Rıza's stance urging to import from the West exclusively the technological advancements.[90]

Sabahattin was a highly controversial figure, both in historical and political terms. He was either admired as an ideologue and an innovator, or regarded as an idealist who had lost touch with reality, and could not grasp the

100 *Mehmet Sabahattin and social science*

urgency of regime change in the Empire. His difficult character did not make him friends: undoubtedly moved by the love of his country, Sabahattin was uncompromisingly polemical with whomever would oppose his views:[91] he did not wish to discuss with anybody his reforming plan, having it all worked out in his mind. He should be credited with at least attempting to bring economic matters into discussion of reform, but he espoused too enthusiastically British liberalism,[92] and, whether blinded by his faith in it, or simply ill-informed, gave an incorrect picture of the economic situation of the Empire, or else had totally unrealistic expectations of what it could achieve. In terms of the Ottomanist identity question, his recipe to reform the Empire by importing the Anglo-Saxon social model, included a partial dismissal of Ottoman culture, religion, custom and political achievements, and a betrayal of the Ottomanist project that it deprived of anything Ottoman.

Sabahattin and the Ottomanist plan

In the previous chapter, part of the emphasis was on the importance of Ahmet Rıza's version of Ottomanism on finding a philosophical platform that did not oppose the belief in Islam. This came to be his version of positivism. The other major achievement of Rıza was to create a forum, through the establishment of the journal *Mechveret*, where Ottomans and non-Ottomans could discuss the political situation of the Empire and debate its future political shape. Sabahattin, on the other hand, did not need to discuss a future plan, he had it well in mind. This took the shape of a federal empire, within which society would have to be drastically altered to resemble the organisation of the impressive and successful Anglo-Saxon society. This was the outcome of his encounter and adherence to the school of *Science sociale*, which gave Sabahattin an altogether different character from many other Young Turk members. As argued by Bozarslan: "La tradition de Le Play (1806–1822) et de Demolins (1852–1907) permit en effet au Prince de se situer en dehors du positivisme en vogue et du darwinisme social qui influençait la majorité des opposants Jeunes Turcs, pour considérer l'individu comme l'élément décisif de la vie sociale."[93]

A very crucial aspect of Rıza's plan was his approach to religion within a positivist framework; for Sabahattin's writings, this aspect was at best marginal. His position vis-à-vis religion does not feature prominently in the writings analysed here. We do, however, have a telling and somewhat poetic encounter with religion in Sabahattin's memoirs. The way Sabahattin recalls his encounter with the ideas of Demolins is very similar to a religious enlightenment. It is precisely the complex relationship of these two concepts, religion and the Enlightenment as it had taken root in Western Europe that gives us a clue to Sabahattin in particular but also to the Young Turk *Weltanschauung* in general. It is in fact the merging, or synthesis, of the two that all those working abroad under the umbrella organisation of the Young Turk movement were attempting to work out. Sabahattin's encounter with Demolins' ideas resembles closely the experience of religious revelation. Moreover, the choice of finding all the answers in a book can be connected to the textual importance in Islam. We can only speculate about this choice of narrative: it could be an attempt to portray his own ideology as very close to Islam, or approximate a familiar discourse that would make his work on Ottomanism and the future more intelligible and acceptable to others. This seems to be the more plausible explanation, as the majority of the exponents of the opposition were confronted precisely with this task: their main obstacle was popularisation, the enlargement of their ideology. However, other possibilities need to be considered. Another equally probable explanation is tightly linked with the elitism and self-projection that most Young Turks had. In some ways, Sabahattin finds himself so enlightened that he has a direct connection with knowledge (the pages of the book) and compares himself to a messenger: once the truth had been revealed to him the world would, or should, have drastically changed.

The way in which the prince's memories are told gives us an additional idea of the background and self-image that many among the Young Turk organisation shared but which was, undoubtedly, a central feature of Sabahattin's character: the idea of a mission. After all, the narrated encounter that changed his life hints at some sort of predestination: as if another Gabriel[94] had come down to illuminate the masses through a modern, progressive and universalistic prophet. Many of the opponents of the rule of Abdülhamit II were convinced elitists, the products of a specific educational background which highlighted their intellectual and educational superiority in comparison to the rest of the population. Moreover, they also saw themselves as possessing the tools and thus being assigned the mission to reform and save the Empire, through their particular reading of Ottomanism. However, in Sabahattin, the level of elitism borders some sort of predestination, which, for example in the case of Rıza, does not surface in the same manner.

In the end, what emerges most from the ideas of the prince is a very eccentric relationship with culture and religion. Although difficult to explain, it seems that the most plausible explanation for this relationship remains the one put forth in the previous chapter for Ahmet Rıza's dilemmas: the natural outcome of an ideology in the making. However, it is also fair to note that Sabahattin defended Islam by stating that its fanatical aspects, to which the West repeatedly referred, should be seen as an outcome of what he sees as the brutal policies of the West on the East.[95] What can be inferred from the material analysed throughout this chapter is that religion was to have a very individual role, as Sabahattin's plan evolved around the idea of multiculturalism, in an Empire where localities were to be maintained but not allowed to interfere in other localities. To sum up in a few lines, Sabahattin was a thinker ahead of his time and, due to the sense of mission and intellectualism, difficult to grasp and his ideas difficult to be turned into actions. He was also out of touch with life in the Ottoman Empire, not understanding that those who opposed the rule of Abdülhamit II wanted tangible results and that, once the revolution had been carried out, ideas of constitutional rule were soon to be submitted to the decisions of the Unionists who had taken up the tutelary role the Young Turk intellectuals, such as Sabahattin, had thought should have been theirs.

Notes

1 It was during Sultan Abdülmecit's reign that reform of the Empire, as more widely acknowledged, begun. This was officially inaugurated with the *Hatt-ı Şerif* of Gülhane in November 1839, and strengthened with the *Islâhat fermânı* in February 1856. In line with *Tanzimat* ideals, power shifted from the Palace to the Porte.
2 Şemsettin Sami Bey was born in June 1850 in Frashër, southern Albania. He is seen as one of the fathers of both Turkish and Albanian nationalism, and is known by two different names in each of these: Şemsettin Sami in Turkey, Sami Frashëri in Albania. He attended the Greek lycée in Yoannina and studied Turkish, Persian and Arabic. He was the editor of various newspapers, among which were *Tercüman-ı Şark* and *Sabah*, and author of a universal encyclopaedia in Ottoman Turkish, as well as a Turkish-Turkish (*Kamus-ı Türki*) and French-Turkish-French dictionaries. In some of his writings, Şemsettin Sami stressed the importance of the modernisation of the Turkish language, purified of Arabic and Persian words. Bülent Bilmez, "Shemseddin Sami Frashëri (1850–1904) – Contributing to the Construction of Albanian and Turkish Identities," in *We, the People: Politics of National Peculiarity in Southeastern Europe*, edited by Diana Mishkova (New York: Central European University Press, 2009): 341–372.
3 Hamit Bozarslan, "Le Prince Sabahaddin (1879–1948)," *Schweizerische Zeitschrift für Geschichte* 52, (2002), 288; Nezahet Nurettin Ege, *Prens Sabahaddin: hayatı ve ilmi müdafaaları* (Istanbul: Güneş Neşriyatı, 1977).
4 Fesch, *Constantinople aux derniers jours d'Abdul-Hamid*, 350.
5 Murat V reigned as Sultan for about three months, from 30th May to 31st August, 1876. Initially chosen because he was very sympathetic to the ideas of constitutionalism of Mithat Paşa and the Young Ottomans (especially Namık Kemal), he then changed his mind and tried to reform much more cautiously. Because of this, he was made to abdicate on the excuse that he was mentally ill. He was followed on the throne by his brother Abdülhamit II. Murat V was respected by many Ottomans of different backgrounds (one of his closest associates was the Greek Freemason Cléanthi Scalieri) because he was seen as an enlightened liberal. He became the champion of the Young Turk opposition and claimed, among other things, that Abdülhamit II had repeatedly attempted to kill him. He died while in captivity at the Çırağan Palace on 29th August 1904.
6 Demetra Vaka was an Ottoman Greek born in 1877 on the island of Büyükada, in the Sea of Marmara. At her mother's death, when she was 11, she was left with no support and decided to leave for New York. She married the American writer Kenneth Brown and with his help, started publishing books on Turkey. Reina Lewis, *Rethinking Orientalism – Women Travel and the Ottoman Harem* (London: I.B. Tauris, 2004). Vaka met Sabahattin at an unspecified time during the occupation of Istanbul and published an account of her meetings with him in three articles in the journal *Asia*.
7 Demetra Vaka, "An Imperial Enemy of Turkish Despotism," *Asia* 24 (January 1924), 36.
8 Ibid., 72.
9 Ibid., 73.

10 Date set at 16th December according to a telegram transcript held by the French Police, bearing no date. Another document, a report, dated January 1902, put their departure on the 14th. "Rapports divers sur le sujets ottomans pendant la guerre de 1914, Mahmoud Pacha (beau-frère du sultan de Constantinople)," *Préfecture de Police de Paris* – BA1.169. Joseph Denais puts the date at 14th; Joseph Denais, *La Turquie nouvelle et l'ancien régime* (Paris: Rivière, 1909), 44.
11 This letter was, in reality, addressed to the Sultan, as it explained the reasons for the three's departure. Seniha Sultan and Sabahattin's pregnant wife had been aware of the plan since the beginning and had participated in the decision. See Fesch, *Constantinople aux derniers jours d'Abdul-Hamid*.
12 Denais, *La Turquie nouvelle*, 44.
13 Vaka, "An Imperial Enemy of Turkish Despotism," 120.
14 Ibid.
15 Denais, *La Turquie nouvelle*, 38.
16 Ibid., 44. There is evidence of Mahmut Paşa having endeavoured to establish, or having established, close links with the British authorities. Hanioğlu, *Young Turks in Opposition*, 146.
17 We know that Lutfullah was one year younger than Sabahattin and thus making him 22 years old at the time. *Mecheroutiette*, instead, sets their age at 26 and 22, "Les états de service du Comité Union et Progrès," *Mecheroutiette* 5, no. 43 (June 1913), 31.
18 Le Figaro, 20th December 1899; "Rapports divers sur le sujets ottomans pendant la guerre de 1914, Mahmoud Pacha (beau-frère du sultan de Constantinople)," *Préfecture de Police de Paris* – BA1.169.
19 "Rapports divers sur le sujets ottomans pendant la guerre de 1914, Mahmoud Pacha (beau-frère du sultan de Constantinople)," *Préfecture de Police de Paris* – BA1.169.
20 "Lettre de Mahmoud Pacha," *Mechveret Supplément Français* 5, no. 89 (January 1900), 1.
21 "Le Princes Sabaheddine et Loutfoullah," *Mechveret Supplément Français* 5, no. 89 (January 1900), 2.
22 "Lettre de Mahmoud Pacha," 1.
23 "Le Princes Sabaheddine et Loutfoullah," 2.
24 "Lettre au Sultan Abdul-Hamid II," *Mechveret Supplément Français* 5, no. 91 (February 1900), 1–2. The letter, dated 21 January 1900, was also published in *L'Aurore*, *L'Eclair*, *La Libre Parole* (where it was attributed to a *Comité Révolutionnaire Turc*). Newspaper cuttings. "Rapports divers sur le sujets ottomans pendant la guerre de 1914," *Préfecture de Police de Paris* – BA1.169.
25 "Lettre au Sultan Abdul-Hamid II," 1–2. It is interesting to note here Mahmut Paşa's elitist conception of political activism, in line of the attitude of the whole Young Turk movement.
26 "Rapports divers sur le sujets ottomans pendant la guerre de 1914, Mahmoud Pacha (beau-frère du sultan de Constantinople)," *Préfecture de Police de Paris* – BA1.169.
27 Hanioğlu, *Young Turks in Opposition*, 143.
28 "Rapports divers sur le sujets ottomans pendant la guerre de 1914, Mahmoud Pacha (beau-frère du sultan de Constantinople)," *Préfecture de Police de Paris* – BA1.169.
29 *L'Aurore*, 25th December 1899.
30 *Le Matin*, 20th January 1900.
31 *Le Libre Parole*, 3rd February 1900.
32 On one occasion, as much as 50,000 Turkish lira, Hanioğlu, *Young Turks in Opposition*, 143.
33 Denais, *La Turquie nouvelle*, 47.

104 *Mehmet Sabahattin and social science*

34 Fesch, *Constantinople aux derniers jours d'Abdul-Hamid*, 359–360.
35 "Les états de service du Comité Union et Progrès," 31.
36 Dispatch of February 1902. "Rapports divers sur le sujets ottomans pendant la guerre de 1914, Mahmoud Pacha (beau-frère du sultan de Constantinople)," *Préfecture de Police de Paris* – BA1.169.
37 Sabaheddin to the Président du Conseil, Paris, 13 January 1902. "Rapports divers sur le sujets ottomans pendant la guerre de 1914,," *Préfecture de Police de Paris* – BA1.169.
38 Vaka, "An Imperial Enemy of Turkish Despotism," 121.
39 Mahmut Paşa would be buried in the Père Lachaise Cemetery.
40 Hanioğlu, *Preparation for a Revolution*, 27.
41 Pierre-Guillaume-Frédéric Le Play (1806–1882) was a French sociologist recognised by many as the "creator of social science." He regarded England as a model nation and maintained that social laws can only be ascertained by observation. In one of his most important works, *La Réforme Sociale*, he put forth a classification of families: the patriarchal, the stock and the stable families, mainly identified according to the level of entrepreneurial ethos encouraged by the leader of the family. Le Play was an advocate of freedom, enterprise, private initiative and self-government. Henry Higgs, "Frédéric Le Play." *The Quarterly Journal of Economics* 4, no. 4 (July 1890): 408–433; Michel Dion "Science sociale et religion chez Frédéric Le Play," *Archives de sociologie des religions* 12, no. 24 (July–December 1967): 83–104.
42 Henri de Tourville (1843–1903), French sociologist, considered the intellectual heir to Le Play, he became the leading theoretician and organiser of a dissenting cluster of Le Play's disciples, and organised a journal, *Science sociale*, which was supposed to produce more in-depth studies and observations of those of Le Play. He provided a system of categories of the family, Nomenclature, which was to give a place to every relevant observation and allow a reorganisation of Le Play's work. Paul Lazarsfeld, "Notes on the History of Quantification in Sociology – Trends, Sources and Problems," *Isis* 52, no. 2 (June 1961): 277–333; Antoine Savoye, "Les continuateurs de Le Play au tournant du siècle," *Revue française de sociologie* 22, no. 3 (July–September 1981): 315–344.
43 Edmond Demolins (1852–1907). He was also a disciple and follower of Frédéric Le Play. Demolins was chief editor of *La Réforme Sociale*, and the founder of *l'École des Roches*, where he wanted to apply educational models tailored on the Anglo-Saxon system, as he observed this in the English schools of Bedales and Abbotsholm and compiled in his book, *A quoi tient la supériorité des Anglo-Saxons?* Henri Marty, "L'Ecole des Roches," *The School Review* 20, no. 1 (January 1912): 27–33; Savoye, "Les continuateurs de Le Play au tournant du siècle."
44 Ege, *Prens Sabahaddin*, 36.
45 The English translation, by Lois Bertram Lavigne, *Anglo-Saxon Superiority – to What Is It Due?*, would be published in 1920 (London: Leadenhall Press).
46 Bozarslan, "Le Prince Sabahaddin," 290.
47 The translation in the text is "communistic." I, however, will use communitarian, as it renders a better idea of what Edmond Demolins really meant: not a communist society (to which one could be led to think due to the translation) but one ordered around the community (either intended as family or the state) and thus communitarian.
48 I will refer to the societies of individualistic formation as individualist societies.
49 Edmond Demolins, *Anglo-Saxon Superiority – to What Is It Due?* (London: Leadenhall Press, 1920), 42–43.
50 Ibid., 27.
51 Ibid.
52 Ibid., 35.

53 Ibid., 27.
54 Ibid., 50.
55 Notably, Sabahattin's admiration for Great Britain was reciprocated, as shown by the local press regarding him as "a rare Turk." Vaka, "An Imperial Enemy of Turkish Despotism," 32.
56 Sabahattin, *Türkiye nasıl kurtarılabilir?*, 100–102.
57 Ibid., 22. In all quotations from Sabahattin's book here translated in English, the original stress indicated by a switch from typeset to handwriting has been rendered into italic.
58 Ibid., 77–78.
59 Ibid., 58.
60 Ibid., 59.
61 Comparing France with Great Britain he noted: "When compared to the French, English youth leave their schools as almost half ignorant. Whereas, when they enter the stage of working life how the latter compared to the former manifest their ability!" Ibid., 32.
62 Ibid., 61–62.
63 Ibid., 27.
64 Ibid., 28.
65 Ibid., 77.
66 It is interesting to note the way in which Sabahattin used the word 'progress', which Comte had made fashionable, but attributing to it an altogether different meaning: while for Comte, progress related to humanistic development, for Sabahattin it related to economic development.
67 Vaka, "An Imperial Enemy of Turkish Despotism," 32.
68 Ibid., 32.
69 Sabahattin, *Türkiye nasıl kurtarılabilir?* 34. Sabahattin's claim that the 'trial and observation' method utilized in conducting scientific investigations and uncover 'universal truths' was 'a by-product of individualism' rather than of the wide acceptance of Newton's method suggests a principled position in defence of the liberal ideology on his part.
70 Ibid., 104.
71 Ibrahim Yalimov, "The Bulgarian Community and the Development of the Socialist Movement," 89–90.
72 Interestingly, the efficacy of Sabahattin's recipe for economic development is challenged by comparative studies between wage levels in the last decades of the Empire and current ones, which reflect the implementation on a global scale of the (neo)liberal economic paradigm: "The absolute difference between the wages of the most industrialized country in the capitalist world-system and the peripheral Ottoman economy turns out to be significantly less than comparable wage levels in present-world economy," in Korkut Boratav, Gündüz Ökçün and Şevket Pamuk, "Ottoman Wages and the World-Economy, 1839–1913," *Review* VIII, no. 3 (Winter 1985), 393.
73 He blamed the reforms of the *Tanzimat* period for, taking a highly centralised country as France as model, re-enforcing in the peoples a sense of affiliation to the government and the administration, while taking away freedom and personal responsibility.
74 Fesch, *Constantinople aux derniers jours d'Abdul-Hamid*, 398.
75 Sabahattin, *Türkiye nasıl kurtarılabilir?* 86.
76 Ibid., 96.
77 Ibid., 96–97.
78 Ibid., 88–89.
79 Ibid., 89–90.
80 Ibid., 91–92.

106 *Mehmet Sabahattin and social science*

81 Fesch, *Constantinople aux derniers jours d'Abdul-Hamid*, 401.
82 Sabaheddin, *Türkiye nasıl kurtarılabilir?* 36.
83 Ibid., 36.
84 Fesch, *Constantinople aux derniers jours d'Abdul-Hamid*, 402.
85 Ibid., 383–388.
86 In an open letter published in the revue *La Presse associée* in February 1905, Sabahattin even compared the Armenian bombing of the Ottoman Bank in 1903 to the brutal policies of Abdülhamit. Fesch, *Constantinople aux derniers jours d'Abdülhamid*, 385–387.
87 Bozarslan, "Le Prince Sabahaddin," 300.
88 Sabahattin, "The Turks and Progress," *The Review of Reviews* 32 (1906), 48. *The Review of Reviews* was a monthly journal founded in January 1890 by W.T. Stead.
89 Sabahattin, *Türkiye nasıl kurtarılabilir?* 39–40.
90 It is interesting to mention here, by way of contrast with Sabahattin's stance, the interest and joy aroused among Young Turks by Japan's victory over Russia and the subsequent peace treaty in 1905. Young Turks and other reformers alike saw in Japan an example of a late moderniser that had managed to defeat not only a superpower, but also the superpower that had been the nightmare of the Ottomans. Japan had reformed, in the eyes of many Ottomans, precisely by synthesising Western technological advancement with traditional aspects, creating a hope for the Empire, to become the "Japan of the Near East." Renée Worringer, "'Sick Man of Europe' or 'Japan of the Near East'?, Constructing Ottoman Modernity in the Hamidian and Young Turk Eras," *International Journal of Middle East Studies* 36, no. 2 (May 2004), 213.
91 See his exchanges with Unionist members through the pages of *Terakki* reported in Ege, *Prens Sabahaddin*.
92 Sabahattin was righly called "un révolutionnaire de droite," Bozarslan, "Le Prince Sabahaddin," 291.
93 Ibid., 291.
94 The archangel Gabriel plays an extremely important role in Islam, as it is he who brings the revelations to Muhammad.
95 Fesch, *Constantinople aux derniers jours d'Abdul-Hamid*, 401.

5 The end of an idea, the 1902 Congress of Ottoman Liberals in Paris

Organisation and attendance

The need to convene a meeting between all the opposition parties gathered under the umbrella of the Young Turk movement had been felt for some time. The Ottoman Revolutionary Party (*Osmanlı İhtilâl Fırkası*), formed in 1897 by Tunalı Hilmi Bey, had taken steps towards organising one under the aegis of the *khedive* of Egypt, to be held either in Brindisi, southern Italy, or on the island of Corfu. However, opposition from the *Mechveret* group on the grounds that the regent, Abbas Hilmi, and his associates, were too close to Freemasonry and the British government,[1] together with difficulties in finding a venue, had led to the abandonment of the plan.[2] Furthermore, the Ottoman diplomatic service admitted that it had co-opted the Italian government into blocking all possible contacts between Young Turk members on Italian soil. Eventually, Mahmut Paşa and his sons took on responsibility for organising the meeting in the form of a proper Congress and chose Paris as the place to hold it. This was for a series of reasons: the relatively large concentration of Young Turk members, the relative tolerance of the French government, a public opinion sympathetic to the Young Turk cause, and the knowledge that the Ottoman government had persuaded the Swiss, German, English, and Italian governments to expel Mahmut and his sons if caught on their soil.

As plans for the organisation of the Congress went ahead, the Ottoman authorities, somehow informed, requested the French to prevent its taking place, claiming that the organisers were "revolutionaries" and "anarchists."[3] The French authorities gave in to the request, and the police put Sabahattin's house under close watch, on Boulevard Malesherbes, where the meeting was believed to be scheduled for 17th or 20th January. Nothing of notice was recorded on either day, apart from a visitor, probably Paul Fesch or Joseph Denais,[4] staying for about ten hours on the 17th.[5] However, M. Lepine, General Prefect of the Paris Police, summoned Sabahattin and Lutfullah to his office on 24th January to inform them that he would not authorise a big meeting of Ottoman opponents of the Sultan on any day.[6] In the meantime, the rumour that a meeting of Ottoman opponents was in preparation had spread through the French press: according to *L'Eclair*, around 50 Ottomans were expected to arrive from Turkey, Egypt, Mesopotamia, Romania, Rumelia, Albania, London, Rome, Geneva and Athens to discuss an agenda roughly consisting in the following points:

1 Dévouement et loyalisme envers la dynastie;
2 Honorer la religion musulmane ainsi que la civilisation moderne. Protéger toutes les autres religions ou cultes;
3 Faire de la Constitution ottomane promulguée en 1876 la base du gouvernement et le pivot de l'entente et de l'union entre tous les Ottomans sans distinction de religion ni de race;
4 Proclamer l'égalité politique entre musulmans et non musulmans et les faire bénéficier également des avantages matériels et moraux du gouvernement du pays.[7]

Le Temps spoke of a proposition among Young Turk members to hold the meeting in London, if the Parisian authorities had insisted upon the ban, and featured an interview with Sabahattin and Lutfullah who expressed the intention to discuss "un projet de constitution nouvelle à donner à leur pays,"[8] which would guarantee equal rights to all ethnic groups living under the Ottoman sultanic banner.

The French press having done its bit, so did the politicians: five French deputies of different political leanings, sympathetic to the position aired in *Mechveret*, approached the French authorities presenting the aims of the meeting the Young Turk members intended to hold as totally peaceful.[9] Not long afterwards, the cabinet director of the President of the Council summoned Rıza and some of his followers to confirm lifting the ban provided the attendees would refrain from discussing revolutionary options or using language that might harm the public image of the Sultan. Rıza obliged:

> Nous avons expliqué au distingué chef du cabinet que nous sommes ni anarchistes ni révolutionnaires, et cela non pas par crainte d'aucune sorte, mais par conviction ferme que les changements brusques, obtenus par des moyens violents, nous paraissent dangereux pour le salut de la Patrie. Nous remercions ici le Gouvernement français d'avoir tenu compte de notre déclaration et d'avoir dissipé ainsi le nuage d'incriminations et de calomnies.[10]

It is possible that the French politicians' intervention was crucial in bringing about the authorities' change of heart, as the *Mechveret* account from which the quote above is taken indicates. If this was so, public opinion, which had rallied in defence of freedom of expression and the Young Turk cause at the time of the *Mechveret*'s trial in 1896, and had come to perceive Young Turk members as victims, not as conspirators, is likely to have played a role in bringing about the French politicians' intervention, and the French authorities' decision. Strategic considerations related to the diplomatic race between the French and British governments for influence in the Ottoman Empire may also have contributed to the lifting of the ban in fear that, otherwise, Young Turks would move their meeting to London or somewhere else in Great Britain, and, from then on, choose the British government as their main interlocutor.[11]

Once the French authorities had given the go-ahead to the Young Turk Congress, albeit still without formal authorisation, Sabahattin and Lutfullah circulated a letter inviting a number of selected delegates to discuss how best to gather morale, and join forces among all Ottomans, regardless of race and religion, in defence of freedom and justice. They indicated that securing unity of action was paramount to saving the Empire, and that only once unity of action had been achieved, discussion should start to try and identify the causes for the backward and dire economic, social, and political situation the Empire was in, and remedy it, first of all, by reinstating the constitutional regime and establishing a solid and modern educational system.[12]

The Young Turk Congress took place from the 4th to the 9th of February 1902; the venue chosen for it was not Sabahattin's house but the neutral environment of a house in Avenue du Trocadéro provided by a member of the *Institut de France*, Monsieur Lefèvre-Pontalis, upon Joseph Denais's intervention.[13] The honorary presidency was awarded to Mahmut Paşa, while Sabahattin himself chaired proceedings; this arrangement, which clearly favoured Sabahattin's faction against Rıza's, had apparently been orchestrated by İsmail Kemal.[14] Forty seven delegates from most ethno-religious components of the Empire – Albanians, Arabs, Armenians, Circassians, Greeks, Kurds, Jews, and Turks – attended the Congress;[15] however, only the Armenians were invited as representatives of their community, while the representatives of the Albanian, Greek, Jewish, and other minorities were invited on account of their personal role in the movement.[16]

The first day: great expectations

The Congress was inaugurated at 9 o'clock with Lutfullah's brief welcoming address to the attendees; expectations on the part of the Congress delegates were very high: "Et c'est de ce jour-là surtout, on peut le dire, que la Turquie put entrevoir, prochaine, l'aurore de la liberté,"[17] and reflected on Sabahattin's opening speech:

> [T]his evening's meeting is a valuable and colourful chapter of our nation's history. That night, close to fifty invited attendees on a mission, with the insignia of the proud crown of Ottomanism on their heads and on their faces manifesting sincere cheerfulness, were received one by one in the hall[.] From the wall was hanging, together with the French flag – worthy to mention the three colours of humanity – the Ottoman flag, consisting of a star taking shelter in the crescent [symbol] of justice of the

nation, [which] was filling with the light of joy the eyes of the Ottomans present there, who were longing to embrace independence.[18]

Throughout his speech, Sabahattin insisted on the need to introduce full respect of the rule of law and allow freedom of religious opinion in the Empire, and emphasised that Ottomanism was alive, that it was, actually, the most important inspiring principle, and objective, for the Congress to achieve:

> the reforms that we shall try to apply and implement today in our fatherland are not in the name of something related to religion or a party, but in the name of the common Ottomanism ... Until yesterday, the different elements that make up the noble Ottoman nation were working separately and have not been able to unite at [any] one place. While all these things are a sign of regret and reflect a painful image to friends and foes alike, today these divided communities of people, with mutual brotherhood and respecting and honouring their law which they had acquired, are coming together as members of the same family gathering ready for united action, in order to strive for an immediate cure against these unbearable injustices that since 25 years have been plundering the Ottoman nation through whirlwind[. This] fact is a source of gratitude.[19]

The next task was drafting a resolution listing the points around which the Ottomanist project revolved:

1. Reject any kind of affiliation between the Ottoman nation and the current despotic, corrupt, and evil, administration;
2. Establish the full upholding of the rights of its various ethnic/religious communities – as mentioned in the Imperial edicts (*Gülhane* and *Islahat Fermanı*) – confirmed by international treaties;
3. Provide the means to fully satisfy the legitimate aspirations of all to be part of the municipal and provincial administrations;
4. On the basis of the equality of rights and duties for all, instil in the citizens a feeling of faithfulness and loyalty towards the throne and the Ottoman dynasty;
5. Strive to direct all Ottomans towards the accomplishment of a threefold aim: maintain the integrity and indissolubility of the Ottoman nation; respect its fundamental laws, in particular the 1876 Constitution, the most important, precious, and effective instrument for protecting the rights and political liberties of the peoples against arbitrary rule; and re-establish internal order and peace.
6. Up-hold international treaties, in particular the Treaty of Berlin, and extend the regulation on the internal order to all provinces.[20]

As soon as the resolution was put to the vote, serious problems emerged: the delegates of two Armenian groups, *Dashnak* and *Henchak*,[21] and two independent Armenian delegates, decided to abstain: the much sought after unity between all delegates had already evaporated.

The reason for the Armenians' decision is not entirely clear. Apparently, the bone of contention was the distribution of administrative power in the reformed Empire, with Rıza and his followers pursuing a centralised policy which revived and reaffirmed the role of Istanbul, while the Armenians wished to see the establishment of local councils and local administrations. The majority of those present, and certainly Sabahattin, who favoured a quasi-federal structure for the Empire, sided with the Armenians, suggesting adding a paragraph to the resolution, to promise the creation of a permanent Committee of opposition groups to oversee its implementation, having the signatories of the Paris Treaty of 1856 and of the Berlin Treaty of 1878 as guarantors. The reference to the 1856 Treaty of Paris, issued following the Congress, in the suggested addition was relevant in that all its signatories had promised to uphold the integrity and independence of the Ottoman Empire;[22] that to the 1878 Berlin Treaty was also important, though in a different way. This is because the Treaty had sanctioned, among other things, the independence of Romania, Serbia and Montenegro, the coming into existence of Bulgaria as an autonomous entity, and the occupation of Bosnia-Herzegovina by Austria and of Cyprus by Great Britain.[23] However, Rıza had authored several articles expressing utter disbelief in the possibility that the European powers would disinterestedly intervene in matters internal to the Ottoman Empire;[24] he held the signatories of the Berlin Treaty responsible for the territorial losses the Empire had suffered, sometimes to their own benefit, as in the case of Austria and Great Britain.[25] He had also clearly stated that he and his followers were "complètement opposés à toute ingérence des Puissances dans les affaires intérieures de notre pays."[26] The addition to the resolution suggested to meet the Armenians' requests had thus an explosive nature, and Sabahattin could not have failed to foresee the consequences of pushing forward with it; he may have been bound to do so by a promise made to İsmail Kemal to persuade him to attend the Congress. Kemal had linked his participation to two conditions, as he himself would recall: the first was that all ethnic groups should be represented, as stated in his memoirs: "[i]t was essential, in my opinion, to show that those who were against Abd-ul-Hamid were acting simply and solely with a view to creating a national Government that should be equally impartial and beneficent to all the peoples of the Empire."[27] The second condition was that, since the signatories of the Paris and Berlin Treaties had manifested the intention to put pressure on the Ottoman government to push forward with reform, the Young Turk movement, through its Congress, should find a way to officially acknowledge them as allies.[28] Given that Kemal did attend the Paris Congress, Sabahattin must have given assurances on both those conditions, and the two must have been working in unison at the Congress, where they could count on a good number of delegates, among whom Lutfullah, the Albanians (who would follow Kemal), the Armenians (inspired by Sisyan Efendi), and the Greeks. On the opposite side stood only "Halil Ganem, Hodja Kadri, Férid Nazim, Hamdi, capitaine d'état-major et Ahmet Rıza."[29]

The matter of Great Powers' involvement with the Young Turk struggle became the main bone of contention with Rıza condemning the idea of accepting it under any guise, and issuing the following statement:

> The Constitution is the guarantor of the felicity and salvation of all the different Ottoman subjects, we have no need for the acts of assistance of the great powers and asking for such assistance is impossible. Even if it could be envisaged, it could act not in favour, but rather against us. Such help would damage our national feeling. Let us work on our own, let us trust and rely on our powers.[30]

At which the majority group replied with a fairly long declaration stating that foreign intervention was inevitable:

> The European intervention will happen sooner or later ... We will request help from Europe together with all the Ottoman peoples in harmony; this way, the intervention would not be against us, we want to turn it to our favour. Yesterday, the interventions were made for Serbia, Montenegro, Bulgaria, Eastern Rumelia and Crete; [if we do not act], tomorrow they will be carried out in the heart of Anatolia, in front of our capital's door.[31]

The first day of proceedings ended with the suggestion that the delegates should give the resolution further consideration, and constructively debate it the following day. Incidentally, in the meantime, the French authorities had given the Congress the formal go ahead, and proceedings had transferred to Sabaheddin's house in Boulevard Malesherbes.

The second day and after: things fall apart

Both *Mechveret* and *Osmanlı* reported that the second day of the Congress started with the two sides already distant in their aims and prepared to raise more issues rather than work towards reaching a compromise; it would close with the interests of the various ethnic and religious groups making up the Empire appearing objectively irreconcilable. In a polemic vein, the *Mechveret* group asked Sabahattin to clarify, in his capacity as president, on what grounds he and his brother had chosen the delegates to invite to the Congress to represent the different factions of the movement or the various ethnic groups of the Empire. The target of the *Mechveret* group's inquiry was the Armenian delegation, whose refusal to sign the resolution in its initial form constituted evidence in their eyes that the Armenians were trying to manipulate the Young Turk movement to their own benefit.

In the past, through the pages of *Mechveret*, Rıza had denounced the Sultan's divisive policies aimed at dividing the opposition and exhorted the minorities that had most suffered from those policies to stick with the Ottomanist project and, by doing so, inflict the Sultan a serious blow.[32] Accordingly, Rıza had urged Albanians, Armenians, Macedonians, and all other minorities to see themselves first and foremost as Ottomans, and refrain from attempting to acquire independence, or special status, if they wished to be part of the Young Turk movement, denouncing such attempts as counter-productive.[33] Hence, at the Congress, he attacked the Armenians head-on: "Ils ne veulent s'entendre, y disent-ils, avec les Jeunes-Turcs que pour renverser le régime actuel. C'est donc un mouvement révolutionnaire seul auquel ils sont prêts à concourir, et rien de plus."[34] Personal antipathies between the delegates became manifest,[35] and the aim of each individual faction took primacy over the communal goal of making Ottomanism a reality. So, for instance, the fact that Rıza had publicly and forcefully denounced the Sultan's aggressive policies in Armenia was overlooked,[36] and so was the fact that Rıza's and Sabahattin's factions had jointly signed a letter denouncing the atrocities committed by the Sultan on the Armenians, as Joseph Denais reported:

> les deux Comités libéraux ottomans, à Paris, le Comité d'initiative privée, 'Constitution et décentralisation' (fondé par le prince Sabaheddine) et le comité 'Union et Progrès' communiquèrent ensemble à la presse la note suivante: 'les partis Turcs d'opposition protestent avec indignation contre les atrocités commises dans les diverses provinces de l'empire ottoman, notamment à Van, et contre les tortures infligées dans les prisons d'Erzeroum aux Turcs et aux Arméniens qui réclament le régime représentatif.'[37]

At this juncture, Ganem made an attempt to reconcile the two positions with the suggestion to alter the planned addition to the resolution so as to characterise any acceptable foreign involvement as *action bienveillante*, more specifically, as *concours moral*:

> le Comité permanent qui sera constitué aura pour mission de se livrer aux démarches nécessaires auprès des Puissances signataires du traité de Paris, de l'année 1856, et du traité de Berlin, de l'année 1878, afin d'obtenir leur action bienveillante pour faire prévaloir les susdits principes et pour mettre en exécution les traités internationaux concernant l'ordre intérieur de la Turquie, ainsi que tous les actes internationaux découlant des susdits traités, et pour les faire appliquer à tous les *vilayets* de l'Empire.[38]

Although, as the passage above shows, Ganem had put the matter of foreign involvement rather well, giving it prominence while keeping it within well-designed borders, the majority of the delegates thought his suggestion did not go far enough towards binding the European powers into providing the movement with active support. Given that the Armenian delegation persisted in the unwillingness to vote for the resolution without the addition on the matter of European powers' involvement, Rıza and his followers accused them of having allied themselves with the Macedonian-Bulgarian Committees to pursue the pan-Slavic project:

> Les Arméniens, qui se déclarent hautement eux-mêmes être un comité révolutionnaire et réclament l'intervention active des Puissances étrangères, tendront la main droite au Comité révolutionnaire bulgare, et la main gauche au nouveau Comité ottoman que nous attendons à l'œuvre et que nous jugerons d'après ses actes.[39]

The profound rift between the *Mechveret* group and the other delegates put before everyone's eyes that the Congress was going to fail on its main objective: achieving the Ottomanist goal of reconciling the interests of all ethnic and religious groups in the Empire that, only two days earlier, all delegates had vigorously advocated. Rıza went as far as accusing the presidency of having allied itself with the Armenian delegates, perhaps on the basis of secret arrangements, and had harsh words of condemnation for the latter's refusal to compromise: "Les patriotes ottomans ne manqueront pas de juger sévèrement l'acte qui consiste à ne point adhérer à un programme qui proclame si largement l'égalité politique entre musulmans et chrétiens."[40] The delegates of the Armenian organisations *Dashnak* and *Henchak* replied that, although they intended to work towards achieving the aims set out in the resolution, they felt entitled to pursue their own particular goals, which they did not see as a threat to the integrity of the Empire but as a challenge to the Sultan for not abiding by Article 61 of the Berlin Treaty of 1878, which stated:

> The Sublime Porte undertakes to carry out, without further delay, the improvements and reforms demanded by local requirements in the provinces inhabited by the Armenians, and to guarantee their security against the Circassians and Kurds. It will periodically make known the steps taken to this effect to the Powers, who will superintend their application.[41]

What provoked the rigidity of the Armenians' position was the fact that, although the Porte had indeed failed to comply with Article 61, and the Sultan had committed atrocities against the population, the signatories of the Berlin Treaty, who should have superintended on the application of the Article, failed to do so. It looked to the Armenians as if making explicit reference in the resolution to their possible future involvement was an absolute priority to binding them to their obligations. Officially, the objectives of the main Armenian political parties (the *Armenakan*, *Henchak* and

Dashnak parties) – ensuring that the reforms would take place as promised at Berlin, and schooling the Armenians of the Ottoman Empire in a progressive manner – were modest and unproblematic.[42] But the members and supporters of those parties housed a deep resentment, and were willing to do anything, at whatever cost, to achieve greater autonomy.

As a result of the divisions that emerged among the delegates, the final resolution of the Congress contained only the following undertakings:

1   Reinstate the 1876 Constitution, and so transform the Sultan's despotic regime into one of freedom and justice;
2   Remind the European powers of their duty to ensure respect of the international treaties signed with the Ottoman Empire, from which its ethnic and religious groups would benefit;[43]
3   Work towards reforming the Empire so as to emphasise the role of local administrations;
4   Work towards the active inclusion of European powers, notwithstanding opposition from a minority group of delegates.[44]

The vague and generic character of the final resolution was a preconceived attempt to come up with something that all delegates would agree upon. However, even this very modest goal was not going to be achieved:

> The resolution consisting of the above mentioned four articles only, which were put down in the discussion, ultimately occupied the present people for three–four nights in agitation. The arguments, debates, rejections, answers and defences started coming from all sides. Sometimes over the etymology of a word, or composition ... the time was spent, for hours, exactly like negotiating an agreement with the Great Powers ... Within this powerful agitation and tidal conflicts, two parties were organised, which had one sacred intention but different methods to reach their aim.[45]

On the closing day, the only point on which all delegates could agree was the condemnation of Abdülhamit's rule.

The only tangible result of the Congress was that, once the minority group had basically ruled itself out, the majority group was able to form the Central Committee of the Ottoman Community of Freedom Loving Peoples, *Osmanlı Hürriyetperveran Fırkasının Merkez Komitesi*. This political group led by Sabahattin was to remain in Ottoman political life for a long time and would serve as one of the few voices of dissent during the Unionist regime after 1908. The committee was composed of seven members, who were chosen almost entirely from among those who had backed the idea of foreign intervention. It included three Muslim members: İsmail Kemal Bey, İsmail Hakkı Bey[46] and Ali Haydar Mithat.[47] The three Christian members were: Vasileos Musurus Ghikis Bey,[48] Fardi Effendi,[49] and a third whose name has been purposely omitted by *Mechveret* [50] for security reasons and who instead has been named by *Osmanlı*, as Siret Bey.[51] Prince Sabahattin was nominated president and immediately promised to donate a large sum, apparently 25,000 francs,[52] to the newly formed committee.

The members of the Committee also worked out and established the articles and regulations for the newly formed organisation. The most important parts of the regulations were those stating that unity of intent and common goals were shared by all those who became members, that the headquarters of the Committee were to be in Paris, and that other branches in France were to be soon opened. The aims were, once again, so broad and the membership so loose that the Committee could not have become, and did not become, a pivotal player in the fight against Abdülhamit II and in the promotion of reform throughout the Empire. On its part, the *Mechveret* group dissolved its publication in Ottoman and, immediately after the Congress, in 1902, started publication of a new journal, *Şura-yı Ümmet*.[53] As we know, after 1902, and even more so after 1907 when the Second Congress of Ottoman Liberals was held, the power of the opposition groups rested with the military and activist groups present in the Balkan provinces, and in particular in Manastır, Salonika, and Üsküp.

Consequences of the Congress

In his memoirs, İsmail Kemal summed up the outcome of the 1902 Paris Congress of Ottoman Liberals: "the lack of agreement among the Turkish reformers which became manifest during the Paris Congress prevented any possibility of united political action likely to give reason to hope for a change in Turkish affairs."[54] Similarly, the Congress of Ottoman Liberals was branded as a failure by all the three main sources on the event: Paul Fesch, Ernest Ramsaur and Şükrü Hanioğlu.[55] The only real immediate and tangible success of the Congress was that the organisers managed, for the first and last time, to achieve a gathering of all the opposition movements mirroring the ethno-religious composition of the Empire. The Second Congress of 1907 in Paris, in fact, was much more limited in its ethnic representation,[56] so that the failure of the 1902 Congress seems to have hampered a dynamic of inclusion. This fact led to another indirect but decisive outcome: positions within the opposition groups crystallised so much that the surge of power soon to take place from the intellectuals into the hands of the military constituted a turning point. Without the rupture within the movement, both the actual organisation of such drastic measures as those of 1908, i.e. the military confrontation against the forces of Abdülhamit, and the passing of power to the military wing, the Unionists, may have never materialised. Because of the rupture, the different wings became more extreme in their respective views and less willing to collaborate with others who, from allies, turned into enemies.

An articulation of the argument that the failure of 1902 marked the end of a peaceful course of action – the intellectual phase of the Young Turk movement – and the end of Ottomanism as a valid answer to European ideological intrusion can be found in İsmail Kemal's memoirs:

> the troubles in Macedonia increased, and the directors of Turkish policy at Constantinople, instead of arriving at an understanding with the Powers which would have been interested in maintaining Turkish integrity, adopted a mischievous policy which drove the people to acts of desperation. Having lost all hope of doing anything salutary for Turkey, all my efforts, as well as those of Redjeb Pasha and other Albanian patriots, were devoted to the task of trying to save Albania from the disaster which we now realised was inevitable.[57]

Overall, the failure of 1902 and the political developments after that year and before 1908 appeared to reiterate the unfeasibility of a peaceful Ottomanist plan. The pages of *Mechveret* illustrate the above very aptly, stating clearly that unity of intents was but a myth: "l'expérience ayant montré que toute entente a été jusqu'ici rendue impossible par ce fait que chaque groupement s'acharnait à soutenir son programme politique."[58] The fact that every group within the broader movement worked, ultimately, for its own gain was considered to be one of the main problems of the movement by Rıza, through the pages of *Mechveret*:

> Les groupes politiques qui se trouvent hors de la Turquie pouvaient seuls prêcher librement la solidarité, et c'était, à vrai dire, leur premier devoir. Ont-ils bien rempli ce devoir? Hélas! pas tout à fait. On trouve sans doute, dans les journaux appartenant aux divers groupes, des appels à la solidarité plus ou moins pompeusement présentés. Oui, chacun de ces groupes invite les différentes nationalités à s'unir, mais à s'unir sous son propre drapeau! Il ne faut pas oublier que les divers partis d'opposition ont dans leur poche un remède spécial à l'aide duquel ils prétendent guérir les maux. La malheur est que chaque parti, croyant son remède le meilleur et supérieur à ceux des autres, n'avait pas pensé à soigner le mal après une commune consultation. Une dissidence régnait donc également entre eux.[59]

All in all, the Congress that had been convened to establish a unified front against the rule of the Sultan ended in rupture between Armenians and the rest, and in a split between the two major factions of Sabahattin and Rıza. On the one extreme stood the Armenians and other Christians who pushed for substantial European involvement and envisaged an Ottoman Empire divided very much on the national lines of the various components. In the middle stood Sabahattin, with the plan of "an Ottoman Confederation in which the various nationalities of the Empire would have a great measure of autonomy and in which the main bond would be the dynasty."[60] On the other extreme was the Ahmet Rıza–Halil Ganem axis, which represented a milder approach to reforming the political entity and, possibly, a bloodless transition to another Sultan. However, the *Mechveret* group represented the section of the Ottoman opposition, grouped under the loose umbrella of the Young Turk movement, which was quicker to abandon plans and hopes for a multi-confessional Ottomanist project. We know that Rıza, after the Congress of 1902, slowly moved towards the idea of Turkism. Proof of this is a document dated 1908 in which an official of the French government reports that the day after setting foot back into the Empire, Ahmet Rıza allegedly proclaimed: "'[l]a Turquie aux Turcs' et à manifester sa méfiance et son aversion envers tous les partis, notamment envers le parti de décentralisation du Prince SABAHEDDINE."[61] Further proof of the fact that the Rıza group was moving towards the Unionist ethos of the post 1908 Revolution political scene is given by another French intelligence report. Written on the 16th of July 1908, shortly after the Young Turk Revolution, the intelligence report claims that the group around Rıza was active in what is described as Eastern Rumelia, placing it geographically close to the section of the army and the organisation that was to become the backbone of the Unionist Turkist policy.[62]

Shortcomings of the Congress

The Congress was a debacle for different reasons that are not limited to the time of the Congress itself but instead have long term repercussions for the history of the Empire and the Republic of Turkey.

The first setback does not concern issues discussed at the Congress and that highlighted a marked difference between the two groups. Rather, it has to do with an aspect which was wholly left out of the discussions, namely religion. Both Sabahattin and Rıza dwelled extensively on the future of religion in their writings, yet did not manage to broach the issue at the Congress. However, Rıza and Sabahattin, while disagreeing on the issue of foreign intervention and on the possibility of a peaceful course of action, had demonstrated until that moment a common ground on religion through their writings. They both considered religion to be a private issue and explained that, what in Europe had been denounced as religious fanaticism of many Muslims in the Empire, was in fact a natural development and the answer to an aggressive European policy that was attempting to break Ottoman society along religious lines.[63] However, they had not reached any more common formulation on the issue of religion than an argumentative defence against another European accusation.

Indirectly, the Congress did somehow clarify further the stance of the two groups on this issue and highlighted even more that, with the failure of the 1902 attempt, the possibility of an inclusive Ottoman proto-nationalism was no longer an option. In fact, only through a highly intellectual and ideological approach could a multi-ethnic and multi-religious Empire have stood the challenges of nationalism in the nineteenth century. The moment that unity among these groups failed to materialise, the religious issue, as embodied in the idea of Ottomanism, collapsed. It is fair to wonder, therefore, if they had discussed this as the first and most important issue, then the Congress could have produced a consolidated group, aware of some differences, but set on preserving religious plurality in the private sphere and, as a consequence, the recognition of equal rights of all citizens, regardless of creed. However, the fate of the Congress, in respect to issues regarding religion, could have been either one that confirmed the intellectual nature of the opposition group, and in doing so tailored a role for religion but remained very vague in the face of practical action; or one that would lose the intellectuality, as it started to do, together with a constructive discussion on religion, for the benefit of political pragmatism and action.

Practical limitations affected the Congress's composition. Many of those coming from abroad had difficulties reaching Paris, since police forces in many countries worked in conjunction with the Ottoman embassies to prevent delegates from travelling. Ethnically and religiously, only the Armenians, as explained earlier, were invited as representatives of their own community, while the Greeks, Jews and other Balkan nationalities were invited on account of their occupational positions. This excluded the Albanians as their opinions were obviously represented, in terms of group, by İsmail Kemal himself, who, as mentioned earlier, was close to Sabahattin and could exercise substantial leverage over the decisions taken. This representational inequality is reflected in the final establishment and composition of the Committee of Freedom Loving Peoples. As mentioned earlier, the president of the committee sanctioned by the Congress was Sabahattin, with Sathas and Sisyan Effendis, who were both from the ethnic minorities, acting as joint vice-presidents. Ali Fahri Bey[64] and Adossidis Efendi,[65] also from the minorities, were the recording secretaries.[66] Since the staunchest supporters of foreign intervention, apart from Sabahattin, were among the exponents of the minorities, the very composition of the committee was biased in favour of this issue as part of the final decisions of the Congress – and this was central to the failure of the Congress itself.

What became clear during the Congress was that the only point all the delegates agreed upon was their hatred for the regime of Sultan Abdülhamit II. This affinity proved to be too abstract to consolidate action. In this light, the Congress was an intellectual effort, which crumbled in the face of pragmatic demands for activism and political organisation. The conclusion of the Congress, the composition of the committee, and the way the minority group was treated, must have been a serious blow for Rıza and his group. The closing of the preface to the minutes of the Congress, as it appeared on *Mechveret,* presented a picture of total separation with the Albanians, Armenians, and Macedonians with Sabahattin himself:

C'est avec le plus vif regret, nous le répétons, que nous nous séparons momentanément de nos compatriotes. Ils ne tarderont pas à nous revenir dès qu'ils auront goûté à l'herbe amère des pâturages diplomatiques, mais ils verront alors qu'ils auront fait le jeu des comités révolutionnaires arménien, macédonien et albanais. La tactique de ces comités, qui est percée à jour, est, à vrai dire, des plus habiles; elle consiste à se présenter devant l'Europe avec un comité ottoman ayant à sa tête un membre apparenté à la dynastie et sollicitant l'intervention de l'Europe pour le même objet. Toutefois les Puissances ne se laisseront pas éblouir, croyons-nous, par cette coalition éphémère qui aura contre elle l'opinion publique en Turquie.[67]

Thus, the Congress resulted mainly in "the accentuation of the difference of views of Sabaheddin and Ahmet Rıza into a rift."[68] This divergence seems to have produced an ideological impasse for the exponents of the Young Turk movement: it impeded on the vision of unity among the opposition groups, it frustrated the ambitions that Ottomans alone could remodel their country upon modern lines and, most significantly, it challenged the belief that, somehow, *Osmanlılık* – Ottomanism – was still a viable option for the coexistence of the various ethno-religious realities of the Ottoman Empire. This multi-layered breakdown led the various exponents of the different currents, and especially the ethnic and religious minorities, to realise that nationalism, as it had been intended in Western Europe, constituted a direct threat to the survival of the Ottoman Empire and, at the same time, the almost inevitable future of its political development.

Transition from intellectualism to activism

As a result of the failed attempt to unite the opposition in 1902 and of the marked differences among the groups that the Congress made manifest, both Turkish and non-Turkish Ottomans opted for an ethnically, religiously or linguistically founded nationalism – I will discuss this further in the next chapter. This, in turn, inaugurated the period culminating with the 1908 Revolution that was, in the eyes of many, doomed to fail precisely because of these factors. In the end, the loss of feasibility of a project based on Ottomanism and the crystallisation of nationalist tendencies made the chances for the existence of a multi-ethnic and multi-religious empire extremely slim. By the time of the Second Congress of Ottoman Liberals, held, as mentioned, from 27th to 29th of December 1907, participation was extremely limited, hinting clearly at a diminished chance of feasibility of the idea of Ottomanism.

The conclusion of this second Congress signalled the dismemberment of an already disjointed opposition. The second attempt should in fact be seen as the formal acknowledgement of divisions that had ended the intellectual phase of the Young Turk movement five years earlier. Some of the most emblematic figures within the organisation decided to withdraw their membership from the Young Turk organisation even prior to this second Congress.[69] Of the ten men who made up the core group that led the revolution, seven had not been prominent in the 'intellectual' phase.[70] The remaining members formed a society, in Salonika in 1906, with the name of *Osmanlı Hürriyet Cemiyeti* (The Ottoman Freedom Committee). The society had strong military affiliations and clearly diverged from the intellectualism of earlier years. The *Osmanlı Hürriyet Cemiyeti* sought, right from the start, a new type of membership and alliance, with military elements and a provincial base in the Manastır and Edirne area. Furthermore, as Erik Zürcher has pointed out, "[a]t the time of the revolution, the CUP had about 2,000 members, of whom about two thirds or more seem to have been military men."[71] The development of such committees as the *Osmanlı Hürriyet Cemiyeti*, is yet another sign of a transition from the intellectual phase of the opposition to the activism of the revolutionary option. The names of some of these organisations, in fact, were themselves distinct from those of the earlier phase, when references were made to science, philosophy and intellectual movements. The Revolutionary Society (*Cemiyet-i İnkılâbiye*),[72] to which both Fesch and Hanioğlu refer, chose to establish a 'watchdog' under the name of *Comité de Salut publique* in Istanbul;[73] this gesture links this phase of the Ottoman struggle to the drastic one of the Reign of Terror in the French experience. Another noteworthy as well as striking difference between the two phases was the type and the source of help envisaged to bring about political transformation. Up until 1902, the Young Turk organisation had debated the extent of Western moral, physical and financial help desired or needed. But when the organisation transited onto a new phase, potential links to Britain were abandoned in favour of Germany – especially during the preparation for the First World War. This shift coincided with an internal move towards Turkism within the Empire, and the drastic change in the environment was clearly felt by contemporaries.[74]

After intellectualism: the trajectory of Ahmet Rıza and Mehmet Sabahattin after the Congress

The Congress of 1902 was a turning point, not only in the history of the Ottoman Empire and modern Turkey, but also more directly in the lives of Sabahattin and Rıza. After the Congress – and the brief attempt at reaching some agreement between the various groups in 1907 – Sabahattin retired from active politics for three years, which he spent in solitary confinement. During this time, he convinced himself even more so that the Ottoman Empire needed social reform as opposed to political solutions.[75] It seemed for a while that he would not be willing to go back to politics and that he had abandoned any plan to constitute or influence an intellectual elite that would lay out a path to modernity. This has also been argued by Şükrü Hanioğlu, who wrote that:

[a]s we have seen, Edhem Ruhi and Abdullah Cevdet [two influential members of the umbrella organisations, and the second, incidentally, one of the four founders of the Ottoman Union Society] could not induce Sabahaddin Bey to work with them. Apparently the prince had no desire to work with members of the old CUP organisation and thus adopted a wait-and-see policy before launching a new campaign against both the Ottoman government and the coalition.[76]

Ahmet Rıza, on the other hand, embittered as much as the prince, was drawn away from active involvement in Ottoman politics and dedicated himself, at least for some time, to reading and contributing to positivist philosophy as well as being part of this circle.[77] Neither of the two, however, would remain outside of politics for long. On the one hand, the path taken by Sabahattin is not so surprising: he remained in the opposition to the CUP, maintaining a resistant attitude. This was due to his political stance as well as his desire to represent an enlightened elite, who could understand better what the population at large actually needed. The most surprising move was that of Rıza. In 1904 Halil Ganem died, severing the link that tied Rıza with non-Turkish groups in the Empire. From then on, the Rıza group, or what was left of it, gradually moved closer and closer to the idea of centralisation of power within a Turkish-oriented Empire. Especially after the revolution of 1908, relying on the Turkish component, Rıza saw an opportunity to promote a new role for religion in politics and push forth the positivist plan that he had in mind once the revolution had taken place. This agenda had been entrusted to him by the Positivist Society in Europe.[78] After the revolution, he went back to the Ottoman Empire and became the Unionist President of the Chamber of Deputies. Once in Istanbul, he was seen as fiercely opposed to religion and one of the most radical elements within the CUP, to the extent that he was among those whose removal from office was demanded by the counter-revolutionaries of 1909.

It seems that after 1902 Sabaheddin distanced himself from organised politics of a large scale, except for a few instances. For example, he remained close to the Balkan minorities and, together with İsmail Kemal, travelled to Britain to follow up on institutional help that had been promised by some within the British government in order to push his own plan ahead. However, as İsmail Kemal himself recalls:

[a]fter the Congress, without interrupting my residence at Brussels, I kept a *pied-à-terre* in Paris, where, in association with the two Princes and other political friends, I continued to push plans for reforms, which I must say were based on and supported by nothing but our own hopes.[79]

It is after the failure of the Congress that Sabahattin's idea of forming a proper committee really picked up some momentum. In 1906, Sabahattin's group, which until then had no 'official' name, took the name of the Society for Administrative Decentralisation and Private Initiative (*Teşebbüs-i Şahsi ve Adem-i Merkeziyet-i İdari Cemiyeti*). The organisation had a central branch in Paris and carried out some activities in Eastern Anatolia and the Black Sea coast. The main aim of the Committee inside Ottoman lands was to use the Turkish component of the population positively as the engine through which ethnic and religious differences would be overcome.[80] Even though some links have been highlighted between the events leading up to the revolution of 1908 and the activities of the Society, as Hanioğlu reports, its members prepared a report in which they underscored the role of their organisation in these events.[81]

The following extract informs us of how programmatically Sabahattin was to envisage the future after the Congress; this extract recalls aspects that made up his earlier ideological approach to reform treated in Chapter 4. Sabahattin claimed that most of the problems of the Empire resided in the fact that the sultan could act freely and impose anything upon a population that would not be ready to oppose him due to acute social paralysis. This paralysis was attributed to lack of education and private initiative, which undermined the emergence of an entrepreneurial class, engaged in agriculture, commerce, and industry. This situation was also fostered by the unwillingness of most people within the Turco-Muslim component to change a status-quo in which the larger part of their productive population was absorbed by the state through employment in the public sector. In the words of Sabahattin:

> [p]our conjurer le péril que menace la nation, notre jeunesse intellectuelle doit se tourner vers les carrières indépendantes et productives. Nous devons unir nos forces pour remplacer l'autocratie absolue par une monarchie constitutionnelle et viser à la décentralisation qui satisfaira [sic] à la fois les éléments chrétiens et musulmans de l'Empire.[82]

Sabahattin quit his exile and went back to the Empire in July 1908, after the revolution. What he would not abandon was his devoted opposition to the constituted powers, which were now represented by the Unionist government. It is in this government that Sabahattin saw, in many instances, a repetition of the repressive regime that the government's members themselves had supposedly combated for years. It was for this reason, in fact, that he was constantly harassed with accusations of plotting to overthrow the Second Constitutional regime. Sabahattin was even accused of having taken part in the 1909 counter-coup. Through the pages of *Terakki*, he constantly debated with editors of newspaper such as *Tanin*, and Unionist members[83] and challenged the regime through the foreign press.[84] An emblematic passage, from *Terakki*, is the following:

> Although a long time has passed since the deposition of Sultan Abdülhamid and the ruler of the former era, the new government finds itself

needing to apply a very harsh rule. This shows that Turkey has not walked on a very sound and developing path.[85]

This obviously set him against the CUP and in very good light with liberals both in the Empire and in the rest of Europe, which explains his hermit-like lifestyle back in Istanbul.[86]

Epilogue: Reflecting on Ottomanism

As just discussed, the failure of the 1902 Paris Congress implied erasing Ottomanism from the Young Turk movement's agenda not just as a political project to implement, but also as an idea to draw inspiration from. Although at the end of the nineteenth century, Ottomanism might have been an outdated and idealistic proposition, it had appealed to a large group of the Empire's citizens (many of whom were from the provinces) who, in its name, had embarked on a journey abroad, devoting a substantial part of their life to intellectual activism in the face of hardship, constant confrontations with Ottoman diplomatic pressure, and ambivalent European governments.

The question of whether Ottomanism had, at the time, any chance of being implemented as a political project is a moot one; the charge levelled by some historians, first to the Young Ottomans, and then to the members of the Young Turk movement, of being quite simply naïve in thinking it possible to turn a fractured, imbalanced Empire into a multi-cultural, cohesive nation, and so avoid its disintegration,[87] being addressed from an early twenty-first-century perspective, appears, at first sight, anachronistic. However, in the light of discussion at the 1902 Congress, the charge to the Young Turks of having been naïve in believing Ottomanism would suffice to save the Empire, appears well-grounded.

The accusation of ingenuity stands as, though Rıza was right in seeing the self-interested motives of the great powers in involving themselves with internal affairs of the Empire, he was naïve in failing to see that, given the strategic position of the Empire, not least in terms of trade routes, combined with its increased military weakness, the Great Powers would have found ways to interfere with its internal affairs whether the Young Turk movement liked it or not. Conversely, though Sabahattin was right in appreciating that the great powers would, at some point, intervene in matters internal to the Empire, he was naïve in failing to see that such intervention would have been motivated exclusively by the powers' desire to make gains – economic or territorial – (and with serious conflicts of interests among them), and that the Young Turk movement would not have had the faintest chance to benefit from it.

Summing up the meaning and standing of Ottomanism among other competing political projects and ideas of the time, arguably, its best historical and moral vindication is to be found in Justin McCarthy's comment:

1902 Congress of Ottoman Liberals in Paris 125

Until the final years of the empire, peoples of different religions lived together who have been unable to live together since … The Ottomans, who could not reform their Empire quickly enough to save it, have a share of responsibility … but guilt falls mainly on the nationalists and imperialists, who did not count the cost when they destroyed the Ottoman Empire.[88]

Rıza and Sabahattin dedicated their life abroad and their intellectual capabilities to an attempt at finding a suitable working idea of Ottomanism. However, as discussed, positions were too distant to be reconciled and their endeavour failed.

Notes

1 Hanioğlu, *Young Turks in Opposition*, 40. See also Anduze, *La Franc-maçonnerie de la Turquie ottomane*, 77, Fesch, *Costantinople aux derniers jours d'Abdul-Hamid*, Denais, *La Turquie nouvelle*, René Lay, *Bibliographie de la Franc-maçonnerie et des sociétés secrètes* (Paris: Société Bibiliographique, 1912).
2 Hanioğlu, "Der Jungenturkenkongress von Paris (1902) und seine Ergebnisse," *Die Welt des Islam* 33, no. 1 (April), 25.
3 "Sabaheddine-Loutfoulah/Comité Liberal Ottoman," *Préfecture de Police de Paris* – BA1653-17154. Apparently, according to the Ottoman authorities, the meeting included discussing plans to assassinate the Sultan. Hanioğlu, "Der Jungenturkenkongress von Paris," 34.
4 Paul Fesch was a Catholic priest who befriended a number of Young Turks (among whom Sabahattin); he authored a first-hand account of events related to the movement, *Costantinople aux derniers jours d'Abdul-Hamid*. Joseph Denais, also a Catholic, was at the time secretary of the *Association des Journalistes Parisiens*, Hanioğlu, *Preparation for a Revolution*, 124, a close associate of Sabahattin's, and an eye witness of events related to the Young Turk movement in Paris that he related in his *La Turquie nouvelle*.
5 "Sabaheddine-Loutfoulah/Comité Liberal Ottoman," *Préfecture de Police de Paris* – BA1653-17154.
6 Ibid.
7 *L'Eclair* 26th January, 1902. "Sabaheddine – Loutfoulah/Comité Liberal Ottoman," *Préfecture de Police de Paris* – BA1653-17154.
8 *Le Temps* 27th January, 1902. Ibid.
9 "Le Congrès des libéraux ottomans," *Mechveret Supplément Français* 8, no. 126 (February 1902), 2.
10 Ibid.
11 Denais, *La Turquie nouvelle*, and Hanioğlu, "Der Jungenturkenkongress von Paris."
12 Fesch, *Constantinople aux derniers jours d'Abdul-Hamid*, 365–367.
13 Denais, *La Turquie nouvelle*, 40.
14 "Paris'te Osmanlı Hürriyetperveran Kongresi," *Osmanlı* 5, no. 104 (April 1902), 3. İsmail Kemal (1844–1919) was born in Valona (Vlora), in today's Albania. He was a civil official in the first years of Abdülhamit's reign and became Governor General of Tripoli in the late 1890s. From 1892 on, he sided with Mithat Paşa's faction within the Young Turk movement. He and Sabahattin developed a close friendship and agreed on almost everything: that Rıza had emphasised too much the role of France with respect to other European players, most notably, Great Britain, as a

potential ally of Ottoman reformers, and that political and administrative centralisation was counterproductive as it encouraged tensions between ethnic and religious minorities. The only point of disagreement between them regarded the evaluation of the reforms of the *Tanzimat* period, which for Sabahattin was only cosmetic, while for Kemal had "inaugurated the era of equality and justice for all the people in the Empire ... [and was] of great and far reaching importance." William M. Fullerton, *The Memoirs of Ismail Kemal Bey* (London: Constable, 1920), 1–2. Kemal was "extolled in the British press and praised by British diplomats in Istanbul," Hanioğlu, *Young Turks in Opposition*, 148.

15 The turn-up would have been higher if police forces in many countries had not worked in conjunction with the Ottoman embassies to prevent Young Turks from reaching Paris.
16 For example, Albert Fua was invited as editor of *Mechveret Supplément Français*, not as representative of the Jewish community; similarly, Halil Ganem was invited for his involvement with *Mechveret*, not to represent the Maronites. Sabahattin's choice to call for the holding of the Congress through as personal a means as a letter would also attract criticism from Rıza and his followers. "Le Congrès des libéraux ottomans."
17 Denais, *La Turquie nouvelle*, 40.
18 "Paris'te Osmanlı Hürriyetperveran Kongresi," 1.
19 Ibid., 3.
20 The resolution is similarly reported in: Fesch, *Constantinople aux derniers jours d'Abdul-Hamid*; Hanioğlu, "Der Jungenturkenkongress von Paris," "Le Congrès des libéraux ottomans," and "Paris'te Osmanlı Hürriyetperveran Kongresi."
21 *Henchak* was a radical Armenian nationalist organisation, formed in 1887 by émigré students in Geneva. It moved its headquarters several times, to Paris, then Athens and, finally, London. *Dashnak* was one of the Armenian revolutionary movements and had been established in 1890 in Tiflis. See Ter Minassian, *Nationalism and Socialism in the Armenian Revolutionary Movement*.
22 The Congress of Paris, which gave way to the Treaty signed in March 1856 following the Crimean War, was attended by the Ottomans, Russia, England, Austria and France. Its outcome was the demilitarisation of the Black Sea and the end of Russian influence on Moldavia and Wallachia, Zürcher, *Turkey, A Modern History*, 56. It is worth remembering that the *Islahat Fermanı* was then issued by the Ottomans as an internal response to what had been set in Paris.
23 "It was a disastrous but unavoidable treaty," Zürcher, *Turkey, A Modern History*, 79.
24 See, for instance, La Rédaction, "Notre Programme," 1, and Rıza, "Les Missionnaires en Turquie," 2.
25 In his evaluation, Rıza overlooked the fact that the Berlin Treaty had mitigated the San Stefano Treaty, which closed the disastrous Russian war, restoring some degree of Ottoman rule in the Balkan provinces while promising administrative reforms.
26 "L'intervention des étrangers," 1.
27 Fullerton, *Ismail Kemal Bey*, 306
28 Ibid.
29 "Le Congrès des libéraux ottomans," 3.
30 "Paris'te Osmanlı Hürriyetperveran Kongresi," 4.
31 Ibid.
32 See Chapter 4 for details on these articles.
33 Rıza, "Pourquoi l'Europe ne réclame pas le Rétablissement de la Constitution en Turquie," 3–4.
34 "Le Congrès des libéraux ottomans," 3. Notably, Rıza's denouncing the Armenians' position as 'revolutionary' was a bold and potentially dangerous step, given

1902 Congress of Ottoman Liberals in Paris

the assurances given to the French authorities about the peaceful nature of matters discussed at the Congress.

35 Rıza also accused Sabahattin of not having submitted a preparatory agenda with the invitation to attend the Congress, when there was still time for the delegates to work towards reaching an agreement. A preparatory meeting, in fact, was organised by the *Mechveret* group at Halil Ganem's house; it offered some rather vague indications, such as loyalty to the dynasty of Osman, reconciling Islam with modern civilisation, the need to safeguard all religious beliefs, giving equal rights to all Ottomans, and, above all, reinstating the 1876 Constitution. Ibid.

36 See, for instance, "Soumission ou Déposition," 1. Back in 1895, Rıza had admired the courage of the Armenians: "It is well-known that the demonstrations organized by the Henchaks in Istanbul in May 1895 – the so-called Bab-ı Âli demonstrations – made quite an impression on Ahmet Rıza. This former French student, positivist and member of the Committee of Union and Progress (CUP) was given a fright by the audacity of the Armenian revolutionaries, the first Christians to dare to defy the sultan in the capital since the fall of Byzanthium." Ter Minassian, "The Role of the Armenian Community," 136.

37 Denais, *La Turquie nouvelle*, 22. The letter, distributed to the French press, was a reaction to a wave of arrests of Muslims, 90 in total, a Mufti among them, who, at the time of the most serious clashes between the Sultan's army and the local population – 1894 to 1896 – had sided with the Armenians.

38 "Le Congrès des libéraux ottomans," 3.
39 Ibid., 4.
40 Ibid., 3.
41 Jacob C. Hurewitz, *Diplomacy in the Near and Middle East*, 2nd edn (Princeton, NJ: Van Nostrand Company, 1958), 190.
42 Ter Minassian, "The Role of the Armenian Community," 112.
43 "Le Congrès des libéraux ottomans," 4.
44 I put together the last two clauses from the various discussions in "Paris'te Osmanlı Hürriyetperveran Kongresi;" "Le Congrès des libéraux ottomans;" and Fesch, *Constantinople aux derniers jours d'Abdul-Hamid*.
45 "Paris'te Osmanlı Hürriyetperveran Kongresi," 4.
46 Former Lieutenant-Colonel of the Ottoman Army. Hanioğlu, *Preparation for a Revolution*, 9.
47 Ali Haydar Mithat, the son of Mithat Paşa.
48 An Ottoman Greek, Ghikis Bey, was "the son-in-law of Musurus Paşa, former Ottoman ambassador to London, [Ghikis] had once been a member of the State Council and had fled to Europe on the heels of Damat Mahmut Paşa and his sons." Hanioğlu, *Young Turks in Opposition*, 183. He was to become, together with İsmail Kemal, one of the closest associates of Sabahattin. Hanioğlu, *Preparation for a Revolution*.
49 Georges Fardis, an Ottoman Greek.
50 It is interesting to note that *Mechveret*, omitting the name of this third member, also specifies that this person, who himself asked *Mechveret* not to be named, had received a strong majoritarian vote. This indicates that he was the most favoured of all those elected. According to the journal, this member was also a staunch opponent of foreign intervention and probably the only one with these ideas within the newly formed committee. "Le Congrès des libéraux ottomans," 4.
51 "Paris'te Osmanlı Hürriyetperveran Kongresi," 7.
52 "Le Congrès des libéraux ottomans," 4.
53 Kaynar "Ahmed Rıza," 383.
54 Fullerton, *Ismail Kemal Bey*, 314.
55 Hanioğlu, "Der Jungenturkenkongress von Paris."
56 Denais, *La Turquie nouvelle*, 41.

57 Fullerton, *Ismail Kemal Bey*, 314–315.
58 "Le Congrès des libéraux ottomans," 1.
59 Ibid., 5.
60 Ramsaur, *The Young Turks*, 73.
61 "Sabaheddine – Loutfoulah/Comité Liberal Ottoman," *Préfecture de Police de Paris* – BA1653–17154.
62 Ibid.
63 See, among other things, the response of Sabahattin to Sir Edward Grey, British minister of foreign affairs, in relation to the latter's claim of a Pan-Islamic and fundamentalist revival. Fesch, *Constantinople aux derniers jours d'Abdul-Hamid*, 401–405.
64 Ali Fahri had been a central figure of the CUP branch in Egypt. Hanioğlu, *Young Turks in Opposition*.
65 Konstantinos Sathas and Anastase Adossidis, two Ottoman Greeks.
66 Hanioğlu, "Der Jungenturkenkongress von Paris," 50.
67 "Le Congrès des libéraux ottomans," 2.
68 Ramsaur, *The Young Turks*, 75.
69 Among these, Ali Aydar Mithat who, in a letter addressed to the director of the *Mémorial Diplomatique* on 8th March 1907, stated: "Je vous serais très obligé de vouloir bien informer vos lecteurs que je me suis retiré depuis le 1er février du Comité 'Union et Progrès', dont fait partie Ahmed Riza Bey." Fesch, *Constantinople aux derniers jours d'Abdul-Hamid*, 396 n. 2.
70 The other three were Mehmet Talat, Mithat Şükrü and Evranoszade Rahmi. Zürcher, *The Young Turk Legacy*.
71 Ibid., 101.
72 This organisation, for which sources are extremely scant, has been labelled by Hanioğlu as a student group which, after merging with another secret society, and being based at the Military Academy, attempted between 1905 and 1907 to align itself with one or the other factions within the CUP. Hanioğlu, *Preparation for a Revolution*, 91.
73 Fesch, *Constantinople aux derniers jours d'Abdul-Hamid*, 409.
74 See, for example, Mehmet Arif Ölçen, *Vetluga Memoir*, Gary Leiser (ed.) (Gainesville: University Press of Florida, 1995).
75 It is, in fact, after the end of the Congress that Sabahattin wrote his monograph, *Türkiye nasıl kurtarılabilir?* first published, as mentioned before, in 1918.
76 Hanioğlu, *Preparation for a Revolution*, 82.
77 See, for example, his dedicated contribution to *The Positivist Review*.
78 Şerif Mardin, "The Mind of the Turkish Reformer, 1700–1900," in Sami A. Hanna and George H. Gardner (eds), *Arab Socialism: A Documentary Survey* (Leiden: Brill, 1969), 43.
79 Fullerton, *Ismail Kemal Bey*, 308.
80 Fesch, *Constantinople aux derniers jours d'Abdul-Hamid*, 398.
81 Hanioğlu, *Preparation for a Revolution*, 93.
82 Gilles Roy, *Abdul-Hamid: le Sultan Rouge* (Paris: Payot, 1936), 210.
83 See Ege, *Prens Sabahaddin*, 193–201.
84 Vaka, "Imperial Enemy."
85 Ege, *Prens Sabahaddin*, 193–201.
86 This emerges clearly from Demetra Vaka's article. Vaka, "Imperial Enemy of Turkish Despotism."
87 McCarthy, *The Ottoman Peoples*, 30.
88 Ibid., 219.

Conclusion

The intellectual phase of the Young Turk movement

This book has explored the issue of reform in the Ottoman Empire in the period between 1895 and 1902. It first analysed reforms as conceived, in broad terms, by Sultan Abdülhamit II, then, and in much more detail, by two leaders of the Young Turk movement, who were seen by many as its ideologues at the time, Ahmet Rıza and Mehmet Sabahattin. This period represented a specific phase in the history of the Young Turk movement – which is labelled the 'intellectual phase' – one that departed sharply from the previous one as well as the one following.

Prior to the defeat of the opposition movement in 1896, the Young Turk émigrés represented the external branch of the movement, which was subordinated to the internal branch, consisting, for the most part, of military officers and bureaucrats who favoured pragmatism in their day-to-day struggle to gain political influence. Up until 1896, the internal branch of the opposition movement had exerted a mitigating influence on the intellectual aspirations of the émigrés of the external branch; matters changed following the defeat of the movement internally, and its activists in exile, mainly in Europe, became entirely free to express their own vision of how to reform the Empire.

The writings of the two leaders of the Young Turk movement living in Paris, Ahmet Rıza and Mehemet Sabahattin, provide an excellent opportunity to examine the pros and cons of the type of intellectual activism characteristic of the external branch, and, in this way, explore a territory hitherto insufficiently covered in the historical literature. Exploiting the opportunities offered by a press that was fairly uninhibited by the Sultan's censorship, Rıza, Sabahattin, and many more Young Turk activists in exile in Europe, succeeded in publishing the books and journals they wanted, and in using the political language they thought was most effective to garner support within the Empire and the international community. They also had the opportunity to contribute to intellectual transnational projects by writing for international journals such as *The Positivist Review* and *La Revue Occidentale*. In this way, they turned the disadvantage of being far from the place of their interest, such as that of living in exile, into an advantage, which, if fully exploited, might have resulted in a formidable weapon in the struggle to overcome the Sultan.

Figures of the stature of Rıza and Sabahattin, however, aspired not just to make their views on reform, circulate and influence the political debates that animated the last decades of the Empire; they also aspired to penetrate, and gain the recognition of, the European intellectual elite. Accordingly, Rıza enjoyed the company of many philosophers – specifically, of Gustave Le Bon, during *les déjeuners du mercredi* – while Sabahattin met with Edmond Demolins and the group of *La Science Sociale*. The affiliation, and personal acquaintance, with Western intellectuals gave the two more than visibility; it offered a feeling of spiritual and social belonging and the opportunity to reach a level of theoretical synthesis that matched the dynamism and richness of the Parisian intellectual life. Possibly, living in exile made Rıza and Sabahattin somewhat remote from the world of action and the real challenges inherent in reforming the Empire. Moreover, they were surely the subject of an 'excessive' exposure to philosophers and intellectuals. However – and probably because of these two factors – they developed an approach to social and political reform that was as daring and ambitious as it was, at times, unrealistic, while thinking of themselves as charged with the 'mission' of saving the Empire from impending collapse.

Ahmet Rıza devoted a substantial part of his time finding a space for himself among the positivist groups, joining in the ranks of Parisian writers which elevated his position to that of an intellectual of world standing. As to Sabahattin, his recollection of his initiation into social science was linked to an almost mystical experience that, allegedly, occurred in a bookshop, after which he felt to be the 'chosen one', and saw himself as a quasi-messianic figure.[1] Rıza's and Sabahattin's affinity with the Parisian intellectual circles was a double-edged sword; on the one hand, it enabled them to reach a level of self-consistency and abstractness in their thinking that would influence, and resonate in, future debates, which, as discussed later, reached well-beyond after their times in Paris. On the other hand, it blinded them to the fact – which would have benefited the Young Turk's cause – that their project lacked a strategy to promote circulation among wider audiences than those of the intellectual circles. This was the case not only for their intellectualism but also for the marked elitism that Rıza, Sabahattin, and most of the members of the Young Turk movement in general took up in their vision of the self. For the Young Turk movement as a whole, their self-perception was that they constituted an intellectual elite that would spread knowledge to the masses, capable of assuming specific political roles, as agent of change, on behalf of the population at large. Here, intellectualism and elitism fuse, giving the Young Turk movement in exile the idea that they also served a social purpose, by filling a space outside the institutionalised powers and serving as a channel for the transmission of specific and modern synthesised ideas. In order to be acclaimed as intellectuals, Paris was seen as the perfect place: it was in France, in fact, that the press had worked as an effective means of dissemination of elite ideas to the masses and the 'culture of the journal'[2] represented the basis for the formation of a new elite. Moreover, the press was seen as the basis of cultural legitimacy in the Empire. In this way, the likes of Rıza and Sabahattin could be seen not only as Ottoman intellectuals but as intellectuals recognised by the West and, thus, modern.

As mentioned before, great inspiration regarding the positive and pivotal role of the elites came from Gustave Le Bon.[3] In his book, Le Bon provides the perfect ideological source for the role that many Young Turk members wanted to take up and for the group's decision for doing this in such specific terms:

> Civilisations as yet have only been created and directed by a small intellectual aristocracy, never by crowds. Crowds are only powerful for destruction. Their rule is always tantamount to a barbarian phase. A civilisation involves fixed rules, discipline, a passing from the instinctive to the rational state, forethought for the future, an elevated degree of culture – all of them conditions that crowds, left to themselves, have invariably shown themselves incapable of realising.[4]

In Le Bon, Young Turk intellectuals also found an explanation as to why this role cannot be held by the population at large, since:

> [t]he part of the people has been the same in all revolutions. It is never the people that conceives them nor directs them. Its activity is released by means of leaders. ... new ideas penetrate the people very slowly indeed. Generally, it accepts a revolution without knowing why, and when by chance it does succeed in understanding why, the revolution is over long ago.[5]

This view undoubtedly captured the imagination of the Young Turk leaders who saw themselves as equals to their French counterparts in bringing modernity and reform, although not necessarily through the same revolutionary means that the French had employed. According to many, the latter became also the view of Young Turks of the Ottoman population at large: "Le peuple se présente non seulement comme ignorant et distant de la science et de l'Occident qui incarne la science et le progrès, ma aussi comme étrange à la raison en tant que telle. Le peuple est une foule irrationnelle."[6] Le Bon's approach also highlighted the ethical underpinnings of its perspective. Le Bon claims that the new elite needs to be open to dialogue since, to be successful, it needs to be tied both to tradition as well as to change, a stance characterised by both rigidity and malleability. Rigidity provides a historical and cultural justification for change, while malleability provides the readiness to adapt to changes resulting from general progress. Clear proof of the impact of Le Bon's ideas on the movement is given by Halil Ganem in an article published in *Mechveret*.[7] In the article, Ganem not only explains the importance of elites in processes of change, but also contextualises the specific type of elite that the *Mechveret* group was intending to constitute:

> Si elle [the elite] se recrute exclusivement dans une aristocratie, c'est le gouvernement monarchique dans toute sa beauté; si elle se recrute exclusivement dans une démocratie, c'est le gouvernement oligarchique. Le mieux serait évidemment qu'elle prît sa source dans les deux classes, voire dans toutes classes de la société, sans distinction; car l'Élite est partout.[8]

From this emerges something that is in between a justification for acting as proto-elite and a new definition of aristocratic elite. Ganem claims that the strength of an elite is its eclectic background, which both justifies a multi-ethnic and multi-confessional composition. Thanks to the already mixed composition of the Young Turk movement, the opposition had the rightful claim to become the elite that would act as agent of change. The elite that emerged for the organisation itself was primarily an intellectual one:

> Ce que nous appelons nous l'Élite, c'est l'Élite intelligente et pensante, l'Élite qui demande à la foi ses hautes inspirations, à la raison ses lumières, à la science ses expériences les plus concluantes et ses brillantes découvertes. L'Élite pour nous, c'est la glorieuse phalange des hommes qui ont souffert pour leurs propres convictions et de ceux qui ont combattu pour la liberté et la justice. L'Élite pour nous, ce sont les hommes qui ont du [sic] et de la fermeté, les courageux, les vaillants, les incorruptibles, ceux qui osent penser haut et élever la voix en faveur de la vérité.[9]

Accordingly, this type of elite would also occupy, rightfully, the place of the aristocracy and, by doing so, it would represent the engine for progress and the bulwark to safeguarding critical moral values:

> Elle dirigeait le peuple, lui servait d'exemple; elle constituait une autorité intermédiaire entre le souverain et la nation; elle tempérait, mitigeait l'omnipotence de l'un et les exigences de l'autre; aux heures de crise, elle les relevait et leur donnait l'élan. Leur maison était le refuge des talents, le foyer commun de l'hospitalité, les archives vivantes des traditions et de la constitution morale de la nation.[10]

In the end, the convergence of intellectualism and elitism produced the final upshot: the impossibility to translate into action Rıza's and Sabahattin's powerful intellectual contributions, to which the Congress of Ottoman Liberals held in Paris in 1902 would, disappointingly for its participants, testify.

The Congress was the first, and the last, instance, in which Ottoman representatives of the various ethnic and religious communities gathered together with a view to co-operate and join forces to try and create a united front. And it was there and then that the intellectual phase of the Young Turk movement showed all its limitations, specifically, its inability to face up to the pressing needs and realities of the moment, most notably, the removal of Sultan Abdülhamit II. The Congress sealed the fate of Rıza's rather unrealistic conceptualisation of Ottomanism as a frame of belonging that was supposed to overcome ethnic and religious divisions while being sanctioned only by already existing laws, as well as the fate of Sabahattin's abstract idea of a total restructuring of the Ottoman society along individualistic principles modelled on British liberalism. Finally, the Congress also confirmed to observers the accusations made towards the Young Turk movement throughout its existence: an intransigent and authoritarian group which lacked diplomatic skills.[11]

The appeal of Ottomanism to ethnic and religious minorities

Rıza's and Sabahattin's contributions on reform came under attack also from intellectual minorities in the Empire. These, keen as they were on preserving their cultural heritage, picked on, and exposed, the internal tensions and contradictions in those contributions, which referred, in particular, to the treatment of the role of religion in the politics and practices of the Empire, whether Muslim or non-Muslim. As a result, slightly paradoxically, the appeal of Rıza's and Sabahattin's thinking on the reform of the Empire, which, irrespective of their differences, both stemmed from the idea (or ideal) of Ottomanism, became as problematic in terms of a supra-national discourse to elitist minorities as it was to the Turkish component. This was revealed rather unambiguously at the 1902 Congress, where the various ethnic and religious communities that made up the Empire were well represented.

In asking the historical question 'Was Ottomanism in the late nineteenth century an entirely utopian vision born and bred in exile, or did it encapsulate the hopes and agendas of some of the Empire's components?' the views of those communities on whether Ottomanism represented a viable option for their political and social future at the time should be taken into account. The Albanian, Arab, and Jewish, minorities offered interesting insights. At the beginning of 1900, the Albanian committees, though ultimately geared towards the formation of an independent state, still seemed to operate under the banner of Ottoman unity. So much so, that, when İsmail Kemal toured Europe looking for allies, whether within the Young Turk movement or among European circles, his firm intention was to defend the rights of the minorities while working towards a federal re-organisation of the administration away from Istanbul. At the 1902 Congress of Ottoman Liberals in Paris, he sided with Sabahattin in favour of the federalist option. Later on, in 1912, in a letter of 29th January to the citizens of Valona, he seemed to have relinquished federalism in favour of secession: "for the Albanian cause it is necessary to pursue a different course of actions [independence]."[12] Elsewhere, though, he noted:

the deep rooted habit of respect towards the Empire, the persuasion that none of the national communities, which like a mosaic constituted the Empire itself, would not yet be ready to acquire by itself economic independence, the understanding that the time was not yet ripe for the division of the Empire, whose survival, for similar or different reasons, was at the heart of all the European powers, all these considerations induced people [Albanians and other minorities] not to rush events and limit aspirations to what was realistic and actually achievable.[13]

But Kemal kept an apprehension that cultural and religious pluralism, central to the activism of the minorities, would not be a central part of the Young Turk agenda:

Upon his experience as careful and devoted administrator and from his liberal and modern background, Ismail Kemal became convinced that it would have been necessary to abolish the absolute centralisation as a sole administration could not have satisfied the needs of peoples so different among each other in culture, religion, customs and climatic and geographical realities. In brief, the concept that Ismail Kemal would have accepted as a first step would have been that of the transformation of the Empire in a federation, maybe vaguely resembling the Swiss system, in which each different community would administer itself autonomously within the same economic and political community.[14]

As to Arab participation in the Young Turk movement, ample evidence is to be found in Hasan Kayalı's *Arabs and Young Turks*; the case of Halil Ganem testifies to the fact that Ottomanism was considered, at the time, a possibility by Turkish and Arab communities alike. Further evidence of a substantially large number of Ottoman Arabs participating in the Young Turk movement is to be found in the following passage:

One of the principal envoys Abdülhamid sent to Europe to contact the Young Turks and win them over was Najib Malhama, his Lebanese Christian security chief. The choice of Malhama undoubtedly had to do with the large number of Arabs, mostly Christian, among the Young Turks in Europe.[15]

Another instance of Arab support for the Young Turks' cause is provided by Amin al-Antaki (a Syrian catholic), who pretended to accept the Sultan's offers to return to the Empire and leave the opposition, while, in fact, gathering information on behalf of the Young Turks in Paris.[16] A certain Ahmet Wardani became the spokesperson of the internal branch charged with liaising with Ahmet Rıza to negotiate and organise the unification of the two branches. Although there is evidence that certain groups that formed in the Arab provinces from the 1880s onwards were opposed to the Istanbul-based

Young Turk movement, "these initiatives remained restricted to a small group and did not constitute the basis of an Arab movement."[17] The Arab provinces contributed to the Young Turk cause also by providing further recruits who became émigrés in the West, particularly in Paris, as well as offering hiding places back home for Young Turks on the run. The overall picture of the relationship between Young Turks and Arab political activists was thus an intimate one.

While, right at the beginning of the Second Constitutional Period, things seemed to be positive for the maintenance of a multi-religious and multi-ethnic Empire,[18] the turning point came after 1909 and then 1912,[19] when the Unionist government became more authoritarian and Turkist oriented; simultaneously, implementing the Ottomanist project was becoming more and more difficult: "[w]hile it would take longer for Arabism and Turkism to find political expression, a meaningful synthesis of the two under a redefined Ottomanism (such as the Young Turks would attempt) was prejudiced by the modes of expression of the two trends [Arabism and Turkism]."[20] It is after these two dates and the taking of power on the part of the Unionists, then, that signs of the difficulty to overcome the ethnic, linguistic and cultural differences between the various components of the Ottoman Empire emerged from a background that had previously appeared to be one of relative cohesiveness, as an astute French commentator of the time noted:

> Les Arméniens ne le revendiquaient pas au lendemain des massacres d'Anatolie. Les Grecs seront loyalistes, si les Turcs les traitent avec justice et leur attribuent la part à laquelle ils ont droit. Le patriotisme de chacun dépendra de la manière dont la nouvelle patrie ottomane se comportera avec tous les enfants.[21]

At that point in time, the minorities of the Empire became crucial in debating the question of Ottomanism, with several individuals offering evidence of the persistence of the latter's appeal.

Many have studied the support that minorities gave to the CUP at the onset of the Second Constitutional Period.[22] Among these, for instance, is the case of Shlomo Yellin, also known as Süleyman, who devoted a good part of his life after the 1908 Revolution to the attempt to alert the Jewish community, to which he belonged, to the danger that Zionism would undermine the idea of Ottomanism.[23] More in general, Jewish local leaders in the Empire were working hard to mould their community into good Ottoman citizens and adopt Ottomanism throughout the nineteenth century, through long articles in local Jewish newspapers.[24] Another case in point, this one coming from the Greek minority, is provided by Pavlos Carolidis, born in a village near Kayseri in 1848; he studied history at the universities of Athens and Tübingen and was elected deputy for Izmir in the Ottoman Parliament in 1908. He took this appointment seriously, and invested in the possibility of working within an Ottomanist framework on account of his "strong belief that the new regime would open the ground for a sincere understanding between the Greek and the Turkish element."[25]

The point worth highlighting is that, if in 1908 the Ottomanist vision still enjoyed a degree of support, it is reasonable to assume this to have been a lot stronger in the period 1895 to 1902, when Ottomanism was at the forefront of the agenda of the opposition movement. If its spirit had prevailed in 1902, and the Young Turk delegates at the Congress had rallied around the federalist option – that Sabaheddin had forcefully advocated – they might, perhaps, have ensured survival of the house of Osman, at least for some time: "a constitution providing universal and equal citizenship combined with ethnic and territorial autonomy might just have saved the Empire and avoided the excesses of nationalism and of the nation-state."[26] This is because the federalist option would have maintained the much sought-after unity of the Empire without requiring an unrealistic degree of affiliation among its various components, which would, in fact, enjoy a good degree of self-government. After the revolution, more and more members of the CUP, who had at different times and to varying degrees been members of the Young Turk movement, turned from Ottomanism to Turkish nationalism, leaving those who did not very little room for manoeuvre. Accordingly, the federalist option became more unlikely, even though some commentators claimed that, in spite of the results of the rigged elections of 1912, which led the Unionists to power, Sabahattin's federal plan was still popular:

> In the Arab provinces of Syria, Beirut, and Aleppo, and the sanjak of Jerusalem, twenty-four of the thirty deputies had already switched to the Entente [Sabaheddin's party], and, before the CUP began to use state resources to manipulate the campaign, the urban vote seemed poised to bring in the Liberals as the majority party.[27]

Having established that Ottomanism represented a valid, and a viable, sociopolitical option in 1908 – and, by extension, more so in 1902 – in addressing the question why the 1902 Congress failed, the definition of the phase the Young Turk movement was undergoing as 'intellectual' reveals itself as rather helpful. This is because, in terms of social and political transformations, it was the intellectualism characteristic of Rıza's and Sabahattin's positions that crystallised their respective factions as if in direct opposition with one another, making them incapable of devising a way to, either unite under one, or else, reach a temporary, partial, compromise between the two, and swiftly implement its main tenets. In the circumstances, an intellectual approach to programming became irrelevant precisely in the urgency of political action. This explains why more activist regimes, such as the Unionists first and Kemalism later, exploiting their authoritarian or pragmatic skills, succeeded in allowing drastic changes to take place.

The last consideration also points to the fact that the failure of the intellectual phase is testament to a discrepancy between the content of the intellectual work of the Young Turk émigrés and the actual process of political and social transition. The spirit of the time, unfortunately for the likes of Sabahattin and Rıza, was one in which positions were crystallising so much that the various components of the Empire needed an active practical approach, not a forum for intellectual debates. However, if on the one hand, the intellectual exercise carried out failed, as it was ill-equipped to respond to the specific demands of the moment, it was nonetheless successful in terms of its legacy as it showed itself instrumental for the emergence of later conversations and discussions. As much as the short-lived First Constitutional Period served as a source of inspiration for many Young Turks, so did the intellectual and ideological work of the organisation carried out abroad between 1895 and 1902 impact on the future statesmen of the Ottoman Empire and early Republic.[28] The dilemmas that are still being discussed nowadays in Turkey on issues such as the role of religion in the public sphere, the appreciation of the Ottoman past, and the place of Turkey in the geopolitical space, are connected to this period, which was a vital part of both the 'longest century' of the Ottoman Empire and, I contend, the most formative era of the Turkish Republic. In conclusion, what has been highlighted is that the story of the intellectual phase of the Young Turk organisation is somewhat ironic and decisively poignant: it was doomed to fail in order to allow for tangible outcomes, but was crucial to the formation of the future ideological, practical and social developments of the Ottoman Empire and the Turkish Republic.

Notes

1 See the account of Sabahattin's encounter with Demolins' book, on display in a bookshop window, as reported in Chapter 4.
2 See Erdal Kaynar's discussion on this. Kaynar, "Ahmed Rıza."
3 Hanioğlu, *Young Turks in Opposition*; and Fesch, *Constantinople aux derniers jours d'Abdul-Hamid*, among others.
4 Gustave Le Bon, *The Crowd, a Study in the Popular Mind*, 19th edn (London: Ernest Benn Limited, 1947), 18.
5 Ibid.
6 Kaynar, "Ahmed Rıza," 326.
7 Halil Ganem, "L'Élite," 1.
8 Ibid.
9 Ibid.
10 Rıza, *La Faillite morale de la politique occidentale*, 135.
11 Kaynar, "Ahmed Rıza," 402.
12 Renzo Falaschi, *Ismail Kemal Bey Vlora – Il pensiero e l'opera attraverso i documenti italiani* (Roma: Bardi, 1985), 25–26.
13 Ibid., 22.
14 Ibid., 22.
15 Hasan Kayalı, *Arabs and Young Turks: Ottomanism, Arabism and Islamism in the Ottoman Empire, 1908–1918* (Berkeley: University of California Press, 1997), 44.
16 Kayalı, *Arabs and Young Turks*, 45.
17 Ibid., 33–34.

18 The outcome of the opening of parliament was, among other things, the emergence of an elite made up of Albanians, Arabs, Armenians, Greeks and Macedonians. Keyder, for example, wrote the following: "[f]or the first time in its history, the Empire appeared to be genuinely multiethnic." Çağlar Keyder, "The Ottoman Empire," in Karen Barkey and Mark Von Hagen (eds), *After Empire: Multiethnic Societies and Nation-building: The Soviet Union and the Russian, Ottoman, and Habsburg Empires* (Oxford: Westview Press, 1997), 35.
19 1909 was the year of the 13th April Incident (*31 Mart Vakası*) and the counter-coup by the Unionists; 1912 is the year of the outbreak of the Balkan Wars.
20 Kayalı, *Arabs and Young Turks*, 38.
21 Alfred Berl, "Jeune Turquie," *La Revue de Paris* 4, no. 6 (November–December 1908), 600.
22 For a number of these studies, see: Arsen Avagyan and Gaisz Minassian, *Ermeniler ve İttihad ve Terakki: işbirliğinden çatışmaya* (Istanbul: Aras yayınları, 2005) and Vangelis Kechriotis, "On the Margins of National Historiography. The Greek İttihatçı Emmanouil Emmanouilidis – Opportunist or Ottoman Patriot?" in Amy Singer, Christoph K. Neumann and Selçuk Akşin Somel, *Untold Histories of the Middle East, Recovering Voices from the 19th and 20th Centuries* (New York: Routledge, 2011), 124–142.
23 Michelle Campos, *Ottoman Brothers: Muslims, Christians and Jews in Early Twentieth-century Palestine* (Stanford, CA: Stanford University Press, 2011). Incidentally, but noticeably, Shlomo's brother, David, was a staunch supporter of Zionism.
24 Julia Cohen Phillips, *Becoming Ottomans – Sephardi Jews and Imperial Citizenship in the Modern Era* (New York: Oxford University Press, 2014). Even though Cohen does not treat the links with Young Turk groups.
25 Vangelis Kechriotis, "Greek-Orthodox, Ottoman Greeks or just Greeks? Theories of Co-existence in the Aftermath of the Young Turk Revolution," *Études Balkaniques* 1 (2005): 56.
26 Keyder, "The Ottoman Empire," 30–44.
27 Ibid., 39.
28 This argument will be developed further on, however, for a discussion of the Ottoman legacy in Republican Turkey see Roderic Davison, "Atatürk's Reforms: Back to the Roots," in Roderic Davison, *Essays in Ottoman and Turkish History*, 243–264.

Afterword

The enduring legacies of the Young Turk intellectuals

The previous chapter discussed how the intellectualism and elitism characteristic of the Young Turk movement during its 'intellectual phase' (1895–1902) had two contradicting, yet, at close scrutiny, foreseeable outcomes. On the one hand, uncompromising adherence of the leaders of the two main factions to their own positions and ideas coupled with an incapability to connect with the more pressing and practical needs of the people, produced a rupture among the *Mechveret* group of Ahmet Rıza and that of Mehmet Sabahattin, revolving around the concept of administrative decentralisation. This rupture sealed the fate of the intellectuals within the broader history of the movement. On the other hand, it was precisely their membership to an elitist and enlightened circle, a sense of intellectual superiority, and self-imposed exile that granted Young Turk intellectuals, like Rıza and Sabahattin, liberty to conceptualise solutions for issues that had ceased to be their daily realities. Furthermore, it allowed them to deeply articulate debates that had until then only been partially formulated and discussed, and that would live well past their time into the Unionist, Kemalist, and, even, contemporary eras. However, their legacy has not yet been acknowledged, in general because it fitted within the broader scope of an Ottoman past that was being eliminated from each of its successor states, and in particular because their intellectual legacy stood in stark contrast to the conceptual understanding of a modern, homogenous, nation-state.

Ottoman legacy in the modern period had long been side-lined, misunderstood or negated because it represented a past that challenged the foundations of modern nation-states that emerged out of former Ottoman domains. In fact, a large component of the state-building process for post-Ottoman states was based on a harsh juxtaposition with the historical 'other'. In the case of Greece, the Ottoman past has long been represented as a period of foreign occupation, that of the Turks, and is usually recorded as a negative interlude in a continuum of Greekness and referred to as Turcocracy (*Turkokratia*). At best, the period is recalled as one of benevolent occupation by the Turks, whose self-recognised cultural inferiority led to a respect for Greek civilisation.[1] A similar approach of negation and misinterpretation was also the fate of the Ottoman past in the case of what used to be the Arab provinces of the Empire. Tales of Turkish robbery of Arab gold overlapping with accusations directed at Istanbul for corrupting the true version of Islam have stayed until today in the hearsay stories that one can easily pick up in street conversations from Syria and Jordan to Palestine. Academically speaking, this perception was expounded by Albert Hourani who spoke of how Ottoman history was seen as no history by many of his Arab colleagues.[2] In the case of Turkey, the Ottoman past was used as the example of everything that 'was' and represented negativity, against the new, positive (and positivist) outlook of Kemalism. Binary distinctions were made between modernity and backwardness, between stagnation and progress, between religious fanaticism and scientific knowledge. The Turkish History Society, founded in 1931, was entrusted with the task of reformulating the past according to these distinctions. It presented the Ottoman past as a dark age for the Turks and the Sultanate culpable for the decadence and corruption of the Turks, prior to the emergence of the Republic. Recognising a positive legacy of the Ottoman time was not a viable option in the construction of the new Turkish nation.

The field has progressed, however, and Ottoman legacy has started to emerge in the historiography. In the last 20 to 30 years, studies of various kinds have discussed, in depth, the importance of the Ottoman legacy for the post-Ottoman lands: in the Balkans, in Turkey, and in the Arab world.[3] The imperial legacy had been unearthed and links across periods were made, enabling the field to grow. The Young Turk period, however, has not yet received its rightful acknowledgement in Ottoman legacy debates, and it is in this discursive space that this section locates itself. Here, a distinction needs to be made. There are important works that do recognise the Young Turk legacy in the Second Constitutional Period (1908–1919) and in the Kemalist Republican era, such as, for example, Eric Jan Zürcher's *The Young Turk Legacy and the National Awakening*, among others.[4] However, these take the Young Turk legacy to mean mostly the activist, militarist organisation that carried out the Revolution of 1908 and that transformed itself in the rule of the Unionists. An active military presence has been a constant factor in Unionist and Turkish politics. Since the counter-coup of 1909,[5] the Unionist period was marked by frequent intervention on the part of a military that held great power in what should have been civilian political dynamics. The role of the army in politics was obviously clear in Republican times with successive coups at almost constant intervals: 27th May 1960, 12th March 1971, 12th September 1980, and 28th February 1997 (i.e. the 'post-modern coup'). In these instances, the military stepped in, replaced the ruling party – most times actually abolished the party – and sometimes carried out executions. It claimed to represent and safeguard the Republican values of the Turkish nation as they had been set out by Mustafa Kemal Atatürk and, which, they cited were entrusted to them by the Constitution. These were clear parallels with the military intervention of 1909, when the army allegedly stepped in to save the Constitution, but in reality to protect the Unionist regime.[6] In recent years, the trend of military intervention in political affairs had seemed to have stopped, until April 2007, on the eve of the Presidential elections, when Abdullah Gül, the openly religious candidate of Erdoğan's Justice and Development Party (*Adalet ve Kalkınma Partisi* – AKP), was set to become the first president of the Turkish Republic. On 27th April, the website of the Chief of the General Staff posted an 'e-memorandum' which, among other things read as follows:

> It is being observed that some circles ceaselessly engaged in the endeavour to abrade the foundational values of the state of the Turkish Republic, with the preeminent one being laicism, have recently intensified their efforts. The indicated activities, continuously presented to the attention of relevant authorities in pertinent settings, represent a wide spectrum, the extent of which varies from desires to question and redefine fundamental values to the organisation of celebrations that are alternatives to our national holidays,[7] which are the symbols of the independence of our state and of our national unity and solidarity. Those who engage in these activities, in their lack of hesitation to exploit the sacred religious sentiments of our people, are attempting to conceal their true intentions by hiding these efforts, which have turned into an open challenge to the state, behind the guise of religion. … The issue that has come forth in recent days with the presidential elections is such that the topic of debating laicism has become a focal point. This situation is being observed with concern by the Turkish Armed Forces. It should not be forgotten that the Turkish Armed Forces is partisan in these debates and is categorical protector of laicism. Moreover, the Turkish Armed forces is absolutely opposed to the debates that are being carried out and interpretations that take a negative standpoint; when it becomes necessary, it will openly and clearly put forth its attitude and actions. It is necessary that no one should doubt this. In short, everyone who is opposed to the understanding of 'how happy he is who calls himself a Turk' of our Republic's founder, the great leader Atatürk, is the enemy of the Turkish Republic and will remain as such.[8]

What seemed to be yet another interference did not have the same outcome as the previous military interventions. As mentioned before, earlier interventions of the army had never been opposed to a degree that would have inhibited their capacity to carry out a change of government following the military taking over powers for some time,[9] and, in many cases, with prison or even death sentences being passed. This time, Erdoğan replied with a public statement on the following day, stating that the office of the Chief of General Staff is directly responsible to the office of the Prime Minister and that the former should abide by the law. This was, more or less, the end of the event and, maybe, the end of the military factor of the Young Turk legacy in Turkish politics.[10]

While the military legacy was more visible, harder to negate, and helped reaffirm the militarist nature of the Kemalist state, the intellectual legacy was more subtle and dangerous. During the Kemalist era, ideas of multi-ethnicity, multiculturalism and religious coexistence that were advocated by Rıza and Sabahattin clashed with the Turkish nationalism that was being formulated and held as the pillar of the new political entity. The attempt of the Young Turk intellectuals to frame a new role for religion, away from the public sphere and into the private one, was also in stark disagreement with the ideas of the new Republic. Religion could not become something owned by the individual, it had to be possessed, owned and controlled by the state.[11] In a similar way, in contemporary Turkey, advocates for the reinstatement of Islam in the public sphere and in the political domain have recognised and reconstructed part of the Ottoman legacy, however again excluding the intellectual phase.

The last decade of the 1980s and the early 1990s saw the emergence of what has been referred to as neo-Ottomanism. If, by name, this approach could lead one to think that the Ottoman past was to be reinstated and its legacy rightly assessed, reality was one of nostalgia and mythologisation of an Ottoman legacy. For a state in which Islam occupied an extremely important position, the Ottoman past was corrupted and presented as a supposed utopia of extreme religious tolerance. The upholders of neo-Ottomanism, among whom Prime Minister, and then President, Turgut Özal[12] was one of the main figures, "had selectively reconstructed Ottomanism as an identity in religio-ethnic (Muslim-Turkish) terms seemingly contrary to the nineteenth century's Ottomanism that ... entailed the coexistence of non-Muslims and Muslims under a modern state system."[13] Similarly, the new political players of the AKP, although making a rapprochement with Turkey's Ottoman past, have also done this in an extremely selective way. *Fatih* Sultan Mehmet[14] and Sultan Süleyman II, now more frequently *Muhteşem* (the magnificent) than *Kanuni* (the lawgiver), are two figures whose memories have effectively transcended the Ottoman–Turkish break in history to become celebrated components of contemporary Turkish culture.

In terms of the Young Turk intellectuals, the persistence in the negation of legacy rests, most probably, on the fact that the likes of Rıza and Sabahattin have historically, yet, wrongly, as the present book has attempted to argue, been assessed as irreligious. Therefore, highlighting the positive contribution of such thinkers seems to be far from what the present Turkish governing elite would be willing to do. On the contrary, and despite prevailing assumptions about Rıza and Sabahattin's religiosity, they both attached great importance to religion and defended Islam in the face of Western accusations.

Having said the above, however, the intellectual legacy is, nonetheless, present and visible. Rıza and Sabahattin, among other Young Turk intellectuals, began conversations that were pertinent in the final days of the Empire and the early days of the Republic and still resonate today. The first, tangible, legacy[15] left by the intellectual phase of the Young Turk organisation is the carrying of political ideas from the realm of the speculative (where they rested before the Revolution) into the corporeal through their articulation in the constitution of a proper political party. This was the case of the short-lived experience of Sabahattin's Ottoman Liberal Party (*Fırka-i Ahrar*, or *Osmanlı Ahrar Fırkası*). Established at the beginning of September 1908, the party was a "Pro-Prince Sabaheddin's movement."[16] Its promoters were Nurettin Ferruh Bey and the journalist Ahmet Samin Bey.[17] Upon the creation of the party, its members offered Sabahattin the presidency but he refused. Even though short-lived, the *Osmanlı Ahrar Fırkası* reflected in many ways Sabahattin's ideals of practical education and the fostering of private initiative, especially among the youth. It was shaped in accordance to European political parties, especially English ones, and its politics were strongly based on Sabahattin's older organisation, the Society for Administrative Decentralisation and Private Initiative *(Teşebbüs-ü Şahsî ve Adem-i Merkeziyet-i İdari Cemiyeti)*. Sabahattin provided financial and doctrinal help and, because of this, the party was informally known as the *Sabahattin Bey Fırkası*.[18] Nevertheless, the party was dismantled following the events of 13th April 1909 (*31 Mart Vakası*),[19] and never reassembled, as many of its members were arrested and others left the country in order to try and organise a new movement in Athens, Cairo and Paris. The ideals expressed by the party left a legacy and remained alive in the minds of many Turkish politicians, both critical and supportive of the *Ahrar Fırkası*, to such an extent that in the post-1910 parliamentary debates, delegates would still recall the political impact of the *Ahrar* party.[20]

The legacy of Sabahattin's thoughts was mainly felt in the sphere of practical education, schooling, and the promotion of private initiative. In 1910, for example, a journal started publication under the name of "Labour and Intellect" (*Sa`y-ü Tetebbü'*), in which writers featured articles defending Sabahattin's individualistic approach to education, researching the potential effects changes envisaged by the prince would have on Ottoman society, and advocating scouting as an important aspect in children's upbringing. Even though these writers do not feature among the most influential, the fact that a whole publication and a group of people dedicated their efforts to exploring and studying the applicability of Sabahattin's ideas to the Empire makes it worthy of note. Similarly, there is evidence[21] of the application of Sabahattin's ideas within the institutions of the Empire in the establishment of a nursery school by Mustafa Satı Bey (1882–1968).[22] The newly founded school was based on the premise that encouraging development of private initiative within pupils was the crucial role of schooling and, therefore, both education and instruction were based on fostering the abandonment of communitarian ideals, reflecting the experiences of the Anglo-Saxon system where similar weight was given to theoretical and practical learning.

Apart from the more tangible manifestations mentioned above, the legacy of Young Turk intellectuals can be located in discussions that came into the open more forcefully after the 1980s. Broadly, these discussions deal with: first, the meaning of identity, second, the role of religion in politics and society, and third, the positioning between East and West. Specifically, these debates have found increased resonance with the emergence of the Turkish–Islamic Synthesis, which responded to the specific type of nationalism promoted by Kemalism over the course of the Republic's first 50 years. The ideologues of the Turkish–Islamic Synthesis putting forth the concept of neo-Ottomanism, the members of the *Aydınlar Ocağı*, and the upholders of Republicanism, attempting to distance themselves from both the Nationalist Movement Party (*Milliyetçi Hareket Partisi* – MHP) and from the Turkish–Islamic Synthesis itself, dispute issues that must have sounded very familiar to the intellectual Young Turks: the degree of foreign cultural influences considered beneficial, the choice between adoption or adaptation vis-à-vis the West, and the role of the state "as an active agent in engineering cultural and intellectual life."[23] Equally, they negotiate the role of religion in the public sphere and in governance, the meaning of national culture, and the role of the family in society.[24] To some extent, it is ironic to see that the social class that promoted the Turkish–Islamic Synthesis was composed of entrepreneurs, precisely the section of society that Sabahattin thought pivotal for the development of his liberal ideas. He would have repudiated the patronising relationship between state and citizen as well as the family metaphor altogether, but he would certainly agree with the idea of Turkey being composed of multiple realities and affinities that have been its territorial and cultural legacy since the establishment of the Ottoman Empire.

Since the beginning of these discussions in the 1980s and more so in the early 1990s, the reverberation of debates put forth by Rıza and Sabahattin, as well as an overall interest in their life, thoughts and work, have intensified. In general terms, these discussions could be seen as coming not only from Young Turk intellectuals but could well be linked to earlier dynamics: the modernising discourse behind the reforms of Sultan Selim III and Sultan Mahmut II, the *Tanzimat* men and the Young Ottomans are just a few examples. Compared to the actors of these earlier dynamics, however, Rıza and Sabahattin differ in that they evidence, through their literary output, and the nature and scope of their activities, a level of engagement with these conversations that were, until that point, unparalleled, giving them a position in history that was peculiar to them, and the parameters of which were solely defined on the basis of their intellectual quest. Reforms introduced by the sultans initially concentrated on cosmetic and practical changes in the military (for example, uniforms and drills), and education (however, again, limited to the army). The *Tanzimat* bureaucrats and the Young Ottomans, on the other hand, did concentrate their efforts and discussions around themes resembling those that would occupy the Young Turk intellectuals; however, neither group had reached the level of synthesis of Rıza and Sabahattin. On the contrary, they represented the two extremes of Westernisation and Islamic modernism that the intellectual phase attempted to bridge. In intellectual terms, moreover, while the Young Ottomans could be closely compared to the members of the Young Turk movement, the striking difference is that the latter carried out a regime change, in 1908, that the former were never able to achieve.

As mentioned earlier, currently, the Young Turk intellectuals' legacy is mainly felt in three areas: the discussions on identity, the role of religion in politics and society and the idea of belonging to the West or the East. As far as the issue of identity, or national culture (as Binnaz Toprak termed it) is concerned, the debates that Rıza and Sabahattin were having had to do with the idea of Ottomanism as an inclusive ideology that left space for the existence of different ethnic and religious groups within the Empire. This diversity, they thought and discussed, accounted for the richness of the Ottomans and had to be preserved. Yet, as their plans for the unity of intent within the Young Turk movement collapsed, so, too, did their motivation to discourage irredentism through the formulation of blueprints for the co-existence of multiple ethnicities and religions beneath a common Ottoman banner that would grant all of the components within the Empire equal citizenship. In fact, some of those who advocated Ottomanism as participants of the Young Turk movement's intellectual phase, later went on to promote – or, become the leading figures of – other nationalisms.[25] Conversations surrounding these issues are ever so present in today's Turkey: they are still debated and negotiated within a context in which the meaning of what the true essence of Turkey is, is mostly defined by excluding and essentialising the other. This tendency is well described by the example given in Yael Navaro-Yashin's book *Faces of the State: Secularism and Public Life in Turkey*,[26] where the author talks about an encounter between two women: one veiled, the other wearing a skirt and a "trimly fit blouse."[27] Each of them imagines the other to be 'foreign': the veiled woman perceives the woman wearing a skirt and trimly fit blouse to be 'Western' while the woman who is veiled is perceived to be 'Arab'. By imagining the other as an outsider, however, both women are claiming exclusiveness to represent the true values, identity and culture, or as Navaro-Yashin herself terms it, the 'nativeness' (*yerellik*),[28] of a Turkish woman. The encounter described by Navaro-Yashin took place in front of the Ayasofya museum in 1994. This illustrates that 92 years after the Congress of Ottoman Liberals in Paris, the meaning of identity is still being discussed and negotiated in Turkey, as it was during the time Rıza and Sabahattin were in exile.

The second issue present in Turkey today, that Young Turk intellectuals attempted to resolve through their discussions, has to do with the role of religion in the political sphere. In 1970, nearly 50 years after the introduction of the Kemalist doctrine, which kept religion under the control of the state and tried to abolish all possible antagonistic religious traces in the public life of the Republic, the first Turkish political party with clear reference to Islam was established. The existence of the party, the National Order Party (*Milli*

Nizam Partisi – MNP), was short-lived and was closed down by the Constitutional Court less than two years after its establishment. Nonetheless, it set the stage for the creation of subsequent parties that held religion as an important point of reference, and were either directly or indirectly connected to the MNP.[29] However, the share of votes of these parties was fairly negligible, until the local elections of 1994, when the Welfare Party (*Refah Partisi* – RF) managed to reach 19.1% and elect its candidates to the position of Mayor in various cities, including Ankara and Istanbul.[30] At this point, what could have been taken as a limited and marginal political group was transformed into a force to be reckoned with, together with all the conversations and discussions that were to emerge around the subject of the role of religion in Turkish politics. These discussions have turned into heated confrontations between political factions, commentators and citizens, to such extremes that recall the misrepresentation of the 'other' when Young Ottomans accused the men of the *Tanzimat* of over-Westernisation. Instead, Young Turks who intellectualised reform, like Rıza and Sabahattin, with the benefit of time and historical experience, were able to bring forth more sophisticated and nuanced debates regarding what had until then seemed to be a *quid pro quo* between reform and religion.

Sabahattin and Rıza had put emphasis on the need to turn religion into a matter confined to the private sphere, but they had at the same time expressed the view that Islam and modernity were compatible, that Islam was a tolerant religion, and that Western denunciations of Islam as a fanatic religion were nothing more than the result of Western aggression.[31] In sum, they were attempting to create a synthesis between the two poles. It is worth noting that, similarly, when it comes to the role of religion in politics, contemporary discussions between defenders of republican and secular values and the proponents of parties such as the RP and the current AKP have been marked by a juxtaposition of each side – at least in terms of perception and representation of the 'other'. The AKP programme, for example, states that "while religion is one of the most important institutions of humanity, secularism is a *sine qua non* condition for democracy."[32] However, staunch secularists claim that the AKP is engaging in "a game of 'dissimulation' (*takiyye*) in order to gain a legitimate place in the political system and to consolidate its power. Such bitter and heated debates attest to the fact that Turkey is still very far from arriving at a consensus on the true meaning of secularism."[33]

The third topic that was the subject of Young Turk intellectual deliberation that is very much at the centre of discussions and debates today is linked to the idea of regional, and for many cultural, affinity: where did the Empire and where does its successor state Turkey belong to? Rıza and Sabahattin's lives in exile illustrate that they fitted in in the philosophical circles of Paris while maintaining their Ottoman identity and an attachment to Islam (though in different ways, and calling for a reformed role of religion in the public sphere). They both agreed that the West had reached technological and scientific advancements that should be absorbed by the Empire, but they were also careful to distance themselves through clear and harsh criticism of Western oppression of other peoples. However, the two profoundly disagreed, as this book has shown, on the extent of Western material and immaterial penetration that was acceptable within the Ottoman Empire. Issues relating to geographical and cultural belonging and Western involvement in the country's internal affairs are particularly conducible to discussions in modern-day Turkey, they were especially so in the early Republic and the mid-1990s. The Kemalist state based a substantial part of its nation-building policy on the representation of Turkey fully being a part of the West, and any regional "affinity with the Arab world was considered an obstacle in accomplishing this project."[34] This view went fairly unchallenged for some time but since the emergence of the Welfare Party on the political scene, discussions and debates about alternative affinities have come to the surface. Until the efforts of the AKP to change this, the followers of the Welfare Party were highly critical of attempts to join the European Union for fears that this would result in the loss of cultural identity and lack of sovereignty.[35] Simultaneously, the republicans and the opponents of the Welfare Party's ideology worked hard to revive Kemalist memories to show that Turkey's rightful place was in and with Europe.[36] Two exhibitions that were organised in the year of the commemoration of the 75th anniversary of the Republic undertook precisely the aforementioned task of placing Turkey in the West. "Family Albums of the Republic" (*Cumhuriyet'in Aile Albumleri*), which was part of the "Three Generations of the Republic" (*Üç Kuşak Cumhuriyet*) held at the Imperial Mint (*Darphane*), in the Topkapı Palace, on 25th September 1998,[37] and "To Create a Citizen: Introduction to Warfare for Creating a Modern Civilisation," held on İstiklal Caddesi were organised with specific aims: as showcases of modernity, they were to highlight Turkey's belonging to the West and the importance and relevance of Republican ideas and ideals. The exhibitions substantially maintained the opposite stance of what followers of the Welfare Party held to be Turkey's heritage, identity, and, by extension, its future.[38]

The position against accession into the European Union was softened by the Welfare Party's two successor parties, the Virtue Party (*Fazilet Partisi, FP*) and the AKP, with the latter actively pushing, in its first years in power, for membership.[39] If, however, at the institutional and political level the idea of joining what had been seen as a 'Christian club' had been accepted, at the popular level, things have not progressed in the same way. The protraction of membership talks and discussions on granting Turkey membership and the continuous blocking of such a prospect by some European countries,[40] have corroborated the view among some Turks that Turkey should not join the EU, as it does not belong there and instead, it should rather look Eastward, to the regions it severed ties with after the end of the First World War. The debate around regional belonging, then, remains as much a contested topic, as it was during the time of Rıza and Sabahattin.

A testament to the Young Turk intellectual legacy is the interest raised and maintained among the general public and in academia. As far as the latter is concerned, the abundance of scholarship that, in one way or another, tackles the three areas analysed above in the fields of political science, sociology and anthropology with a historical take on their respective subjects, bears witness to the enduring interest that these discussions still arise in researchers. As far as the general public is concerned, interest in the figures of Ahmet Rıza and Mehmet Sabahattin is clearly demonstrated by the publication of books on, and posthumous reprints of works authored by, Rıza and Sabahattin.[41] Rıza's book *La Faillite morale de la politique occidentale en Orient* has been re-published at least four times, in Tunisia in 1979,[42] in Algeria in 1980,[43] in Turkey in 1988[44] and 2004;[45] while two books were published on Ahmet Rıza in 2011[46] and 2012,[47] and his own memoir came out in 1988.[48] Sabahattin's *How Can Turkey be Saved?* has been re-published three times, although in a simplified version; in 1950,[49] 1965[50] and 2002;[51] it has additionally been published as a faithful transliteration from Ottoman into the modern Turkish script,[52] while five publications have come out analysing his works and contribution to political science and sociology.[53]

These last few pages have attempted to link the conversations and discourses about identity, the role of Islam in politics and the debate on the regional and cultural belonging of the Ottoman Empire that so much involved the Young Turk intellectuals with those going on in Turkey, especially after the early 1990s. It is striking that debates on national identity, on religion and its place in society and politics, and the question of regional affinity were present then and are present now. The Young Turk intellectuals, such as Rıza and Sabahattin, started conversations about the future of the Ottoman Empire that both the upholders of secularism and the religious parties in modern-day Turkey have taken up again. However, one last consideration is to be made.

One approach to the evaluation of these conversations is to see them as dilemmas that needed and need to be resolved: the Ottoman Empire then and Turkey today have been searching for one, clear-cut position to follow. According to this view, history bequeaths us a list of successive failures and the contemporary situation is one of a lack of balance and one that has given rise to "various 'identity crises'."[54] The other approach, which is being preferred here and is by far more interesting as an evaluation of the past and the present, is to see these conversations not as dilemmas but, rather, as discussions that, in the nineteenth century, characterised the essence of the Ottoman Empire and, similarly, represent the very essence of Turkey, today. By this, while the Ottoman Empire and Turkey certainly occupy a peculiar position, current labels of 'exceptionalism' and 'liminality' do not apply to them.[55] In fact, the Young Turk intellectuals and those who continue their debates were not and are not in a transitory phase from one definite 'indigenous' identity, or choice, to another external 'modern' one. Rather, they were, and are, in constant negotiations with an identity that is malleable, multifaceted and already encompasses the indigenous and the external, through interaction in a world that has no boundaries in the realm of ideas.[56] According to this latter interpretation, the Young Turk intellectuals were not to find a final answer to their questions regarding the face of the state, the place of religion in politics, and the geopolitical affinity of the Empire, as 'their' Empire evolved around these debates. Their ultimate achievement was, rather, to generate these discussions and bring them to the fore. Similarly, in today's Turkey, one position is not likely to prevail over the other but what can be expected is a continuous process of constant adjusting and reformulation of these positions as an outcome of these debates and discussions.

Notes

1 See, for example, Helen Angelomatis-Tsougarakis, *The Eve of the Greek Revival: British Travellers' Perceptions of Early 19th century Greece* (New York: Routledge, 1990), David Brewer, *Greece, the Hidden Centuries – Turkish Rule from the Fall of Constantinople to Greek Independence* (New York: I.B. Tauris, 2010). On the constructed foundations for the creation of modern Greece, see Michael Herzfeld, *Ours Once More*.
2 Exemplary is the following passage: "the rule of the Ottoman Turks over Arab society prevented Arab and Muslim civilisation from developing further, or even killed the life it had." Albert Hourani, *The Emergence of the Modern Middle East* (London: Macmillan, 1981), 1.
3 Apart from Hourani's title previously mentioned, some of the earliest and most important in this field are, just to mention a few: Ergun Özbudun and Ahmet Evin, *Modern Turkey: Continuity and Change* (Oplade: Leske + Budrich, 1984), Davison, *Essays in Ottoman and Turkish History*; L. Carl Brown (ed.) *Imperial Legacy: The Ottoman Imprint on the Balkans and the Middle East* (New York: Columbia University Press, 1996).
4 Zürcher, *The Unionist Factor and The Young Turk Legacy*.
5 On 13th April 1909, the *At Meydanı* square in Istanbul, "was thronged with soldiers, civilians, students of medreses (softas) and hocas, all of whom were laying siege to the Parliament building." David Farhi, "The Şeriat as a Political Slogan – or the Incident of the 31st Mart," *Middle Eastern Studies* 7 (1971), 275. They were demanding, among other things, the dismissal of the Grand Vizier, of the Minister of War, of the President of the Parliament, and of various Young Turks from influential places, along with the full implementation of the *Şeriat*. The revolt seems to have been mainly the work of the *İttihad-ı Muhammedi Cemiyeti* (Society of Muhammedan Union) angered by a lessening of religious power at government level and a decrease in the appointment of religious figures in the administration. However, there is evidence of active political collaboration between the *İttihad-ı Muhammedi Cemiyeti* and the A*hrar Fırkası*, as "the Young Turks displayed considerable anxiety as a result of the[ir] growing co-operation." Ibid., 288. The rebellion was put down and gave way to the dismantling of the two organisations. It gave the CUP the pretext to arrest political opponents and to start procedures for the deposition of Sultan Abdülhamit II on 27th April on the accusation that he had fostered the uprising.
6 See Erik J. Zürcher, *Turkey*, 100–101.
7 Here, the e-memorandum referred to: the organisation, in Ankara, of a Koran reading competition concurrent with the 23rd April national holiday; the organisation, in Şanlıurfa, of a choir of little girls whose attire was deemed archaic by the e-memorandum; these girls were made to recite specific prayers and pictures of Atatürk were apparently taken down together with the Turkish flag; school

principals had been asked to attend the Holy Birth festival (*Kutlu Doğum Şöleni*) held in Ankara; primary school students were praying in headscarves at some event organised in the Denizli province; and, in the same province, the use of a state school to deliver an Islamic sermon and religious talk directed at women.

8 www.milliyet.com.tr/2007/04/27/son/sonsiy39.asp
9 For example, Kenan Evren, one of the generals who carried out the 1980 coup, was president of the Republic from 1980–1989, with Turkey being under marshal law for his first three years in office.
10 There are other indications that this might be the case, or that at least the relationship between the state and the military is drastically changing. Among a number of changes that started in 2001, in 2004 parliament altered some articles of the Constitution in order to remove representatives of the military from the Education Council and put military spending under the scrutiny of civilian courts. The same year, the presence of military judges was abolished from the State Security Courts. For more details, see especially Chapters 5 and 6 of Hale and Özbudun, *Islamism, Democracy and Liberalism in Turkey*. The decreased role of the military in politics was also a result of EU aversion to the army interfering in the political sphere.
11 Özyürek, *Nostalgia for the Modern*. Olivier Roy, *Secularism Confronts Islam* (New York: Columbia University Press, 2007).
12 Turgut Özal was Prime Minister between 1983 and 1989, and then President from 1989 to 1993.
13 Yılmaz Çolak, "Ottomanism vs. Kemalism: Collective Memory and Cultural Pluralism in 1990s Turkey," *Middle Eastern Studies* 42, no. 4 (2006), 590.
14 A museum, *Panorama 1453*, opened on 31st January 2009, on the site of one of the decisive battles between the Ottomans and the Byzantines, near the *Topkapı* door. The website of the museum has a telling last line in the general description: "with the hope that the enthusiasm for the conquest will remain eternal, and that it will inspire tomorrow's conquerors," http://panoramikmuze.com/panorama-1453/hakk %C4%B1nda.aspx. A blockbuster movie was produced in 2012, on the conquest of the city, with the title of *Fetih 1453* and there are talks on the idea of making the takeover of Istanbul a national holiday, which has actually been discussed for some time now, since the emergence of the Welfare Party in the 1990s.
15 In terms of this tangible legacy, that of Mehmet Sabahattin seems to be more preponderant than that of Ahmet Rıza.
16 Tarık Zafer Tunaya, *Türkiye'de siyasal partiler*, vol. 1, 2nd edn (Istanbul: Hürriyet Vakfi Yayinlari, 1984), 142–143.
17 According to Tunaya, Ahmet Samin was murdered in 1910 by CUP members.
18 Tunaya, *Türkiye'de siyasal partiler*, 151.
19 The *Abide-i Anıt*, the memorial to commemorate those who died as consequence of the *31 Mart Vakası*, is at the *Hürriyet-i Ebediye* hill of Istanbul's Şişli district. The Şişli municipality has taken up the monument as its logo. Thus, the event, even if not explicitly, endures as an Ottoman legacy.
20 Mehmet Sabahettin, *Türkiye Nasıl Kurtarılabilir?* trans. Muzaffer Sencer, ed. Prof. Nurettin Şazi Kösemihal (İstanbul: Elif Yayınları, 1965)
21 Ibid., 11.
22 Mustafa Sati al-Husri, apart from having held important positions in the Ottoman Empire, became one of the fathers of Arab nationalism. Appointed Director of General Education in Iraq in the 1920s, he emphasised the need to start from lower education, in order to mould the new Arab citizens. "The Progress of Pan-Arab Nationalism Between the Wars, a View by Sati' al-Husri," in Robert Landen, *The Emergence of the Modern Middle East: Selected Readings* (New York: Van Nostrand-Reinhold, 1970).

Afterword 151

23 Binnaz Toprak, "Religion as State Ideology in a Secular Setting: The Turkish-Islamic Synthesis," in *Aspects of Religion in Secular Turkey*, Malcolm Wagstaff (ed.) Occasional Paper Series 40 (1990), 12.
24 Ibid., 11.
25 See, for example, the figure of İsmail Kemal.
26 Yael Navaro-Yashin, *Faces of the State: Secularism and Public Life in Turkey* (Princeton, NJ: Princeton University Press, 2002).
27 Navaro-Yashin, *Faces of the State*, 19.
28 Ibid., 20.
29 The list of these parties is: the National Salvation Party (*Milli Selamet Partisi*), the Welfare Party (*Refah Partisi*), the Virtue Party (*Fazilet Partisi*) from which the Felicity Party (*Saadet Partisi*) and the Justice and Development Party (*Adalet ve Kalkınma Partisi*), the contemporary ruling party, were born.
30 Hale and Özbudun, *Islamism, Democracy and Liberalism in Turkey*, 3.
31 See Chapter 3 and 4 for details on Rıza's and Sabahattin's views on religion.
32 Hale and Özbudun, *Islamism, Democracy and Liberalism in Turkey*, 22. A similar distrust and construction of the 'other's' essence can be observed through the description of the extreme fears expressed by the opponents of the Welfare Party in the days immediately following the elections of 1994 in Chapter 1 of Navaro-Yashin, *Faces of the State*. A similar technique of selective representation is used by the other side as well. For example, members of the Virtue Party took pains to show that religion had always been part of Turkish politics, that during the first years of Mustafa Kemal's rule, religion was thought to have an important role in the definition of the nation, and that the claims of their political opponents were based on a corrupted view of history; Özyürek, *Nostalgia for the Modern*, 154. Those who pushed for this reinterpretation of Kemalism were, to some extent, right. Yavuz, in fact, presenting a sound argument, wrote that "At a fundamental level, ... Turkish identity, even during the Republican period, could not escape its religious basis." Hasan Yavuz, "Turkish Identity and Foreign Policy in Flux: The Rise of Neo-Ottomanism," *Critique: Critical Middle Eastern Studies* 7, no. 12 (1998), 26. It is understandable, moreover, that the opponents of the Welfare Party were anxious of a possible extremisation of politics. So much the debates around the place of religion in politics had not been settled that they feared a reverse of the extremisation that had taken place after 1923, during the Kemalist years. A similar claim, to the fact that the issue of religion and politics is yet to be solved, is the main topic of Özyürek, *Nostalgia for the Modern*.
33 Hale and Özbudun, Islamism, *Democracy and Liberalism in Turkey*, 22. Similar fears and suspicions about the 'other' are recounted by Berna Turam. In the 1990s, each side would have imagined a scenario of doom, had the other prevaricated: "[i]n the first scenario, the secular institutions would wipe out the Islamic social forces. In the second one, Islamists would conquer and defeat secular institutions and the state." Berna Turam, *Between Islam and the State*.
34 Navaro-Yashin, *Faces of the State*, 50.
35 Hale and Özbudun, *Islamism, Democracy and Liberalism in Turkey*, 6.
36 During the Prime Ministry of Admiral Bülent Ulusu, under the post-coup military-led interim government of 1980–1983, steps were taken to include Islam as part of the political identity of the state in both domestic and international policy. This, however, was a strategic choice to prevent the growing influence of leftist elements and to reinforce social cohesion, therefore differing from what is argued here in the case of the Welfare Party. For more on this, see Çolak, "Ottomanism vs. Kemalism: Collective Memory and Cultural Pluralism in 1990s Turkey," Yavuz, "Turkish Identity and Foreign Policy in Flux: The Rise of Neo-Ottomanism," and Lerna K. Yanık, "Constructing Turkish 'Exceptionalism': Discourses of

152 Afterword

Liminality and Hybridity in post-Cold War Turkish Foreign Policy," *Political Geography* 30 (2011).

37 The exhibition was organised by the *Tarih Vakfı*, the History Foundation. For more on the exhibition itself, see the official website: www.tarihvakfi.org.tr/cms/index.php/cumhuriyetin-75-yili/item/212-uc-kusak-cumhuriyet-sergisi?tmpl=component&print=1.

38 Esra Özyürek interviewed Professor Zafer Toprak from Boğaziçi University and curator of the exhibition. In the interview, he pointed out that his main goal in putting up these exhibits was to prepare the Turkish public to become part of the European Union. Özyürek, *Nostalgia for the Modern*, 79.

39 It is debateable, however, whether the AKP sees accession to the EU as a natural process for Turkey, or whether "the sudden pro-Western and pro-EU turn of Turkish Islamists ... can be considered a protective shield against the repressive actions of the secularist establishment." Hale and Özbudun, *Islamism, Democracy and Liberalism in Turkey*, 27.

40 In 1997, for example, Wilfried Martens speaking on behalf of the Christian Democrats, said in the European Parliament that "the EU is in the process of building a civilisation in which Turkey has no place," see Yavuz, "Turkish Identity and Foreign Policy in Flux: The Rise of neo-Ottomanism," 28.

41 Here the issue is that interest in their works is present but the two do not seem to be discussed within the topic of the legacy of Young Turk intellectuals.

42 *La Faillite morale de la politique occidentale en Orient* (Tunis: Éditions Bouslama, 1979).

43 *La Faillite morale de la politique occidentale en Orient* (Algiers: Societe d'Edition et de la communication, 1980).

44 *Batı'nın doğu politikasının ahlâken iflası* (Ankara: Kültür ve Turizm Bakanlığı yayınları, 1988).

45 *Batının politik ahlâksızlığı: Batı'nın doğu politikasının ahlâken iflası* (İstanbul: Boğaziçi Yayınları, 2004).

46 Mustafa Gündüz and Musa Bardak, *Eğitimci bir Jön Türk lider: Ahmet Rıza Bey ve vazife ve mesuliyet eserleri; padişah ve şehzadeler, kadın, asker* (İstanbul: Divan Kitap, 2011).

47 Erdem Sönmez, *Ahmed Rıza: bir Jön Türk liderinin siyasi-entelektüel portresi* (İstanbul: Tarih Vakfı Yurt Yayınları, 2012).

48 *Ahmed Rıza Bey'in Anıları* (İstanbul: Arba Yayınları, 1988).

49 Nezahet Nurettin Ege (ed.) *Türkiye nasıl kurtarılabilir?* (İstanbul: Türkiye Basımevi, 1950).

50 Muzaffer Sencer (ed.) *Türkiye nasıl kurtarılabilir?* (İstanbul: Elif Yayınları, 1965).

51 İnan Keser (ed.) *Türkiye nasıl kurtarılabilir?* (İstanbul: Liberte Yayınları, 2002).

52 Fahri Unan trans., *Türkiye nasıl kurtarılabilir? Ve İzahlar* (Ankara: Ayraç Yayınevi, 1999).

53 Cavit Orhan Tütengil, *Prens Sabahattin* (İstanbul: Geçit Yayını, 1954); Nezahet Nurettin Ege, *Prens Sabahaddin: hayatı ve ilmi müdafaaları* (İstanbul: Güneş Neşriyatı, 1977); Rukiye Akkaya, *Prens Sabahaddin* (Ankara: Liberte, 2005); Mehmet Alkan, *Gönüllü sürgünden zorunlu sürgüne: bütün eserleri* (İstanbul: Yapı Kredi Yayınları, 2007); Cenk Reyhan, *Türkiye'de liberalizmin kökenleri: Prens Sabahaddin* (Ankara, İmge Kitabevi, 2008).

54 For this approach, see Joshua W. Walker, "Turkey's Imperial Legacy: Understanding Contemporary Turkey through its Ottoman Past," *Perspectives on Global Development and Technology* 8 (2009), 506.

55 For a discussion on liminality in the case of Turkey, see Yanık, "Constructing Turkish 'Exceptionalism': Discourses of Liminality and Hybridity in post-Cold War Turkish Foreign Policy," 80.

56 This is exemplified by the fact that both Rıza and Sabahattin regarded the intellectual, philosophical and technological achievements that were geographically found in the West as the product and belonging of humanity as a whole, not the prerogative of one civilisation or culture.

References

Period publications

Denais, Joseph. *La Turquie nouvelle et l'ancien régime*. Paris: Rivière, 1909.
Depont, Octave and Xavier Cappolani. *Les Confréries Religieuses Musulmanes*. Algiers: Adolphe Jourdan, 1897.
Engelhardt, Edouard. *La Turquie et le Tanzimat*. Paris: A. Cotillon, 1882.
Fehmi, Youssouf. "L'Amnistie et les Jeunes Turcs," *La Petite Republique*, 8873, 31 Juillet (1900), 1.
Fehmi, Youssouf. *Tablettes Revolutionnaires d'un Jeune Turc*. Paris: A. Michalon, 1903.
Fesch, Paul. *Constantinople aux derniers jours d'Abdul-Hamid*. 2nd edn. New York: Burt Franklin, 1971.
Fesch, Paul, Joseph Denais, and René Lay. *Bibliographie de la Franc-maçonnerie et des sociétés secrètes*. Paris: Société Bibiliographique, 1912.
Ganem, Halil. *Les Sultans Ottomans*. 2 vols. Paris: Chevalier-Marescq: 1901–1902.
Léouzon Le Duc, Louis Antoine. *La Turquie est-elle incapable de réformes?* Paris: E. Dentu, 1876.
Midhat, Ali Haydar. *The Life of Midhat Pasha*. London: John Murray, 1903.
Mourad Bey. *Le Palais de Yildiz et la Sublime Porte – Le Véritable Mal d'Orient*. Paris: Imprimerie Chaix, 1895.
Procès contre le Mechveret et La Jeune Turquie. Paris: Chevalier-Marescq, 1897.
Rıza, Ahmed. *Tolérance Musulmane*. Paris: Clamaron-Graff, 1897.
Rıza, Ahmed. *La Faillite morale de la politique occidentale en Orient*. Paris: Librairie Picart, 1922.
Sabahattin, Mehmet. *Türkiye nasıl kurtarılabilir?* İstanbul: Kader Matbaasi, 1334/1918.
Scalieri, Cléanthi. *Appel a la justice internationale des grandes puissances par rapport au grand process de Constantinople par suite de la mort du feu Sultan Aziz*. Athens: Imprimerie l'Union, 1881.

Period journals and newspapers

English Supplement to the Osmanlı, 1898.
L'Aurore, 1899.
La Dépêche, 1896.
La Revue Occidentale, 1899–1903.

Le Figaro, 1899.
Le Libre Parole, 1900.
Le Matin, 1900.
Mecheroutiette, 1908–1913.
Mechveret Supplément Français, 1895–1908.
Osmanlı, 1898–1902.
Şûra-yı Ümmet, 1902–1903.
Osmanlı Supplément Français, 1898–1899.
The New York Times, 1894–1901.
The Positivist Review, 1900–1913.
The Review of Reviews, 1900–1906.
The Times, 1895–1908.

Police archives

"Rapports divers sur le sujets Ottomans pendant la guerre de 1914." *Préfecture de Police de Paris* – BA 1.169.
"Rapports divers sur le sujets Ottomans pendant la guerre de 1914, Mahmoud Pacha (beau-frère du sultan de Constantinople)." *Préfecture de Police de Paris* – BA 1.169.
"Rapports divers sur le sujets Ottomans pendant la guerre de 1914." *Préfecture de Police de Paris* – BA/1653–1109.700–702-A.
"Sabaheddine – Loutfoulah/Comité Liberal Ottoman." *Préfecture de Police de Paris* – BA/1653-(17154).

Publications

Abu Manneh, Butrus. "The Sultan and the Bureaucracy: The Anti-Tanzimat Concepts of Grand Vizier Mahmud Nedim Pasa." *International Journal of Middle East Studies* 22, no. 3 (1990): 257–274.
Abu Manneh, Butrus. "The Islamic Roots of the Gülhane Rescript." *Die Welt des Islam* 34 (1994): 173–203.
Ahmad, Feroz. *The Young Turks, the Committee of Union and Progress in Turkish Politics, 1908–1914*. Oxford: Oxford University Press, 1969.
Ahmad, Feroz. "Some Thoughts on the Role of Ethnic and Religious Minorities in the Genesis and Development of the Socialist Movement in Turkey: 1876–1923." In Mete Tunçay and Erik J. Zürcher (eds), *Socialism and Nationalism in the Ottoman Empire 1876–1923*. London: I.B. Tauris, 1994.
Akarlı, Engin and Gabriel Den-Dor (eds). *Political Participation in Turkey: Historical Background and Present Problems*. İstanbul: Boğazici Universitesi, 1975.
Akçura, Yusuf. *Üç Tarz-ı Siyaset*. Ankara: Türk Tarih Kurumu Basımevi, 1976.
Akkaya, Rukiye. *Prens Sabahaddin*. Ankara: Liberte Yayınları, 2005.
Alkan, Mehmet. *Gönüllü sürgünden zorunlu sürgüne: bütün eserleri*. İstanbul: Yapı Kredi Yayınları, 2007.
Alkan, Necati. "The Eternal Enemy of Islam: Abdullah Cevdet and the Baha'i Religion." *BSOAS* 68, no. 1 (2005): 1–20.
Anderson, Benedict. *Imagined Communities*. 2nd edn. New York: Verso, 1991.
Anduze, Eric. *La Franc-Maçonnerie de la Turquie Ottomane 1908–1924*. Paris: L'Harmattan, 2005.

References

Angelomatis-Tsougarakis, Helen. *The Eve of the Greek Revival: British Travellers' Perceptions of Early 19th Century Greece*. New York: Routledge, 1990.

Ansari, M. Ali. *Iran, Islam and Democracy – The Politics of Managing Change*. London: Royal Institute of International Affairs, 2000.

Anscombe, Frederick F. "Islam and the Age of Ottoman Reform." *Past and Present* 208, no. 1 (2010): 159–189.

Aslan, Taner. "İttihad-ı Osmani'den Osmanlı İttihat ve Terakki." *Bilig/Türk Dünyası Sosyal Bilimler Dergisi* (2008): 79–120.

Avagyan, Arsen and Minassian, Gaisz. *Ermeniler ve İttihad ve Terakki: işbirliğinden çatışmaya*. İstanbul: Aras Yayınları, 2005.

Barkey, Karen, and Mark Von Hagen (eds). *After Empire*. Oxford: Westview Press, 1997.

Berkes, Niyazi. *The Development of Secularism in Turkey*. New York: Routledge, 1998.

Berl, Alfred. "Jeune Turquie." *La Revue de Paris* 4, no. 6 (November–December 1908): 599–600.

Bilmez, Bülent. "Shemseddin Sami Frashëri (1850–1904) – Contributing to the Construction of Albanian and Turkish Identities." In Diana Mishkova (ed.) *We, the People: Politics of National Peculiarity in Southeastern Europe*. New York: Central European University Press, 2009.

Blaisdell, C. Donald. *European Financial Control in the Ottoman Empire*. New York: Columbia University Press, 1929.

Boratav, Korkut, Gündüz A. Ökçün and Şevket Pamuk. "Ottoman Wages and the World-Economy, 1839–1913." *Review* VIII, no. 3 (Winter 1985): 379–406.

Boyar, Ebru. "The Press and the Palace: the Two-Way Relationship Between Abdülhamid II and the Press, 1876–1908." *BSOAS* 69, no. 3 (October 2006): 417–443.

Bozarslan, Hamit. "Le Prince Sabahaddin (1879–1948)." *Schweizerische Zeitschrift für Geschichte* 52 (2002): 287–301.

Bridges, John Henry. *Illustrations of Positivism*. 2nd edn. New York: Burt Franklin Reprints, 1974.

Brewer, David. *Greece, the Hidden Centuries – Turkish Rule from the Fall of Constantinople to Greek Independence*. New York: I.B. Tauris, 2010.

Brown L. Carl (ed.) *Imperial Legacy: The Ottoman Imprint on the Balkans and the Middle East*. New York: Columbia University Press, 1996.

Campos, Michelle. *Ottoman Brothers: Muslims, Christians and Jews in Early Twentieth-century Palestine*. Stanford, CA: Stanford University Press, 2011.

Choueiri, M. Youssef. *A Companion to the History of the Middle East*. Malden, MA: Blackwell, 2005.

Cohen, Phillips Julia. *Becoming Ottomans – Sephardi Jews and Imperial Citizenship in the Modern Era*. New York: Oxford University Press, 2014.

Çelik, Zeynep. *The Remaking of Istanbul: Portrait of an Ottoman City in the Nineteenth Century*. Seattle: University of Washington Press, 1986.

Çelik, Zeynep. *Displaying the Orient. Architecture of Islam at Nineteenth Century World's Fairs*. Berkeley: University of California Press, 1992.

Çelik, Zeynep and Leila Kinney. "Ethnography and Exhibitionism at the Expositions Universelles." *Assemblage* 13 (December 1990): 34–59.

Cevdet, Abdullah. "Les Prisonniers politiques en Turquie." *Mechveret Supplément Français* 3, no. 56 (May 1898): 5.

Çolak, Yılmaz. "Ottomanism vs. Kemalism: Collective Memory and Cultural Pluralism in 1990s Turkey." *Middle Eastern Studies* 42, no. 4 (2006): 587–602.

Comte, Auguste. *Système de politique positive*. Paris: L. Mathias, 1851–1854.
Comte, Auguste. *Cours de philosophie positive*. Paris: Ballieres et Fils, 1864.
Clayer, Nathalie, Alexander Popovic, and Thierry Zarcone. *Presse Turque et presse de Turquie Varia Turcica XXIII*. İstanbul: Isis, 1992.
Davison, Roderic. *Reform in the Ottoman Empire, 1856–1876*. Princeton, NJ: Princeton University Press, 1963.
Davison, Roderic. "Nationalism as an Ottoman Problem and the Ottoman Response." In William Haddad and William Ochsenwald (eds), *Nationalism in a Non National State – the Dissolution of the Ottoman Empire*. Columbus: Ohio State University, 1977.
Davison, Roderic. (ed.) *Essays in Ottoman and Turkish History, 1774–1923: The Impact of the West*. Austin: University of Texas Press, 1990.
Demolins, Edmond. *Anglo-Saxon Superiority, to What Is It Due?* Translated by Lois Bertram Lavigne. London: Leadenhall Press, 1920.
Deringil, Selim. "Legitimacy Structures in the Ottoman State: The Reign of Abdulhamid II (1876–1908)." *International Journal of Middle East Studies* 23 (1991): 345–359.
Deringil, Selim. "The Invention of Tradition as Public Image in the Late Ottoman Empire, 1808–1908." *Comparative Studies in Society and History* 35 (1993): 3–29.
Deringil, Selim. *The Well-Protected Domains*. London: I.B. Tauris, 1998.
Devereux, Robert. *The First Ottoman Constitutional Period – A Study of the Midhat Constitution and Parliament*. Baltimore, MD: The John Hopkins Press, 1963.
Dion, Michel. "Science sociale et religion chez Frédéric Le Play." *Archives de sociologie des religions* 12, no. 24 (July–December 1967): 83–104.
Dubois, Philippe. "Expulsion de M. Ahmed-Riza." *L'Intransigeant* (April 1896). Reproduced in *Mechveret Supplément Français* 1, no. 9 (April 1896): 5.
Dumont, Paul. "Freemasonry in Turkey: A By-product of Western Penetration." *European Review* 13, no. 3 (2005): 481–493.
Duman, Hasan. *A Biography and Union Catalogue of Ottoman Yearbooks*. Ankara: Foundation for Information and Documentation Services, 2000.
Ege, Nezahet N. (ed.) *Türkiye nasıl kurtarılabilir?* İstanbul: Türkiye Basımevi, 1950.
Ege, Nezahet N. (ed.) *Prens Sabahaddin: hayatı ve ilmi müdafaaları*. İstanbul: Güneş Neşriyatı, 1977.
Emin, Ahmet. *The Development of Modern Turkey as Measured by Its Press*. New York: Longmans, 1914.
Esposito, John, and John Donohue (eds). *Islam in Transition – Muslim Perspectives*. New York: Oxford University Press, 2007.
Falaschi, Renzo. *Ismail Kemal Bey Vlora – Il pensiero e l'opera attraverso i documenti italiani*. Roma: Bardi Editore, 1985.
Farhi, David. "The Şeriat as a Political Slogan – or the Incident of the 31st Mart." *Middle Eastern Studies* 7 (1971): 275–299.
Faroqhi, Suraya. *Approaching Ottoman History*. Cambridge: Cambridge University Press, 1999.
Findley, Carter V. *Bureaucratic Reform in the Ottoman Empire: the Sublime Porte, 1789–1922*. Princeton, NJ: Princeton University Press, 1980.
Findley, Carter V. "The Advent of Ideology in the Islamic Middle East – Part II." *Studia Islamica* 56 (1982): 147–180.
Findley, Carter V. "Economic Bases of Revolution and Repression in the Late Ottoman Empire." *Comparative Studies in Society and History* 28, no. 1 (1986): 81–106.

158 References

Findley, Carter V. *Ottoman Civil Officialdom: a Social History*. Princeton, NJ: Princeton University Press, 1989.

Fortna, Benjamin C. *Imperial Classroom: Islam, the State, and Education in the Late Ottoman Empire*. Oxford: Oxford University Press, 2002.

Frierson, Elisabeth. "Unimagined Communities: Women and Education in the Late Ottoman Empire, 1876–1909." *Critical Matrix, Princeton Journal of Women, Gender and Culture* 9, no. 2 (1995): 55–90.

Fullerton, William Morton. *The Memoirs of Ismail Kemal Bey*. London: Constable, 1920.

Georgeon, François. *Abdulhamid II, Le sultan calife (1876–1909)*. Paris: Fayard, 2003.

Georgeon, François. "Ottomans and Drinkers: The Consumption of Wine and Alcohol in Istanbul in the 19th Century." In Eugene Rogan (ed.) *Outside In. Marginality in the Modern Middle East*. London: I.B. Tauris, 2002.

Goldstein, Robert Justin. "Fighting French Censorship, 1815–1881." *The French Review* 71, no. 5 (April 1998): 785–796.

Göçek, Fatma Müge. "What is the Meaning of the 1908 Young Turk Revolution? A Critical Historical Assessment in 2008." *İstanbul Üniversitesi Siyasal Bilgiler Fakültesi Dergisi* 38 (2008): 179–214.

Gökalp, Ziya. *The Principles of Turkism*. Translated by Robert Devereux. Leiden: Brill, 1968.

Gökalp, Ziya. *Turkish Nationalism and Western Civilisation – Selected Essays of Ziya Gökalp*. Translated and edited by Niyazi Berkes. London: Allen and Unwin, 1959.

Gökalp, Ziya. *Hars ve Medeniyet*. İstanbul: Toker Yayınları, 1995.

Gündüz, Mustafa and Musa Bardak. *Eğitimci bir Jön Türk lider: Ahmet Rıza Bey ve vazife ve mesuliyet eserleri; padişah ve şehzadeler, kadın, asker*. İstanbul: Divan Kitap, 2011.

Hale, William and Ergun Özbudun. *Islamism, Democracy and Liberalism in Turkey, the Case of the AKP*. New York: Routledge, 2010.

Halid, Halil. *The Diary of a Turk*. London: Black, 1903.

Hanioğlu, Şükrü. (ed.) *Kendi Mektuplarında Enver Paşa*. İstanbul: Der Yayınları, 1989.

Hanioğlu, Şükrü. "Notes on the Young Turks and the Freemasons, 1875–1908." *Middle Eastern Studies* 25, no. 2 (April 1989): 186–197.

Hanioğlu, Şükrü. "Der Jungenturkenkongress von Paris (1902) und seine Ergebnisse." *Die Welt des Islam* 33, no. 1 (April 1993): 23–65.

Hanioğlu, Şükrü. *The Young Turks in Opposition*. New York: Oxford University Press, 1995.

Hanioğlu, Şükrü. "Garbcılar: Their Attitudes Toward Religion and Their Impact on the Official Ideology of the Turkish Republic." *Studia Islamica* 86 (1997): 133–158.

Hanioğlu, Şükrü. *Preparation for a Revolution*. New York: Oxford University Press, 2001.

Hanioğlu, Şükrü. *A Brief History of the Late Ottoman Empire*. Princeton, NJ: Princeton University Press, 2008.

Hanioğlu, Şükrü. "The Committee of Union and Progress and the 1908 Revolution." In François Georgeon (ed.) *'L'Ivresse de la liberté' La révolution de 1908 dans l'Empire ottoman*. Leuven: Peeters, 2012.

Hanna, A. Sami and George H. Gardner (eds). *Arab Socialism: A Documentary Survey*. Leiden: Brill, 1969.

Hansluck, Frederick W. *Christianity and Islam under the Sultans*. Vol. 2. Oxford: Clarendon Press, 1929.
Herzfeld, Michael. *Ours Once More: Folklore, Ideology and the Making of Modern Greece*. Austin: University of Texas, 1982.
Heywood, Colin. "Review of The Diary of Karl Süssheim (1878–1947): Orientalist between Munich and Istanbul, by Barbara Flemming and Jan Schmidt." *The Journal of the Royal Asiatic Society* 13, no. 2 (2003): 247–248.
Higgs, Henry. "Frédéric Le Play." *The Quarterly Journal of Economics* 4, no. 4 (July1890): 408–433.
Hourani, Albert. *The Emergence of the Modern Middle East*. London: Macmillan, 1981.
Hourani, Albert. "Ottoman Reform and the Politics of Notables." In Albert Hourani, Philip S. Khouri and Mary C. Wilson (eds), *The Modern Middle East: a Reader*. London: I.B. Tauris, 1993.
Hurewitz, Jacob C. *Diplomacy in the Near and Middle East*. 2nd edn. Princeton, NJ: Van Nostrand Company, 1958.
İslamoğlu, Huri (ed.) *Ottoman History as World History*. İstanbul: The Isis Press, 2007.
Karpat, Kemal. "The Transformation of the Ottoman State, 1789–1908." *International Journal of Middle East Studies* 3, no. 3 (1972): 243–281.
Karpat, Kemal. "The Mass Media, Turkey." In Richard Ward and Dankwart Rustow, *Political Modernisation in Japan and Turkey*. Princeton, NJ: Princeton University Press, 1964.
Karpat, Kemal. *The Politicization of Islam*. 2nd edn. New York: Oxford University Press, 2002.
Kayalı, Hasan. *Arabs and Young Turks: Ottomanism, Arabism and Islamism in the Ottoman Empire, 1908–1918*. Berkeley: University of California Press, 1997.
Kaynar, Erdal. "Ahmed Rıza (1858–1930) Histoire d'un vieux jeune turc." PhD diss. École des Hautes Études en Sciences Sociales, Paris, 2011.
Kechriotis, Vangelis. "Greek-Orthodox, Ottoman Greeks or just Greeks? Theories of Coexistence in the Aftermath of the Young Turk Revolution." *Études Balkaniques* 1 (2005): 51–72.
Kechriotis, Vangelis. "On the Margins of National Historiography. The Greek İttihatçı Emmanouil Emmanouilidis – Opportunist or Ottoman Patriot?" In Amy Singer, Christoph K. Neumann and Selçuk Akşin Somel, *Untold Histories of the Middle East, Recovering Voices from the 19th and 20th Centuries*. New York: Routledge, 2011.
Keddie, Nikkie. *Sayyid Jamāl ad-Din 'al-Afghāni' – A Political Biography*. Berkeley and Los Angeles: University of California Press, 1972.
Kerslake, Celia, Kerem Öktem, Philip Robins (eds). *Turkey's Engagement with Modernity: Conflict and Change in the Twentieth Century*. Basingstoke: Palgrave Macmillan, 2010.
Keser, İnan (ed.) *Türkiye nasıl kurtarılabilir?* İstanbul: Liberte Yayınları, 2002.
Keyder, Çağlar. "The Ottoman Empire." In Karen Barkey and Mark Von Hagen (eds), *After Empire: Multiethnic Societies and Nation-building: the Soviet Union and the Russian, Ottoman, and Habsburg Empires*. Oxford: Westview Press, 1997.
Kieser, Hans-Lukas. *A Quest for Belonging*. İstanbul: Isis Press, 2007.
Kieser, Hans-Lukas. *Türklüğe ihtida: 1870–1939 İsvicre'sinde Yeni Türkiye'nin öncüleri*. İstanbul: Iletisim, 2008.

Koçak, Orhan. "'Westernisation against the West': Cultural Politics in the Early Turkish Republic." In Celia Kerslake, Kerem Öktem and Philip Robins (eds), *Turkey's Engagement with Modernity – Conflict and Change in the Twentieth Century.* New York: Palgrave, 2010.

Koloğlu, Orhan. "La Formation des intellectuels à la culture journalistique dans l'Empire Ottoman et l'influence de la presse étrangère." *Varia Turcica XXIII.* İstanbul: The Isis Press, 1992.

Kuran, Ercüment. "The Impact of the Turkish Elite in the Nineteenth Century." In William Polk and Richard Chambers (eds), *Beginnings of Modernisation in the Middle East.* Chicago, IL: University of Chicago Press, 1968.

Kurzman, Charles (ed.) *Modernist Islam, 1840–1940: A Sourcebook.* New York: Oxford University Press, 2002.

Kurzman, Charles (ed.) *Democracy Denied 1905–1915: Intellectuals and the Fate of Democracy.* Cambridge, MA: Harvard University Press, 2008.

Landen, Robert. *The Emergence of the Modern Middle East: Selected Readings.* New York: Van Nostrand-Reinhold, 1970.

Landen, Robert. "The Young Ottoman: Namık Kemal's 'Progress', 1872." In Camron Amin, Benjamin Fortna, Elizabeth Frierson, *The Modern Middle East: A Sourcebook for History.* New York: Oxford University Press, 2006.

Lazarsfeld, Paul. "Notes on the History of Quantification in Sociology – Trends, Sources and Problems." *Isis* 52, no. 2 (June 1961): 277–333.

Lewis, Bernard. "The Impact of the French Revolution on Turkey." *Cahiers d'Histoire Mondiale* 1, no. 1 (1953): 105–125.

Lewis, Bernard. *The Emergence of Modern Turkey.* London: Oxford University Press, 1961.

Lewis, Bernard. "Ottoman Observers of Ottoman Decline." *Islamic Studies* 1, no. 1 (1962): 71–87.

Lewis, Reina. *Rethinking Orientalism – Women Travel and the Ottoman Harem.* London: I.B. Tauris, 2004.

Le Bon, Gustave. *La Civilisation des Arabes.* Paris: Fermin-Didot, 1884. http://classiques.uqac.ca/classiques/le_bon_gustave/civilisation_des_arabes/civilisation_arabes.html. Accessed on 18 March 2005.

Le Bon, Gustave. *The Crowd, a Study in the Popular Mind.* 19th edn. London: Ernest Benn Limited, 1947.

Le Bon, Gustave. *The Psychology of Revolution.* www.gutenberg.org/cache/epub/448/pg448.html. Accessed on 30 January 2010.

Mango, Andrew. *Atatürk.* 8th edn. London: John Murray, 2004.

Mardin, Şerif. *The Genesis of Young Ottoman Thought: A Study in the Modernisation of Turkish Political Ideas.* Princeton, NJ: Princeton University Press, 1962.

Mardin, Şerif. "Libertarian Movements in the Ottoman Empire 1878–1895." *The Middle East Journal* 16, no. 2 (1962): 169–182.

Mardin, Şerif. "The Mind of the Turkish Reformer, 1700–1900." In Sami A. Hanna and George H. Gardner (eds), *Arab Socialism: A Documentary Survey.* Leiden: Brill, 1969.

Mardin, Şerif. *Religion, Society and Modernity in Turkey.* New York: Syracuse University Press, 2006.

Marty, Henri. "L'Ecole des Roches." *The School Review* 20, no. 1 (January 1912): 27–33.

Mauss, Marcel. *The Gift.* New York: Norton, 1990.

McCarthy, Justin. *The Ottoman Turks: An Introductory History to 1923.* London: Longman, 1997.
McCarthy, Justin. *Ottoman Peoples and the End of Empire.* London: Arnold, 2001.
McDougall, James. *History and the Culture of Nationalism in Algeria.* Cambridge: Cambridge University Press, 2006.
Midhat, Ali Haydar. *Midhat Paşa'nın hatırları.* İstanbul: Temel Yayınları, 1997.
Miller, William. *The Ottoman Empire and its Successors, 1801-1927.* Cambridge: Cambridge University Press, 1927.
Mitchell, Timothy. *Colonising Egypt.* Cambridge: Cambridge University Press, 1988.
Navaro-Yashin, Yael. *Faces of the State: Secularism and Public Life in Turkey.* Princeton, NJ: Princeton University Press, 2002.
Ochsenwald, William. *The Hijaz Railroad.* Charlottesville: University Press of Virginia, 1980.
Ölçen, Mehmet Arif. *Vetluga Memoir*, Gary Leiser (ed.). Gainesville: University Press of Florida, 1995.
Osmanoglu, Aïché. *Avec mon père le Sultan Abdulhamid.* Paris: L'Harmattan, 1991.
Özbudun, Ergun and Ahmet Evin. *Modern Turkey: Continuity and Change.* Oplade: Leske + Budrich, 1984.
Özbudun, Ergun. *The Constitutional System of Turkey, 1876 to the Present.* New York: Palgrave Macmillan, 2011.
Özdalga, Elisabeth (ed.). *Late Ottoman Society – the Intellectual Legacy.* London: Routledge, 2004.
Özyürek, Esra. *Nostalgia for the Modern: State Secularism and Everyday Politics in Turkey.* Durham, NC: Duke University Press, 2006.
Özyürek, Esra (ed.). *The Politics of Public Memory in Turkey.* New York: Syracuse University Press, 2006.
Piscatori, James P. (ed.). *Islam in the Political Process.* Cambridge: Cambridge University Press, 1984.
Polk, William and Richard Chambers (eds). *Beginnings of Modernisation in the Middle East.* Chicago, IL: University of Chicago Press, 1968.
Ramsaur, Ernest E. 'The Bektashi Dervishes and the Young Turks." *The Moslem World* 32, no.1 (January 1942): 7–14.
Ramsaur, Ernest E. *The Young Turks: Prelude to the Revolution of 1908.* 2nd edn. New York: Russell & Russell, 1970.
Ramsay, William Mitchell. *Impressions of Turkey during Twelve Years' Wanderings.* London: Hodder & Stoughton, 1897.
Reyhan, Cenk. *Türkiye'de liberalizmin kökenleri: Prens Sabahaddin.* Ankara: İmge Kitabevi, 2008.
Rıza, Ahmet. *La Faillite morale de la politique occidentale en Orient.* Tunis: Éditions Bouslama, 1979.
Rıza, Ahmet. *La Faillite morale de la politique occidentale en Orient.* Algiers: Société d'Edition et de la communication, 1980.
Rıza, Ahmet. *Batı'nın doğu politikasının ahlâken iflası.* Ankara: Kültür ve Turizm Bakanlığı yayınları, 1988.
Rıza, Ahmet. *Ahmed Rıza Bey'in Anıları.* İstanbul: Arba, 1988.
Rıza, Ahmet. *Batının politik ahlâksızlığı: Batı'nın doğu politikasının ahlâken iflası.* İstanbul: Boğaziçi Yayınları, 2004.
Rogan, Eugene (ed.) *Outside In: On the Margins of the Modern Middle East.* London: I.B. Tauris, 2002.

162   References

Roy, Gilles. *Abdul-Hamid: le Sultan Rouge*. Paris: Payot, 1936.
Roy, Olivier. *Secularism Confronts Islam*. New York: Columbia University Press, 2007.
Ryan, Andrew. *The Last of the Dragomans*. London: Geoffrey Bles, 1951.
Sabahattin, Mehmet. *İttihad ve Terakki Cemiyetine açık; mektublar: Mesleğimiz hakkında üçüncü ve son bir iz Sabahattin*. İstanbul: Mahmud Bey Matbaası 1327/1911.
Sabahattin, Mehmet. *Türkiye Nasıl Kurtarılabilir?* Translated by Muzaffer Sencer, edited by Prof. Nurettin Şazi Kösemihal. İstanbul: Elif Yayınları, 1965.
Sabahattin, Mehmet. *Türkiye nasıl kurtarılabilir? Ve İzahlar*. Translated by Fahri Unan. Ankara: Ayraç Yayınevi, 1999.
Savoye, Antoine. "Les Continuateurs de Le Play au tournant du siècle." *Revue française de sociologie* 22, no. 3 (July–September 1981): 315–344.
Singer, Amy, Christoph K. Neumann and Selçuk Akşin Somel. *Untold Histories of the Middle East, Recovering Voices from the 19th and 20th Centuries*. New York: Routledge, 2011.
Schayegh, Cyrus. *Who is Knowledgeable is Strong – Science, Class, and the Formation of Modern Iranian Society, 1900–1950*. Berkeley, CA: University of Los Angeles Press, 2009.
Şeni, Nora. "Fashion and Women's Clothing." In Şirin Tekeli (ed.) *Women in Modern Turkish Society: A Reader*. London: Zed Books, 1995.
Shaw, Stanford J. "A Promise of Reform: Two Complimentary Documents." *International Journal of Middle East Studies* 4, no. 3 (July 1973): 359–365.
Sohrabi, Nader. "Illiberal Constitutionalism. The Committee of Union and Progress as a Clandestine Network and the Purges." In François Georgeon (ed.) *'L'Ivresse de la liberté' La révolution de 1908 dans l'Empire ottoman*. Leuven: Peeters, 2012.
Somel, Selçuk Akşin. *Historical Dictionary of the Ottoman Empire*. Oxford: The Scarecrow Press, 2003.
Sönmez, Erdem. *Ahmed Rıza: bir Jön Türk liderinin siyasi-entelektüel portresi*. İstanbul: Tarih Vakfı Yurt Yayınları, 2012.
Stavrianos, Stavros L. *The Balkans since 1453*. London: Hurst, 2000.
Tekeli, Şirin. *Women in Modern Turkish Society: A Reader*. London: Zed Books, 1995.
Temo, İbrahim. *İbrahim Temo'nun İttihad ve Terakki Anıları*. 2nd edn. İstanbul: Arba, 1987.
Ter Minassian, Anahide. *Nationalism and Socialism in the Armenian Revolutionary Movement, 1887–1912*. Cambridge, MA: The Zoryan Institute, 1984.
Ter Minassian, Anahide. "The Role of the Armenian Community in the Foundation and Development of the Socialist Movement in the Ottoman Empire and Turkey, 1876–1923." In Mete Tunçay and Erik Ian Zürcher (eds), *Socialism and Nationalism in the Ottoman Empire 1876–1923*. London: I.B. Tauris, 1994.
Toprak, Binnaz. "Religion as State Ideology in a Secular Setting: The Turkish-Islamic Synthesis." In Malcolm Wagstaff (ed.) *Aspects of Religion in Secular Turkey, Occasional Paper Series* 40 (1990).
Tunaya, Tarık Zafer. *Türkiye'de siyasal partiler*. Vols 1 & 2. İstanbul: Hürriyet Vakfi Yayinlari, 1984.
Tunçay, Mete and Erik J. Zurcher (eds). *Socialism and Nationalism in the Ottoman Empire, 1876–1923*. London: I.B. Tauris, 1994.
Turam, Berna. *Between Islam and the State: The Politics of Engagement*. Stanford, CA: Stanford University Press, 2007.
Turfan, M. Naim. *Rise of the Young Turks: Politics, the Military and Ottoman Collapse*. London: I.B. Tauris, 2000.

Tütengil, Cavit Orhan. *Prens Sabahattin*. İstanbul: Geçit Yayını, 1954.
Vaka, Demetra. "An Imperial Enemy of Turkish Despotism." *Asia* 24 (January 1924): 32–36: 72–73.
Vaka, Demetra. "Prince Sabaheddine as a Free-lance Liberal." *Asia* 24 (February 1924): 120–123: 150–151.
Vaka, Demetra. "Prince Sabaheddine in the Hour of the Kemalists." *Asia* 24 (March 1924): 208–211: 233–234.
Wagstaff, Malcolm (ed.) "Aspects of Religion in Secular Turkey." *Occasional Paper Series* 40 (1990).
Walker, Joshua W. "Turkey's Imperial Legacy: Understanding Contemporary Turkey through its Ottoman Past." *Perspectives on Global Development and Technology* 8 (2009): 494–508.
Wasti, Tanvir. "The Last Chroniclers of the Mabeyn." *Middle Eastern Studies* 32, no. 2 (April 1996): 1–29.
Worringer, Renée. "'Sick Man of Europe' or 'Japan of the Near East'?: Constructing Ottoman Modernity in the Hamidian and Young Turk Eras." *International Journal of Middle East Studies* 36, no. 2 (May 2004): 207–230.
Yalimov, Ibrahim. "The Bulgarian Community and the Development of the Socialist Movement in the Ottoman Empire During the Period 1876–1923." In Mete Tunçay and Erik Ian Zürcher (eds), *Socialism and Nationalism in the Ottoman Empire 1876–1923*. London: I.B. Tauris, 1994.
Yanık, Lerna K. "Constructing Turkish 'Exceptionalism': Discourses of Liminality and Hybridity in Post-Cold War Turkish Foreign Policy." *Political Geography* 30 (2011): 80–89.
Yavuz, Hasan. "Turkish Identity and Foreign Policy in Flux: The Rise of Neo-Ottomanism." *Critique: Critical Middle Eastern Studies* 7, no. 12 (1998): 19–41.
Young, George. *Constantinople*. London: Methuen & Co. Ltd., 1926.
Zarcone, Thierry. *Secret et sociétés secrètes en Islam*. Milan: Archè, 2002.
Zürcher, Erik J. *The Unionist Factor: The Role of the Committee of Union and Progress in the Turkish National Movement, 1905–1926*. Leiden: E.J. Brill, 1984.
Zürcher, Erik J. *Turkey, A Modern History*. 6th edn. London: I.B. Tauris, 2004.
Zürcher, Erik J. *The Young Turk Legacy and the National Awakening: From the Ottoman Empire to Atatürk's Turkey*. London: I.B. Tauris, 2010.

Websites

Marxist Internet Archive, www.marxists.org/reference/subject/philosophy/index.htm.
Milliyet Haber, www.milliyet.com.tr/2007/04/27/son/sonsiy39.asp.
Panorama 1453 Tarih Müzesi, http://panoramikmuze.com/panorama-1453/hakk%C4%B1nda.aspx.
Tarih Vakfı, www.tarihvakfi.org.tr/cms/index.php/cumhuriyetin-75-yili/item/212-uc-kusak-cumhuriyet-sergisi?tmpl=component&print=1.

Index

Abdülaziz Sultan 2, 39, 65
Abdülhamit II, Sultan 4, 7; and *Mechveret* 62–5; plans for assassination of 37; and reform 16-19, 21; and religion 19–21; and Sabahattin 90, 97, 98; and suspension of the Constitution 54; and the press 40–2; and the Young Turk opposition 6, 7, 23–5, 38, 46, 52, 115, 119
Abdullah Cevdet 29, 30, 32, 34, 122
Abdülmecit, Sultan 2, 61, 80
Abu-Bakr (Caliph) 64
Activism, Young Turk transition to 120–1
Adalet ve Kalkınma Partisi (AKP – Justice and Development Party) 141, 142, 146, 147
Affaire Ahmet Rıza (L') 70
Ahmet Cevdet 40
Ahmet Wardani 134
Al-Bāsir (journal) 54
Ali Fuad 31
Ali Haydar Mithat 39, 115
Ali Rıza 52
Ali Suavi 40
Amin al-Antaki 134
Anglo-Saxon and education 86; and personal initiative 86; society 88, 93, 94, 100; superiority 85, 88
Armenian groups 36, 109, 111, 112, 114; and *Mechveret* 113
Aydinlar Ocağı 144

Berlin, Treaty of (1878) 110, 111, 114, 115
Bertradot, Barchille 80

Carolidis, Pavlos 135
Cemiyet-i İnkılâbiye (Revolutionary Society) 121
Clémenceau, Georges 55

Committee of Union and Progress, CUP *see Osmanlı İttihad ve Terakki Cemiyeti*
Communitarian (communistic) and individualistic formations and religion 97; and Sabahattin 92–33; definition of 86, 87, 88, 91
Comte, Auguste 8, 30, 55, 56, 57, 59, 72
Constitutionalism 3, 5, 35, 36
Counter-revolution of 13th April 1909 (*31 Mart Vakası*) 143

Dashnak 110, 114
De Tourville, Henri 85, 90
Decentralisation 90, 94, 95, 96, 139; and Sabahattin 90, 94, 95, 96
Demolins, Edmond 6, 55, 85, 86, 87, 88, 90; and Sabahattin, 85–9, 90, 92, 97
Denais, Joseph 85, 107, 109, 113
Dubois, Philippe 60, 69

Education, and Rıza 61; and Sabahattin 91, 123; in England and France 87
Elitism 37; and the Young Turk movement 101, 130–33, 139
e-memorandum of Chief of General Staff of Turkish Republic (2007) 141
Enver Paşa 1, 2, 5, 7
Erdoğan, Recep Tayyip 141
Exile, Algerian groups in 37; benefits of 6, 35, 36, 45, 129, 130, 139
Exposition Universelle 6, 53, 54

Fazilet Partisi (FP – Virtue Party) 147
Fesch, Paul 42, 107, 116, 121
First Congress of Ottoman Liberals 5, 6; consequences 116–118; expectations 109–112; failure 112–116, 124;

organisation 107–9; shortcomings 118–120, 132
First Constitutional Period 4, 5, 6, 7, 9, 42, 54, 63, 137
Freemasonry and Abdülhamit II 33; and the Young Turk movement 32; in the Ottoman Empire 32, 107

Greece 14, 25, 42, 139
Grey, Edward (Sir) 96
Gül, Abdullah 141

Halil Ganem 6, 34, 37, 54, 55, 63, 70, 71, 91, 112, 113, 118, 122, 131, 132, 134
Hatt-ı Şerif of Gülhane 2, 14, 110; and Rıza 61; and Sabahettin 95
Henchak 110, 114
Hicaz Railway 21, 22, 23
Hilâl (journal) 54
Hürriyet (journal) 35

İbrahim Temo 29, 30, 34
İbret (journal) 39
İkdam (journal) 40
Intellectualism and the Young Turk movement 120–1, 129–33, 136, 139
İshak Sükûti 29, 30
Islahat Fermanı 2, 14, 110
Islam and *Mechveret* 58–60; and Sabahattin 96, 97
Islamic modernism 145
İsmail Kemal 39, 109, 111, 115, 116, 117, 119, 122, 133, 134
İttihad-ı Osmani Cemiyeti (Ottoman Union Society) 30

Jamal ad-Din al-Afghani 36

Kemalism 136

La Faillite morale de la politique occidentale en Orient 6, 71, 148
La Revue Occidentale 55, 129
Laffitte, Pierre 43, 55
Le Bon, Gustave 55, 72, 130–1
Le Moniteur Ottoman (journal) 39
Le Play, Frédéric 85, 90, 100
Lefèvre-Pontalis, Eugène 109
Legacy, Military 142; and Sabahattin 143; and Young Turk 9, 137, 139, 140, 142, 143, 144, 145, 147
Lutfi Paşa 13
Lutfullah (brother of Sabahattin) 6, 39, 43, 80, 85, 107, 108, 109, 111

Mahmut Celalettin Paşa, *Damat* 6, 39, 44, 80, 81, 82, 85, 107, 109; and Abdülhamit II 80, 83; and Ahmet Rıza 82, 83, 84
Mahmut II, Sultan 2, 30, 60, 144
Mahmut Nedim Paşa (Grand Vizier) 17
Manastır 116, 121
Mechveret, and Abdülhamit II 61, 62–5, 68; composition and content 54–7; trial against 68–71
Mehmel 20
Mehmet II (*Fatih*), Sultan 142
Mehmet Reşit 29
Mekteb-i Sultani 52
Military Medical College (*Mekteb-i Tıbbiye-i Şâhâne*) 29
Milli Nizam Partisi (MNP – National Order Party) 145–6
Milliyetçi Hareket Partisi (MHP – Nationalist Movement Party) 144
Mithat Paşa 31, 32, 39, 41
Mizan (journal) 37, 43
Modernisation, and al-Afghani *see* Jamal ad-Din al-Afghani; and Sabahattin 92
Modernity, and Abdülhamit II 16, 23; and Sabahattin 97; and the Young Turk movement 35, 131, 146
Muhbir (journal) 40
Murat Bey (*Mizancı*) 31, 37, 38, 70
Murat V (Sultan) 32, 80
Mustafa Kemal, Atatürk 5, 140
Münir Bey (also Paşa, Ottoman Ambassador to France) 53, 69, 83

Namık Kemal 31, 35, 36, 39, 40
Naum Paşa (Ottoman Ambassador to France) 44
neo-Ottomanism 142, 144
Nizam ve Terakki 30

Oğuz 13
Osmanlı (journal) 32, 43, 112, 116
Osmanlı Ahrar Fırkası (Ottoman Liberal Party) 143
Osmanlı Hürriyet Cemiyeti (Ottoman Freedom Society) 121
Osmanlı Hürriyetperveran Fırkası (Ottoman Freedom lovers party) 115
Osmanlı İhtilâl Fırkası (Ottoman Revolutionary Party) 107
Osmanlı İttihad ve Terakki Cemiyeti (Ottoman Committee of Union and Progress) 37, 38, 43, 45, 46, 135; constitution of 30; predecessors and

allies 30, 31, 32, 34; and *Mechveret* 57, 66; and Sabahattin 82, 83, 122, 124; and Rıza 122; and Turkish nationalism 136
Osmanlılık (Ottomanism) and *Mechveret* 57, 67, 68, 73; and minorities 135; and Rıza 9, 65, 71–3, 133; and Sabahattin 9, 100–2, 110; appeal of 133–37; as proto-nationalism 3, 14, 24, 32, 36, 46, 145; feasibility and collapse of 117, 119, 120, 124–5, 133, 134, 135, 136
Osmanoglu, Aïché (Ayşe Osmanoğlu) 19
Ottoman Constitution (1876) 4, 14, 24, 25, 31, 33, 40, 42, 54; and Rıza 62, 67; and Sabahattin 92, 102; and the Young Turk movement 40, 43, 109, 110, 115
Ottoman Constitution (1908) 7, 141
Ottoman minorities, and *Mechveret* 65–8; and Ottomanism see *Osmanlılık* (Ottomanism) feasibility and collapse; and Rıza 60, 63, 113; and Sabahattin 95, 96–8, 122; and Abdülhamid II 24
Ottoman press (discussion of) 39–44
Özal, Turgut 142

Pan-Islamism 24, 34, 72, 96, 97
Paris, CUP branch in 37, 38, 39, 45, 57, 68; destination for exiles 44, 130; First Congress of Ottoman Liberals in see First Congress of Ottoman Liberals; Halil Ganem in 54; Rıza in 6, 31, 43, 53–6; Sabahattin in 6, 43, 82–5; Second Congress of Ottoman Liberals in see Second Congress of Ottoman Liberals
Positivism 3, 6, 8, 30, 32, 37, 55, 56, 59, 72
Private initiative 6, 86, 88, 90, 92, 94, 95, 123, 143
Puybaraud, Antoine (Paris Police *Préfecture*) 69

Quillard, Pierre 43, 83

Refah Partisi (RF – Welfare Party) 146
Rifa'a Badawi Rafi al-Tahtawi 35, 36
Russo-Turkish War (1877–78) 4

Sabah (journal) 40
Salonika 116, 121
Scalieri, Cléanthi 32
Science sociale 85, 90, 100, 130
Second Congress of Ottoman Liberals 116, 120

Second Constitutional Period 123, 135, 140
Selânikli Nâzım 30
Selim III, Sultan 2, 61, 144
Şemsettin Sami Bey 80
Sufi orders 33, 34
Süleyman II (*Muhteşem/Kanuni*), Sultan 1, 13, 142
Şura-yı Ümmet (journal) 116

Takvim-i Vekayi (journal) 39
Tanin (journal) 123
Tanzimat 2, 3, 18, 24, 31, 36, 39, 144, 146; and Sabahattin 90, 91, 92, 95
Terakki (journal) 123
Tercüman-ı Ahval (journal) 39
Tercüman-ı Hakikat (journal) 40
Tercüme Odası (Translation Office) 5, 30, 31, 35, 52, 80
Teşebbüss-i Şahsi ve Adem-i Merkeziyet-i İdari Cemiyeti (Society for Administrative Decentralisation and Private Initiative) 123, 143
The Positivist Review 55, 129
Treaty of Karlowitz (1699) 13
Tunalı Hilmi Bey 107
Turkish History Society 140
Turkish Republic (Republic of Turkey) 4, 7, 25, 118, 137, 140, 141, 142, 143, 144, 145, 147
Turkish-Islamic Synthesis 144
Türkiye nasıl kurtarılabilir? (How Can Turkey be Saved?) 88, 148

Unionist(s) 7, 97, 102, 115, 116, 118, 123, 135, 136, 139, 140, 141
Üsküp 116

Valona 133
Vatan 43

Waldeck-Rousseau, Pierre 84
West, and Abdülhamit II 23, 24; and Rıza 5, 6, 7, 8, 57–8, 70, 71, 72; and Sabahattin 5, 6, 7, 8, 94, 97, 98–100, 101; and the Young Turk movement 32, 35, 36, 40, 121, 130, 131, 135, 144, 145, 146, 147
Westernisation 2, 60, 72, 99, 145

Yellin, Shlomo 135
Young Ottomans 3, 4, 5, 6, 25, 31, 33, 44, 45, 52, 63, 124, 144, 145, 146

Young Turk movement and intellectualism 5, 6–9, 32, 35, 36, 40, 44–6, 54, 55, 69, 71, 89, 97, 101, 102, 116, 117, 118, 119, 120, 121, 124, 125, 129, 130, 131, 132, 136, 137, 139, 142, 144, 145, 146, 148

Young Turk Revolution (1908) 5, 7, 102, 118, 120, 121, 122, 123, 135, 136, 140, 143

eBooks
from Taylor & Francis
Helping you to choose the right eBooks for your Library

Add to your library's digital collection today with Taylor & Francis eBooks. We have over 50,000 eBooks in the Humanities, Social Sciences, Behavioural Sciences, Built Environment and Law, from leading imprints, including Routledge, Focal Press and Psychology Press.

Choose from a range of subject packages or create your own!

Benefits for you
- Free MARC records
- COUNTER-compliant usage statistics
- Flexible purchase and pricing options
- 70% approx of our eBooks are now DRM-free.

Benefits for your user
- Off-site, anytime access via Athens or referring URL
- Print or copy pages or chapters
- Full content search
- Bookmark, highlight and annotate text
- Access to thousands of pages of quality research at the click of a button.

Free Trials Available

We offer free trials to qualifying academic, corporate and government customers.

eCollections
Choose from 20 different subject eCollections, including:

- Asian Studies
- Economics
- Health Studies
- Law
- Middle East Studies

eFocus
We have 16 cutting-edge interdisciplinary collections, including:

- Development Studies
- The Environment
- Islam
- Korea
- Urban Studies

For more information, pricing enquiries or to order a free trial, please contact your local sales team:

UK/Rest of World: **online.sales@tandf.co.uk**
USA/Canada/Latin America: **e-reference@taylorandfrancis.com**
East/Southeast Asia: **martin.jack@tandf.com.sg**
India: **journalsales@tandfindia.com**

www.tandfebooks.com